SLEUTHING THE BIBLE

Clues That Unlock the Mysteries of the Text

John Kaltner and Steven L. McKenzie

WILLIAM B. EERDMANS PUBLISHING COMPANY
GRAND RAPIDS, MICHIGAN

Wm. B. Eerdmans Publishing Co.
4035 Park East Court SE, Grand Rapids, Michigan 49546
www.eerdmans.com

25 24 23 22 21 20 19   1 2 3 4 5 6 7

ISBN 978-0-8028-7522-8

Library of Congress Cataloging-in-Publication Data

Names: Kaltner, John, 1954- author. | McKenzie, Steven L., 1953- author.
Title: Sleuthing the Bible : clues that unlock the mysteries of the text /
    John Kaltner and Steven L. McKenzie.
Description: Grand Rapids, Michigan : William B. Eerdmans Publishing Company,
    2019. | Includes bibliographical references and index.
Identifiers: LCCN 2018061361 | ISBN 9780802875228 (pbk. : alk. paper)
Subjects: LCSH: Bible—Hermeneutics. | Bible—Criticism, interpretation, etc.
Classification: LCC BS476 .K35 2019 | DDC 220.601—dc23
    LC record available at https://lccn.loc.gov/2018061361

We dedicate this book

to our fellow Bible detectives, past, present, and future,

*to our predecessors and teachers who laid the foundations
on which our careers have been built,*

*to our contemporaries whose collegiality we enjoy
and from whom we continue to learn,*

*to our successors in anticipation of their new insights
and in the hope that we will have contributed modestly to them.*

Contents

CONTENTS

PART TWO: DUSTING FOR PRINTS

An Initial Walk-Through

The subject of this book is the Bible. But not the Bible as you're used to seeing it. We're investigating the Bible with a chalk outline behind crime-scene tape. We won't be reading the Bible the way most people do, looking for answers, at least not the answers to life's big questions like, What's the meaning of it all? or, How can I be a better person? We're going to bury our noses in the Good Book trying to sniff out the questions it raises, not any answers it might provide. We hunt for the mysteries of the Bible, not its solutions. And not mysteries like, Where is the ark of the covenant? or, Where did Solomon's gold come from? We're interested in figuring out how the Bible came to be the way it is today. That's the kind of chase that excites us the most. We're Bible detectives.

We invite you to join us. We know your type. You're enthralled with the Bible because some of the stories it contains are so preposterous and hard to believe that you can't stop thinking about them. The outrageous nature of some of the most beloved Bible tales raises a host of questions in your mind. "C'mon, a talking snake?" "How can a guy live inside a fish for three days?" "So she cuts his hair and he goes from Superman to a wimp in a matter of seconds?" "How come the only way *I* can walk on water is if the temperature is twenty below?" You may not realize it, but your training as a biblical sleuth is already under way. Of such ponderings Bible detectives are made. You are a Bible detective in the making; your apprenticeship has begun. We only want to help accelerate and refine your sleuthing skills to satisfy your own sense of curiosity. Who knows? Maybe someday you'll decide to suffer the slings and arrows of the police academy (that is, graduate school), and if you do you'll already have a leg up. Asking questions is a necessary part of being a cop on the Bible beat. Inquiring minds want to know, and if you're missing the inquisitorial gene, you're probably not cut out for the force. Then again, if you lacked that gene, you probably wouldn't be reading this book.

One of the things they taught us in the academy was how to make the move from asking questions to looking for clues when reading the Bible. The two activities have much in common, since both entail being an observant and careful reader, and each can uncover mysteries in the text. But searching for clues is a type of inquiry that lets you do something you can't do when you're just asking questions—it allows you to categorize and systematize what you discover. A set of questions that emerge from reading a Bible story is just that, a list of separate and unrelated questions that you generate as you read. But if you're on the lookout for clues when you read that same story, each question that arises becomes identified with a particular type or class of clue. This makes it possible to connect it to other occurrences of the same clue and to compare something you find in one part of the Bible with something you find in another section of it. In other words, you have the big picture in mind and you can now see patterns and tendencies that you weren't aware of before. With that simple shift from asking questions to searching for clues, we took the first step toward earning our badges. Now it's your turn.

The body in question

It may strike you as odd, and perhaps even somewhat scandalous, to treat a religious text as if it were part of a crime scene. As weird as that might seem, it's exactly the way we and most of our fellow investigators relate to the Bible. A careful examination of its contents uncovers countless examples of illegal activities that in another context would be evidence of criminal behavior and grounds for prosecution. Among the violations the Bible is guilty of are the following:

> breaking and entering
> inconsistent testimony
> fraud

tampering
coercion
perjury
impersonation
collusion
robbery

It looks like we could throw the book at the Good Book. Keep in mind that this list is a compilation of some of the offenses Bible detectives have brought to light by reading between the lines of the text. It doesn't include the many violent crimes that are reported within the biblical stories themselves, like murder, rape, terrorism, and assorted acts of mayhem.

The image of the Bible as a body is an apt one for our purposes. Like the body of a person, the body of literature that constitutes the Bible is made up of many different parts that fit together to form a whole. There's an overall connection among the different parts, but each one can still be identified as an entity in its own right. Just as the heart is part of the circulatory system that is part of the whole body, so Genesis is part of the Pentateuch (the first five books of the Hebrew Bible) that is part of the entire Bible. Similar to a body with its many parts, the Bible is a set of texts rather than a single text. (If this paragraph has a familiar ring to it, your powers of perception are firing on all cylinders. We don't want to be brought up on any of the above charges, so we'd like to acknowledge our indebtedness to New Testament author Paul ["the apostle"], who sometimes went by the alias Saul—see 1 Corinthians 12.)

The biblical corpus at the crime scene contains a lot of clues to what has happened, and it's the Bible detective's job to discover those clues and see where they lead. One place they usually do not lead is to the doorstep of the perp. Biblical clues can tell us a great deal, but they hardly ever point to the guilty parties and identify the ones who left them behind. Because the authors of virtually every book in the Bible are anonymous, the many "Whodunits?" that pepper its pages will likely remain unanswered forever. That might make Bible detective work seem pointless and futile to some. But let's face it, even the best detectives seldom close all their cases. Maybe you're like us and in it for the thrill of the chase. We always leave a little food on our plates after we're done eating at our favorite diner just to remind ourselves that there are still questions out there waiting to be answered.

B(u)y the book

If you've picked up this book because you're looking for a run-of-the-mill introduction to the Bible, please put it down now and move along, because there's nothing to see here, folks. What you are holding in your hands is instead a training manual for wannabes, those interested in developing the skills and know-how required to become a Bible sleuth and consequently receive the rights, privileges, and honors thereunto appertaining. Specifically, this manual contains an overview of fifteen of the most common clues Bible detectives look for as they go about their investigative work. (Around the station, they're known as the Pentakaidecalogue.)

Those fifteen clues have been divided into two groups to reflect the fact that some folks are more clued in than others. The first set we've called "smoking guns" because they are relatively easy to spot by anyone with average cognitive abilities and an attention span in the normal range. In a few cases, some tips are provided regarding how to recognize and analyze these clues, but for the most part your own powers of observation and deduction will be the only tools you'll need to get a whiff of the smoking guns.

The second group of clues is found under the heading "Dusting for Prints" because they require more specialized training and a deeper dive into the detective's bag of tricks. Returning to our proverbial corpse at the crime scene, sometimes the cause of death is obvious and sometimes it's not. It's a bit easier to spot a bullet wound than poison in the bloodstream. These clues are present in the latter situation, when the biblical corpus has to be shipped off to the lab for further examination and an autopsy. To crack these cases the investigator usually needs to be proficient in the biblical languages, be familiar with the history and cultures of the ancient world, and have knowledge of a large segment of the biblical literature in order to make comparisons across the corpus. Some of our friends on the force don't have the stomach for that level of detail, and so they avoid the lab at all costs, which can lead to some odd departmental politics.

Like many professions, biblical detective work is inherently hierarchical, and some of our colleagues take tremendous pride in their place in the pecking order. Sometimes their obsession with the next rung up the career ladder leads them to absurd acts and drastic measures. We know of one guy who actually sued his own precinct because he didn't make sergeant, and another who put in for a promotion after he retired and was on his way out the door. To give you a taste of that side of biblical police work, we've instituted our own system of rank in this training manual. If you're able to work your way through all the material and assignments in the "Smoking Guns" section, you will have achieved the level of Detective I, and if you can do the same with the clues in the "Dusting for Prints" section, you'll be immediately promoted to Detective II.

This manual represents a crash course in the basics of Bible detecting. It's a tutorial designed to lay the foundation and get you up to speed for the rigorous workout your gray matter will be put through should you decide to go further and enroll in the police academy. Many clues could be added to the fifteen that make up the Pentakaidecalogue, and the more of them you're able to master the higher you can climb up the chain of command. So, if you're an upwardly mobile type who breezes your way through these clues, keep in mind that there are other peaks to scale. Just don't sue us if you can't make it to the top.

Each chapter in this manual treats a different clue, and they're all laid out in a similar way. (Consistency and precision are essential in police work.) A brief opening section introduces the clue, and then you get up close and personal with it as we parade before you a lineup of some of the most notorious cases related to it that we've been able to dig up from our files (i.e., the various biblical books). Those samples are taken from the two main sets of case files Bible sleuths spend much of their time mucking around in—the Hebrew Bible (a.k.a. the Old Testament) and the New Testament.

To help you navigate the terrain and prevent you from getting lost in the weeds, we're not going to present the details of these cases exactly as they appear in the original files. When we quote the relevant portions of a file, we'll often put the part containing the clue in italics so it will be immediately apparent to you. This will allow you to zoom right in on the incriminating evidence and get your investigative juices flowing, similar to what happens when the murderer uses the victim's blood to scrawl a message on a wall near the body.

After we've briefed you on what the case file contains, we'll explain to you step-by-step how we as Bible detectives examine that particular crime scene before we dash off to the next one. Keep in mind that in each case we're providing you only excerpts from the files, and so it is a good idea to have the entire biblical corpus in the room with you as you're reading, just in case you want to get a sense of the wider context of the crime scene. If you keep your magnifying glass clean, you may notice that we sometimes use the same case to illustrate different clues. That's because evidence comes in lots of forms, from weapons to fingerprints to psychological profiles to DNA. It's rare that a case is solved by just one piece of evidence. Good detectives use every means at their disposal to try to catch the bad guy. Heck, we even consulted psychics a time or two before we learned to rely on more conventional—and more effective—methods.

Detectives like to tie up all the loose ends, so after a meticulous analysis of each clue, we have a section titled "Why This Clue Matters." Here we offer observations on the significance of the clue, and we identify a number of investigative skills and abilities that searching for it will allow you to develop. As an added bonus, you don't have to wait long to flex your muscles and see what kind of shape you're in. If you're going to be a cop, you have to be willing to get your hands dirty, and this will be your chance to play around a bit in the mud. Every chapter concludes with a section called "The Casebook" that asks you to read through some files on your own and wrestle with the clue in a number of biblical passages that weren't discussed in the chapter. By the time you've finished the book, you'll know exactly where you stand: Detective I if you suss out all the "Smoking Guns," Detective II if you can solve all the cases after "Dusting for Prints." If you don't make the grade, you can repeat the course or try to recoup the money you spent on this manual.

Tips for rookies

Treating it as if it's part of a crime scene is not how people are usually taught to read the Bible. You are therefore probably a neophyte at approaching the text in this way, and it will likely take some time to get used to. With that in mind, we'd like to offer a few words of encouragement and advice as you commence your training. Here are a few tips we've learned along the way about how to do the job.

The Bible Detective's Code
1. An open mind is as important as an eagle eye.
2. Forget what you think you already know about the corpus.
3. Don't be squeamish about examining the corpus.

4. Never stop asking questions.
5. Go where the clues lead.
6. Evidence can often be read in more than one way.
7. Teamwork is crucial.

Better than most, we know the importance of that last one. Our mutual fate as Bible dicks was sealed early on, not because we loved to wear deerstalker caps and our parents couldn't pry magnifying glasses out of our hands, and not because we couldn't put down Sir Arthur Conan Doyle or Agatha Christie or turn our eyes away from *Perry Mason*, *Kojak*, or a dozen other TV cop/detective shows. No, we were detectives-in-waiting because we were bookworms, and one of our favorite reads was the Bible (okay, so our nerdiness also manifested itself at a young age). As grown-ups, we've been partners in crime a long time. Each of us sometimes goes his separate way as a lone wolf or in the company of others, but for nearly a quarter-century we've been assigned to the same precinct (Rhodes College), the same division (Religious Studies Department), and the same beat (Biblical Studies). Our offices are even right across the hall from each other, which has saved us a small fortune on shoe leather. Over the years we've worked on a lot of cases together, and it's been our good fortune to have experienced the excitement and fun that come with collaboration. We've written this manual in the hope that future Bible detectives will want to join us in what we think is a very cool, if sometimes misunderstood, profession. On to the clues!

PART ONE

SMOKING GUNS

. . . clues that are easy to spot with normal
powers of observation and deductive skills

1

The Clue of the

INTRUSIVE NARRATOR

Sometimes there's not a doubt in your mind as to what has happened. You come home, and things are just not right. The door is wide open, the place has been ransacked, and the dog is missing. You're standing in the middle of a crime scene, and it's painfully obvious. At other times, it takes a little longer to realize that something is amiss. All seems normal for a while until you find yourself asking, "Hey, where did all this broken glass come from?" Only then does it dawn on you that someone has been there who shouldn't have been.

Welcome to the world of biblical detecting! Both of the above scenarios aptly describe the aftermath of the work of a notorious figure whose fingerprints are found throughout the Good Book—the intrusive narrator. He's a master trespasser and interloper whose presence can be as palpable or as subtle as the person who invades your living room. The only difference is that he's guilty of breaking into and entering a story rather than a house. In fact, the story he enters is the very one he's telling, so it's the equivalent of someone breaking into one's own home. Let's get acquainted with this biblical delinquent and see how he operates by dipping into the files and examining a couple of cases of forced entry that show the intrusive narrator at his disruptive best.

Our first case involves Saul, who goes on to become the first king of Israel. One day, when he was still young, his father asked him to go out with one of the servant boys to look for the family's donkeys that had wandered off. They search far and wide with no luck, and then the following episode is related.

> When they came to the land of Zuph, Saul said to the boy who was with him, "Let us turn back, or my father will stop worrying about the donkeys and worry about us." But he said to him, "There is a man of God in this town; he is a man held in honor. Whatever he says always comes true. Let us go there now; perhaps he will tell us about the journey on which we have set out." Then Saul replied to the boy, "But if we go, what can we bring the man? For the bread in our sacks is gone, and there is no present to bring to the man of God. What have we?" The boy answered Saul again, "Here, I have with me a quarter shekel of silver; I will give it to the man of God, to tell us our way." *(Formerly in Israel, anyone who went to inquire of God would say, "Come, let us go to the seer"; for the one who is now called a prophet was formerly called a seer.)* Saul said to the boy, "Good; come, let us go." So they went to the town where the man of God was. (1 Sam. 9:5–10)

In this passage the intrusive narrator sticks out like a sore thumb and is much easier to locate than Saul's donkeys. The sentence that begins "Formerly in Israel . . ." breaks the flow of the story and actually interrupts the conversation taking place between Saul and the boy. The voice of the narrator suddenly refers to something that was done in the past but is no longer practiced, and only after the narrator has had his say does Saul reply to the boy's suggestion that they visit the man of God. The unexpected appearance of the narrator is jarring and obvious, and it is often easier to identify in English translations of the Bible because narratorial comments like this one are sometimes placed in parentheses, as they are here.

THE CLUE OF THE INTRUSIVE NARRATOR: an interruption of the main story to convey a piece of information

The second case comes from the New Testament and is found at the end of the Gospel of John. That gospel is the only one that reports a scene in which the Roman governor Pontius Pilate dispatches soldiers to break the legs of Jesus and those crucified with him in order to hasten their deaths.

> But when they came to Jesus and saw that he was already dead, they did not break his legs. Instead, one of the soldiers pierced his side with a spear, and at once blood and water came out. *(He who saw this has testified so that you also may believe. His testimony is true, and he knows that he tells the truth.) These things occurred so that the scripture might be fulfilled, "None of his bones shall be broken." And again another passage of scripture says, "They will look on the one whom they have pierced."* After these things, Joseph of Arimathea, who was a disciple of Jesus, though a secret one because of his fear of the Jews, asked Pilate to let him take away the body of Jesus. Pilate gave him permission; so he came and removed his body. (John 19:33–38)

Here the narrator is doubly intrusive because he interrupts the narrative to impart two pieces of information to the reader. After describing how Jesus's side is pierced, the narrator refers to someone who saw these things and speaks the truth. Is the narrator speaking about himself? If so, this is a rare self-referential statement by the biblical narrator that serves as a calling card and says, "Here I am." The other intrusion is a set of two quotations from Scripture that help explain the events that have just been described. Fulfillment citations like these disrupt the flow of the narrative even though they are not in parentheses and are further examples of the hand of the intrusive narrator at work. Only after the narrator has put his two cents in does the story resume with Joseph of Arimathea requesting the body of Jesus.

This, in a nutshell, is the guy we're after. We'll be considering many other cases involving the intrusive narrator in this chapter, and once you know what to look for, it is often one of the easiest clues to recognize in the Bible. The technical term for his offense commonly used in literary studies is "breaking the frame," which refers to any information imparted to the reader that is not a part of the plot of the narrative. When trying to track him down and apprehend him, a good working premise is the following: A break in the flow of a story might mean the intrusive narrator has been up to his old tricks. In some passages, like the two above, it's quite easy to spot him. But sometimes he can sneak up on you like a pickpocket, and you might not realize he's close at hand until you discover your wallet is missing.

We should keep in mind the profile of the culprit we are hunting. Who is this intrusive narrator? What would an artist's sketch of him look like? Could you pick him out of a lineup? What's his m.o.? Like most break-ins, his usually take place at the intersection of motive and opportunity. But he's not motivated by the things that prompt most common criminals, like greed, lust, or vengeance. The intrusive narrator is impelled by a more noble drive—the desire to help. In terms of his motive, then, the Bible's intrusive narrator is more Robin Hood than Jesse James. And his opportunity? It's ever present because he is the one telling the story, and he can pause it and put things on hold to speak in his own voice whenever he likes. Never forget—even when he's not intruding, the narrator is always there and can break in at any moment.

A Pathological Explainer

A dominant trait of the intrusive narrator is his obsession with explaining things, often seemingly insignificant and random things. He often inserts little asides that are meant to fill in the blanks for his audience and therefore lessen the likelihood that they will be confused by something going on in the story. We often see this proclivity to elucidate in observations related to geography and chronology, and these tend to be rather blunt assertions that are easy to detect, but we'll also examine cases in which the intrusive narrator's presence is more subtle and elusive.

Naming names

Place-names are one of the intrusive narrator's specialties, particularly obscure older names that have been replaced by newer ones. Sometimes he refers to a known place and then gives its earlier name, but he also on occasion reverses field by first mentioning the former name of a familiar place. This can be seen in the description of Abram's return from doing battle with enemy forces when he is greeted by the ruler of the city of Sodom. "After his return from the defeat of Chedorlaomer and the kings who were with him, the king of Sodom went out to meet him at the Valley of Shaveh (*that is, the King's Valley*)" (Gen. 14:17). The parenthetical clarification—the parentheses are not in the Hebrew original—gives an alternative name to the valley, but we're not sure if this is an older (or newer) name for it. It might be that they were two contemporaneous ways of referring to the same place, like "New York City" and "the Big Apple."

A similar thing can be seen in reference to a town mentioned in Genesis 35:6. "Jacob came to Luz (*that is, Bethel*), which is in the land of Canaan, he and all the people who were with him." This time we know that Luz is actually the older name of the place because an intrusive narrator clears up any confusion about the matter in another biblical book. "The house of Joseph sent out spies to Bethel (*the name of the city was formerly Luz*)" (Judg. 1:23). Over in Genesis there's an especially interesting situation regarding the city of Hebron as the burial place of Abraham's wife, Sarah, because the intrusive narrator engages in a bit of doublespeak by referring to it with two different alternative names. In one place it is stated, "And Sarah died at Kiriath-arba (*that is, Hebron*) in the land of Canaan; and Abraham went in to mourn for Sarah and to weep for her" (Gen. 23:2). But then, later in the very same chapter, we read, "After this, Abraham buried Sarah his wife in the cave of the field of Machpelah facing Mamre (*that is, Hebron*) in the land of Canaan" (Gen. 23:19). So apparently Hebron was known as both Kiriath-arba and Mamre. That's like adding its original name of "New Amsterdam" to "New York" and "the Big Apple."

We do not find many geographical comments from the intrusive narrator in the New Testament. One is possible in Acts 8:26, which sets Philip off on a journey resulting in the baptism of an Ethiopian eunuch. "Then an angel of the Lord said to Philip, 'Get up and go toward the south to the road that goes down from Jerusalem to Gaza.' (*This is a wilderness road.*)" The parentheses around the final sentence indicate that this is understood by the NRSV translator to be an aside from the intrusive narrator, but that isn't necessarily the case. There are no quotation marks in Greek (or Hebrew, for that matter), and so it is possible that the words from the angel include those in the parentheses; this is the way a number of other English translations understand the verse. This highlights one of the challenges of trying to hunt down and identify the intrusive narrator, who can sometimes prove to be a slippery prey.

How should we analyze and understand these cases in which the intrusive narrator swoops in and reveals his presence on a matter of geography? What do these scenes of forcible entry suggest? They might indicate that the story was written at a later time when people no longer knew the older name of a place, and so the narrator felt the need to step in and clarify things. That appears to be the best way to understand a statement like "The name of the city was formerly Luz." Alternatively, people might have been familiar with both names, even if one of them had already replaced the other. Perhaps there were people alive who knew a place by its former name, and so the narrator used both. In some cases, like the Valley of Shaveh/King's Valley, it is possible that the same place was known by two different names at the same time that were being used more or less interchangeably. This is not unlike the situation with some place-names today, when many people still think of Mumbai, Beijing, and Myanmar as Bombay, Peking, and Burma.

Doing time

The Bible sometimes calls attention to chronological gaps with intrusive narrators. After the people enter the land that will become Israel, Joshua commemorates the occasion in an unusual way. "Joshua set up twelve stones in the middle of the Jordan, in the place where the feet of the priests bearing the ark of the covenant had stood; and they are there *to this day*" (Josh. 4:9). After all the men are circumcised in the next chapter, God reassures Joshua about the significance of that ritual, and the intrusive narrator uses the same expression (copycat alert!). "The LORD said to Joshua, 'Today I have rolled away from you the disgrace of Egypt.' And so that place is called Gilgal *to this day*" (Josh. 5:9). A similar scene is depicted in the Gospel of Matthew to explain how the field bought with the money that Judas received for betraying Jesus got its name. Here the connection between the name of the place and what is happening in the story is apparent even in translation. "But the chief priests, taking the pieces of silver, said, 'It is not lawful to put them into the treasury, since they are blood money.' After conferring together, they used them to buy the potter's field as a place to bury foreigners. For this reason that field has been called the Field of Blood *to this day*" (Matt. 27:6-8). In each of these cases, the action of the plot pauses briefly so the narrator can direct a comment to the audience and remind them that "this day" is different from "that day."

The exact day the narrator is referring to with the expression "to this day" is impossible to know, but some passages allow us to narrow down the range of possible dates a bit and indicate in general terms when the intrusive narrator was operating. An account of the dedication of the temple in Jerusalem by King Solomon, presented in 1 Kings 8, describes the layout and contents of the building. At one point reference is made to the poles used to transport the ark of the covenant from place to place. "The poles were so long that the ends of the poles were seen from the holy place in front of the inner sanctuary; but they could not be seen from outside; they are there *to this day*" (1 Kings 8:8). Although the phrase is identical to the one in the passages we've just looked at, in this case the day it refers to can be dated in relative terms. In 587 BCE the Jerusalem temple was destroyed by the Babylonians in an invasion that began the period known as the Babylonian exile. This means that this verse and the intrusive narrator responsible for its final three words come from a time prior to that tragic and traumatic event.

Sometimes the expression "to this day" is employed by a narrator to help explain why certain people behave the way they do, especially when that behavior might appear eccentric or bizarre. An example of this is found in the aftermath of a marathon wrestling match that lasts an entire night and leaves Jacob hobbled from a blow to the hip delivered by a mysterious opponent. You might think it has something to do with why some people limp, but you'd be barking up the wrong tree. According to the intrusive narrator, the story provides the origin for an unusual dietary practice. "Therefore *to this day* the Israelites do not eat the thigh muscle that is on the hip socket, because he struck Jacob on the hip socket at the thigh muscle" (Gen. 32:32). Another example occurs in the report of an even weirder nighttime injury, this one suffered by a Philistine god named Dagon. The Philistines capture the ark of God and then house it in Dagon's temple, but in the morning they discover Dagon's statue toppled over before the ark and its severed head and hands lying in the doorway. After describing this macabre scene, the narrator breaks the frame with this observation: "This is why the priests of Dagon and all who enter the house of Dagon do not step on the threshold of Dagon in Ashdod *to this day*" (1 Sam. 5:5).

The explanatory nature of these chronological intrusions is obvious, and they have much in common with the Clue of the Etiology discussed in chapter 3. This should come as no surprise, since biblical stories, like crime scenes, often contain multiple clues, and sometimes those clues can be interpreted in more than one way. Beyond their explanatory role, however, these intrusions can sometimes also be attempts to respond to curiosity by the story's author or audience. People are always captivated by things they do not understand or that strike them as strange or peculiar, whether they're rock formations (like Joshua's stones in the river) or the eating habits of others (like the Israelites' avoidance of the thigh muscle), and the Bible's intrusive narrator sometimes steps in to help them make sense of those oddities.

Now you see him, now you don't

In some cases things are a bit more muddled, and it can be hard to determine whether or not the intrusive narrator has actually contaminated the scene. The difficulty is not in determining whether the narrator is present (he's the one relating the story, so he's never absent), but in figuring out if we're dealing with an *intrusive* narrator. It's a Jekyll and Hyde or Bruce Banner and the Hulk situation—Dr. Jekyll and Banner are always there, but at times they're transformed into their evil twin and do things they normally wouldn't do. Like those two laid-back fellows and their more sinister alter egos, the narrator and the intrusive narrator are one and the same. In some biblical passages it's not completely clear if we're hearing from Banner or the Hulk, because what is being said might actually be a part of the story rather than a break in the frame of the narrative. Here's where the real detective work begins.

We saw an example of this in the passage from Acts in which the sentence "This is a wilderness road" could be a comment from the intrusive narrator or just a continuation of the angel's words to Philip as he begins his journey. Another New Testament story is similarly ambiguous in this regard. Only the Gospel of John describes an encounter that Jesus has with a woman at a well in Samaria as he is traveling from Judea to Galilee. After he asks the woman to give him some water, the text continues, "The Samaritan woman said to him, 'How is it that you, a Jew, ask a drink of me, a woman of Samaria?' (*Jews do not share things in common with Samaritans*)" (John 4:9). The parentheses (and our italicized text) indicate that the NRSV believes the last sentence is a statement from the intrusive narrator that explains to the reader why the woman responds as she does. That's possible, but because Greek lacks quotation marks, it's also possible that the woman is still speaking and the last sentence contains her words. One might argue that Jesus would have been well aware that Jews did not share things in common with Samaritans, so there would be no reason for the woman to state the obvious, which

18

would tip the scale in favor of it being a comment from the intrusive narrator. But the other alternative remains a possibility, so we'll never know for sure if the words come from Dr. Jekyll or Mr. Hyde.

The grammar of a passage can occasionally provide important clues about whether or not the intrusive narrator has been working the area, even when you are unable to read it in its original language. A good example can be seen in Acts 23:6–8, where Paul takes advantage of a division within the Jewish council that is hearing his case. "When Paul noticed that some were Sadducees and others were Pharisees, he called out in the council, 'Brothers, I am a Pharisee, a son of Pharisees. I am on trial concerning the hope of the resurrection of the dead.' When he said this, a dissension began between the Pharisees and the Sadducees, and the assembly was divided. (*The Sadducees say that there is no resurrection, or angel, or spirit; but the Pharisees acknowledge all three.*)" At first glance, it might appear that the words in parentheses are advancing the story by identifying what is dividing the group. On the other hand, this could be a comment from the intrusive narrator explaining to the uninformed reader what exactly Sadducees and Pharisees differ over. Careful consideration of the grammar, especially the verbal tenses, makes the latter option more likely. Except for Paul's declaration about himself, all the verbs in the passage prior to the parentheses are in the past tense, but those within the parentheses are in the present tense. In addition, the verbs that follow the parentheses continue in the past tense as the story goes on to describe the chaos that ensues within the council. This highlights the italicized section as an outlier that breaks the frame in order to address the reader directly. Even without knowledge of Hebrew and Greek, the biblical investigator can employ grammar as an important resource in implicating the intrusive narrator.

At times the intrusive narrator's touch is so light that you'll swear he could have been a safecracker. With the stealth and swiftness of a sneak attack he breaks in, has his say, and is back in Jekyll mode in the blink of an eye. Note the way Luke begins his genealogy of Jesus in the third chapter of his gospel. "Jesus was about thirty years old when he began his work. He was the son (*as was thought*) of Joseph son of Heli" (Luke 3:23). There then follows a mind-numbing listing of seventy-five consecutive repetitions of the formula "son of X" that ends with "son of God." (We did the legwork and counted them all, three times. Sometimes being a detective isn't the glamour job people think it is.) As you prepare to work your way through all those generations of fathers and sons with their unusual names, it's easy to skip right over the three words in italics. But there they sit, a testimony to the subtlety and proofreading talent of the intrusive narrator. He well remembers that two chapters earlier he had told his readers that Jesus's mother, Mary, conceived him without having sexual relations with a man, and so to avoid any inconsistency he now informs them that those who weren't in the know naturally assumed that Joseph was his biological father. The insertion clears up the contradiction, but it's introduced with such finesse and understatement that you can easily miss the fact that you've just had a close encounter with the intrusive narrator.

An additional set of texts that highlight an as-yet-unexplored aspect of the subtle voice of the intrusive narrator is the fulfillment citations mentioned earlier in connection with the description of Jesus's death in John 19. These passages linking events in the life of Jesus with some of the prior Scriptures are present in a number of New Testament books, but they are most frequently found in Matthew's Gospel. Here are some examples of prophetic fulfillment citations taken from Jesus's birth story as presented in Matthew's first two chapters:

> *All this took place to fulfill what had been spoken by the Lord through the prophet:*
>   "Look, the virgin shall conceive and bear a son,
>   and they shall name him Emmanuel,"
> which means, "God is with us." (Matt. 1:22–23)

> Then Joseph got up, took the child and his mother by night, and went to Egypt, and remained there until the death of Herod. *This was to fulfill what had been spoken by the Lord through the prophet,* "Out of Egypt I have called my son." (Matt. 2:14–15; see also Matt. 2:16–18, 23)

Like other comments from the intrusive narrator, these put the narrative on pause and do not relate events of the story. Also like ones we've already seen, they are explanatory in nature in that they attempt to fill in some perceived gap in knowledge on the reader's part. But these fulfillment citations have an interpretive dimension lacking in the other comments. The reader is being told how to evaluate the events that have been described, and the narrator has become an interpreter. He is not just telling readers something *about* Jesus, he is telling them what to *think about* Jesus. The repeated references to Jesus as the fulfillment of the earlier prophetic writings introduce a rhetorical aspect to the narrator's role that changes him from merely an explainer to a persuader, and he is an intruder of a different sort because he wishes to influence and shape the reader's beliefs.

In other words

The final piece of the puzzle that completes his psychological and professional profile is the intrusive narrator's talent as a master linguist. He's an international man of mystery who is conversant in more than one language, and he uses that skill to (what else?) explain and clarify things for his audience. Not one to flaunt his abilities in this area, he usually limits his work to a brief translation of a word or a simple phrase that he believes might be unfamiliar to his readers and therefore cause them confusion. He performs his work as a decoder sparingly, and in fact it is almost entirely limited to the New Testament writings. This reflects the unique linguistic circumstances under which the original readers of the New Testament lived. The texts are written in Greek about events that took place in a context in which the primary spoken language was Aramaic. Some readers of the New Testament writings would have been familiar with Aramaic (and the related language of Hebrew), but others would not have been, and so the intrusive narrator occasionally puts on his translator's hat in the service of the latter group.

A rare example of the intrusive narrator functioning as a translator in the Hebrew Bible can be found in the book of Esther. In that tale, set during the reign of a Persian king named Ahasuerus, a member of the king's court named Haman had devised a plot to kill all the Jews living in the area. The text describes the game of chance that was played to determine when Haman's plan would be enacted. "In the first month, which is the month of Nisan, in the twelfth year of King Ahasuerus, they cast Pur—*which means 'the lot'*—before Haman for the day and for the month, and the lot fell on the thirteenth day of the twelfth month, which is the month of Adar" (Esther 3:7). The word *pur* eventually entered the Hebrew language, and its plural form is now used for the Jewish holiday Purim, which has its basis in the events described in Esther. Because the term would have been unfamiliar to many of Esther's readers, the intrusive narrator inserts himself into the text to pause the action of the story and inform them of its meaning before disappearing again so the plot can resume. By the way, that is the briefest disappearance of an intrusive narrator in the Bible, because he's also found at the beginning and end of the passage, when the names of the first and twelfth months of the calendar are identified. That makes this a rare triple play in which the intrusive narrator breaks in and enters a single biblical verse three times.

It's really in the New Testament where the intrusive narrator's translation chops are most evident, and in the Gospels of Mark and John in particular they're on full display. In a teaching of Jesus unique to Mark, the meaning of a term that likely has its origin in Hebrew is given. "But you say that if anyone tells father or mother, 'Whatever support you might have had from me is Corban' (*that is, an offering to God*)—then you no longer permit doing anything for a father or mother, thus making void the word of God through your tradition that you have handed on. And you do many things like this" (Mark 7:11–13).

Similar translation activity occurs in a couple of miracle stories in which Mark has Jesus speak in Aramaic rather than the usual Greek he converses in throughout the Gospels. One describes the resuscitation of a young girl. "He took her by the hand and said to her, 'Talitha cum,' *which means, 'Little girl, get up!'*" (Mark 5:41). The other is an account of the healing of a man with a speech impediment. "Then looking up to heaven, he sighed and said to him, 'Ephphatha,' *that is, 'Be opened.'* And immediately his ears were opened, his tongue was released, and he spoke plainly" (Mark 7:34–35). In his description of Jesus's death, Mark's intrusive narrator intervenes to make sure his readers know the location of the event. "Then they brought Jesus to the place called Golgotha (*which means the place of a skull*)" (Mark 15:22). At the climactic death scene, Jesus's last words are translated from Aramaic. "At three o'clock Jesus cried with a loud voice, 'Eloi, Eloi, lema sabachthani?' *which means, 'My God, my God, why have you forsaken me?'*" (Mark 15:34).

In John the intrusive narrator comes charging out of the gate to put his translational stamp on the initial encounter between Jesus and his earliest followers in the first chapter of the gospel. Three times in the space of five verses he is there to helpfully explain to the reader the nuances of the titles and names that are being used.

When Jesus turned and saw them following, he said to them, "What are you looking for?" They said to him, "Rabbi" (*which translated means Teacher*), "where are you staying?" (John 1:38)

He first found his brother Simon and said to him, "We have found the Messiah" (*which is translated Anointed*). (John 1:41)

He brought Simon to Jesus, who looked at him and said, "You are Simon son of John. You are to be called Cephas" (*which is translated Peter*). (John 1:42)

During a miracle story, the intrusive narrator explains the name of the place where a man born blind will regain his sight. Jesus tells the man, "'Go, wash in the pool of Siloam' (*which means Sent*). Then he went and washed and came back able to see" (John 9:7). In addition, twice in the account of Jesus's trial and death he renders potentially unfamiliar place-names in their more familiar Hebrew versions. One is a scene that is recounted only in John's Gospel. "When Pilate heard these words, he brought Jesus outside and sat on the judge's bench at a place called The Stone Pavement, *or in Hebrew Gabbatha*" (John 19:13). The other is the same explanatory note regarding the location of Jesus's death that is found in Mark (as well as Matthew, whose narrator does not translate as often as Mark's does). "Then he handed him over to them to be crucified. So they took Jesus; and carrying the cross by himself, he went out to what is called The Place of the Skull, *which in Hebrew is called Golgotha*" (John 19:16–17).

WHY THIS CLUE MATTERS

Now that we've observed the intrusive narrator in action and studied how he operates, a big question remains—so what? Countless people read the Bible every day who have never even heard of the intrusive narrator, and their lives are no worse off for it, so what's the point and payoff of searching through the weeds for him? It's a fair question, but as biblical detectives who have spent a fair amount of time knee-deep in those weeds, we'd like to issue an APB for the intrusive narrator and encourage all Bible readers to remain on the lookout for him. This may seem like a trivial and insignificant clue, but here are some reasons why we think pursuing the intrusive narrator is worth your time and effort. Don't forget—sometimes the biggest of mysteries is solved by the smallest of clues.

THE CLUE OF THE INTRUSIVE NARRATOR CAN HELP US . . .

1. Be more careful readers.
2. Pay attention to the role of the narrator.
3. Think about how authors respond to the needs of readers.
4. Be aware of the relationship between a text and its various contexts.
5. Keep in mind the original audience a text was written for.

THE CASEBOOK

Find the Clue of the Intrusive Narrator in the following chapters:

Genesis 36
Deuteronomy 3
Joshua 8
Joshua 9
Judges 1
2 Samuel 18
Daniel 2
Matthew 8
Matthew 28
Mark 3
John 20
Acts 1
Acts 5
Acts 17

2

The Clue of the

PHYSICAL DESCRIPTION

This is a true story of crime-fighting success. In 1927, when ice was sold in blocks for iceboxes, an employee of the Southland Ice Company in Dallas started selling other staple items—milk, bread, and eggs—in addition to ice in his ice house. Since demand for these items was especially great on Sundays and evenings when grocery stores were closed, the move was a raging success, and the convenience store was born. Southland Ice Company picked up on the idea and began carrying grocery items in all its ice houses. The number of stores expanded, as did the inventory. Canned goods, in-season produce like watermelons, and gas pumps were added, then beer and liquor after Prohibition ended. The name changed too, first to Tote'm, because people toted their purchases, then in 1946 to 7-Eleven, reflecting the stores' hours of operation. Under the new name, the company opened stores throughout Texas and then in other states. In 1963, a 7-Eleven in Austin, Texas, found itself so busy after a University of Texas football game that it stayed open all night. Soon other 7-Elevens were open 24/7 nationwide. International expansion followed. Success attracted competition, and other convenience store chains opened. But 7-Eleven remains the largest of them all with some twenty-five thousand stores worldwide.

With the advent of convenience stores came the convenience-store holdup. By the mid-1970s robberies were epidemic. A study devoted to the problem produced a series of recommendations; robberies could be reduced if stores used time-controlled safes, had limited cash on hand, enhanced the lighting indoors and out, and ensured clear visibility of the interior from the outside, and vice versa. 7-Eleven adopted these recommendations nationally, and robberies declined by half over the next decade. The National Association of Convenience Stores started selling to stores a package that included these measures and more because they were so effective. One of the items in the package was height strips for the doors—rulers that marked feet and inches from the ground, beginning at about 5 feet 2 inches and going up to around 7 feet. Their purpose initially was to help convenience store clerks and other witnesses determine the height of a fleeing robber, to help police with descriptions of robbery suspects. They are not really necessary for that purpose any longer because the video from security cameras gives a much clearer and more accurate idea than any description. But they are still included in the security measures for most convenience stores, mainly because they have a psychological impact on prospective robbers. Customers have gotten used to the height markers. A lot of people don't even know what they are for. But criminals notice them, and to them they send the message that the store owners are concerned about safety and have invested in devices that increase the likelihood of apprehension and conviction of anyone who perpetrates a robbery on the premises.

> THE CLUE OF THE PHYSICAL DESCRIPTION: a specific feature mentioned to highlight a role the character will play in the text

Eyewitnesses may have been replaced by video cameras in some quarters, but they both get at the same thing—physical characteristics, which are essential for identifying someone you don't know personally or by name. That's why "What did the person look like?" is the first question asked by investigating officers in everything from purse snatching to murder in the first degree. Physical descriptions are also among the first things you expect to find about a character in a novel or the subject of a biography. The description allows you to imagine what the character looked like or is imagined to look like in the author's mind.

This is where the Bible is different. We have no idea what most of the characters in the Bible looked like. There's no description of Adam. None of Eve. None of Cain or Abel. None of Noah. None of Abraham or

Sarah or Moses or Joshua. There is also no description of Jesus or Paul or any of the other apostles. You get the picture or don't get the picture. There just isn't much interest on the part of the writers as to what these figures looked like. It's not that physical descriptions are all that rare in the Bible. But when they are provided, they usually focus only on a specific feature that highlights a role the character will play in the text. Given this specific function, physical descriptions can be very useful and important clues for understanding biblical literature. The Clue of the Physical Description is among the easiest to recognize. The feature described will typically play a role in the story or have a bearing on its outcome. At the same time, the implications of a physical description are not always clear in a cursory reading of the text.

We went to see Diane, the department sketch artist, before we started this chapter. She has less to do these days with the prevalence of video cameras, so she was happy to sit down with us for a nice, long chat. We asked her if the protocol for physical description that we both learned in the academy is still in use today. She told us that it is, so we're going to follow it as we investigate the clues that the Bible gives in its physical descriptions.

Gender

The first thing to be determined is whether the person we're looking for is male or female. That's not always as easy as you might think, even with video. Crooks sometimes disguise themselves, and baggy clothing can hide a multitude of differences. But in the Bible the matter is pretty straightforward. What is interesting is the role that good looks play in Bible cases.

Handsome men

A good example is Joseph, who is described with two adjectival phrases: handsome of form and handsome of appearance (Gen. 39:6), maybe "well built and handsome," as the Jewish Publication Society (JPS) translation has it. The reason for this description becomes clear in the next verse, which tells how his master's wife was attracted to him and tried to seduce him. The description explains his appeal to her and prepares the way for the next stage of the story, which reads like a scene from a Harlequin romance novel. Not surprisingly, the JPS version calls the male figure in Song of Songs 1:16 handsome for much the same reason, namely, his sex appeal. The female speaker is attracted to him and in love with him. The book, after all, is erotic poetry.

But it's not always about sex. There are other reasons for pointing out a man's handsomeness besides sexual attraction. Physical appearance becomes a motif that expresses suitability for certain offices or roles. Joseph's description not only accounts for his attractiveness to Potiphar's wife but also is part of the typical depiction of the wise young man in the foreign court. It is no accident that Daniel and his friends are also described as handsome and without physical defect (Dan. 1:4), the finest young men of Judah, who were being groomed for positions in the Babylonian court. Another part of the portrait is that God was with them and gave them special abilities and wisdom, as he did to Joseph. Good looks were also an asset for a king. Saul (1 Sam. 9:2), David (1 Sam. 16:12), Absalom (2 Sam. 14:25), and Adonijah (1 Kings 1:6) are all described as handsome. Curiously, all of them except David were failures as kings. Their handsomeness, though, accounts for their popular appeal and the charm that got them to the throne in the first place. Psalm 45 combines motifs in its praise for the king on his wedding day. His good looks (v. 2) are the reason for both his sex appeal to his bride and his popular appeal to his subjects. People like their leaders to be young and vigorous, which is why Americans loved JFK and his "Camelot" presidency.

Beautiful women

Of course, Jackie was also a big reason for the popularity of Camelot. Women's good looks also lie behind their sex appeal in a number of Bible stories, and the language can be identical. For instance, Rachel (Gen. 29:17) is described in exactly the same terms as Joseph—beautiful of form and beautiful of appearance, or "shapely and beautiful" (JPS). And in Song of Songs (4:1, 7; 6:4), the female figure is as beautiful as the male is handsome, using the same Hebrew word. As with Joseph, the description often explains the attraction of another, specific character. Rachel's beauty is the main reason why Jacob falls in love with her, and the beauty of the female in Song of Songs is the reason she appeals to her male lover. The beauty of Abishag, the winner of the "Miss Israel" contest in 1 Kings 1:1-4, serves a specific purpose. It becomes a test of King David's virility. When he does not know her sexually despite her great beauty (v. 4), Adonijah declares himself king (v. 5). Job's three daughters were also the most beautiful in the land in his day (Job 42:15), and this was part of Job's reward for enduring the test God put him through and for speaking rightly of God (Job 42:12-17)

A woman's beauty can be dangerous in Bible stories. Not the beauty per se, but the desire that it fosters in men. Sarah's (Sarai) and Rebekah's beauty were the reason their husbands feared that the foreigners among whom they sojourned would kill them to get their wives. It was the reason that Abraham and Isaac lied and said that their wives were their sisters in the thrice-told story in Genesis 12:10-20, 20:1-18, and 26:6-11. In this case, the husbands' fears proved groundless. It was really their unreasonable fear and lack of faith that caused the problems rather than their wives' beauty or the lust of strangers. Bathsheba's beauty (2 Sam. 11:2) sparked David's desire, which led him to commit adultery and endanger his kingdom. Again, the story makes clear that her beauty was not to blame but his lack of self-control. His son Amnon suffered the same deficiency when he gave in to his lust for his beautiful half sister Tamar (2 Sam. 13:1). He raped her and then cast her off in disgust (2 Sam. 13:14-15), ruining her life (2 Sam. 13:20) and ensuring his own murder in revenge at the hands of Tamar's brother Absalom (2 Sam. 13:22-33).

Beauty can also be an asset. For three women—Rebekah (Gen. 24), Abigail (1 Sam. 25), and Esther (the book of Esther)—beauty is just one attribute in a set of attributes that each of them possessed. Rebekah is described as beautiful and a virgin (Gen. 24:16), Abigail as clever and beautiful (1 Sam. 25:3), and Esther as shapely and beautiful (Esther 2:7, using almost the same language as occurred for Joseph and Rachel). But beauty in each case was just the tip of the iceberg, the feature that attracted the attention of the other characters. The characteristics that really made them shine surface in their words and actions in the stories about them. Rebekah showed herself to be gracious and hospitable as well as a hard worker, when she gave a drink to Abraham's servant and offered to draw water for his camels (Gen. 24:12-20). Drawing water was hard work and camels can drink a lot, so this was a remarkable gesture of hospitality. Rebekah also demonstrated her faith when she agreed to return with the man to be Isaac's wife. This meant leaving her home and family for a strange land because she believed it to be God's will; it was exactly what Abraham had done. Abigail was smart and articulate. She was caught in a bad marriage with a fool. And we mean that literally; the guy's name, Nabal, means "fool" (see chapter 11, "The Clue of the Name"). His rudeness and stupidity angered David to the point that he set off to wipe out all the males in Nabal's household. Abigail, as a woman and the mistress of the house, was the only one who prevented what would have been a tragedy not only for Nabal but also for David and his aspirations to be king. She hurried to take provisions to him and used just the right mix of flattery and reason to talk David out of attacking (1 Sam. 25:18–35). In addition to being the winner of another beauty contest, Esther was courageous and intelligent. She risked her life to save her people, the Jews, from annihilation. She did this by appealing to the king with the right combination of courtly protocol and tact.

Race

Race was not as sharp a distinguishing factor in Bible times as it is today because there were no "white" people in the Bible's stories. They were all "people of color"—Mediterraneans, Middle Easterners, and Africans. Still, there are occasional hints of racial identity in physical descriptions. A great example is in Numbers 12, where Miriam and Aaron, Moses's sister and brother, respectively, complained about him because of his Cushite wife. We don't know the details of his marriage to this woman. We don't even know her name. She was evidently different from Zipporah, the wife who circumcised his son to save his life in Exodus 4:24–26. The only hint about the identity of this new wife is her description as a Cushite. Cush was the name of the country south of Egypt, basically today's Ethiopia. That meant that the woman was black. God supported Moses in the controversy and showed support by giving Miriam, who took the lead in the affair, a skin disease that temporarily made her "white as snow"—a fitting contrast to her complaint against a black woman.

Age

Age is probably the characteristic that is mentioned more than any other for biblical figures. This is because it is a common theme in Bible stories. The advanced years of Abraham and Sarah come up frequently in the stories about them as part of the point that they could not have children, which is the setting for their search for an heir. Moses gets the prize for the sweetest old age. Deuteronomy 34:7 reports that he died at 120 years of age with some of his key faculties still very much intact. Specifically, his eye was not dimmed, that is, his sight was still sharp, and "his vigor had not abated." This is a way of saying that Moses was still sexually active. Even at 120 he did not have David's problem in the bedroom. As Sgt. Harbauer, who has seniority in the department and has been here longer than anyone can remember, puts it, "There's snow on the roof, but the fire's still burning inside." The man who offered lodging to the traveling Levite and his concubine in Judges 19 is described as old (v. 16), which accounts for his powerlessness to resist his fellow citizens who came knocking at his door in the middle of the night wanting him to send out his guest so that they could abuse him. Eli's age (98) explains his feebleness and death when his chair toppled over in shock at the news that the ark had been captured (1 Sam. 4:18). The old man Barzillai, who aided David when he was on the run from Absalom (2 Sam. 19:32-38), declined the rewards offered by David when he returned victorious on the grounds that he was too old to enjoy them, and he astutely requested that they be given to his son instead. David's advanced age occasioned the contest for "Miss Israel" (1 Kings 1:1-4); the lucky winner got to spend her days and nights in the embrace of the decrepit old king, supposedly to keep him warm but really to see if he could still "rise to the occasion" sexually back before the little blue pill. Zechariah and Elizabeth, the proud parents of John the Baptist, are both old when he is born (Luke 1). They are like Abraham and Sarah. Luke also tells about senior citizens Simeon and Anna, each of whom realizes a lifelong ambition of getting to see the Messiah before their deaths (Luke 2:25-38).

There are fewer examples where youth is emphasized. David was the youngest of Jesse's sons when he was chosen to replace Saul (1 Sam. 16:1-13). His youth at this point and against Goliath in the next chapter displayed his faith in God and his success because of that faith despite his youth and inexperience. Solomon called himself a young lad in his prayer asking for divine help with the overwhelming task of ruling the people of Israel (1 Kings 3:7). The best-known passage about a character's youth again belongs to Luke. Right after Luke tells about Simeon and Anna meeting the baby Jesus, he jumps to a point in Jesus's life when he was twelve and went with his parents to Jerusalem (Luke 2:40-52). He got separated from his parents, who found him talking with the religious authorities in the temple and amazing them with his wisdom and insight, all the more because of his age.

Height

Height is a key issue in two of the Bible's best-known and most-beloved stories. The first is the story of David and Goliath. In a detail that is unique to this story, an exact measure is given for Goliath's height—six cubits and a span. A cubit was about eighteen inches (elbow to tip of middle finger), and a span was about six inches (width of the hand), making Goliath about nine and a half feet tall, way above the door frame of the closest 7-Eleven. (Check chapter 14, "The Clue of the Messy Manuscript," though, for an interesting variation on Goliath's height.) David, on the other hand, was short. There is no measure given of his height, but he was the youngest (or smallest) of his brothers (1 Sam. 17:14). The contrast was not just with Goliath but also with Saul, who is described as the tallest man in Israel (1 Sam. 9:2), though he was nowhere near as big as Goliath. David was too small to wear Saul's armor (1 Sam. 17:38–39). All of this sets up the contest in which the small boy David, armed with only his faith and a sling, faces off against the giant warrior Goliath. The contrasting descriptions of size make it the quintessential story of the victory of the underdog.

The other story about height is about Zacchaeus, in Luke 19:1–10. He was a tax collector who lived in the town of Jericho and wanted to get a look at Jesus, who was passing through. But there was a crowd around Jesus, and Zacchaeus was small of stature. So, he climbed up in a tree to get a clear view. When Jesus came by, he called Zacchaeus down and did him the honor of staying in Zacchaeus's house. Zacchaeus was happy to welcome Jesus and so pleased that Jesus would single him out, especially since he was short, that he promised to give half of his wealth to the poor and restore quadruple any amounts he had gotten by fraud. He was a small guy with a big heart.

Weight

The Bible character who gets the prize for size in terms of girth and weight is the Moabite king Eglon (Judg. 3:12–25). He was so hefty that he literally ate the sword that killed him. According to Judges 3:21-22, Ehud thrust his sword into Eglon's belly, and the fat rolled over the hilt and consumed the whole thing. Eglon's appetite also aided Ehud's escape. The inserted blade released the contents of his intestines, euphemistically referred to as "dirt" (NRSV) or "filth" (JPS). The odor from it wafted to the guards stationed outside of the chamber where Eglon and Ehud met. They reasoned that Eglon was using the bathroom, probably a common occurrence, and did not think there was any cause for alarm. Little did they realize the Bible's undisputed heavyweight champ was down for the count. Their lack of response gave Ehud time to rally Israel to victory over Moab and freedom for Israel.

Hair

Samson, as is well known, was all about his hair. He was a Nazirite or "devoted one" from birth (Judg. 13:7). The prophet Samuel was also a Nazirite from birth (1 Sam. 1:11). That meant they were not supposed to drink wine or alcohol, touch a dead body, or cut their hair (Num. 6:2-6). Before it was all over, Samson violated all those requirements. Right off the bat in Judges 14, he ate honey from a beehive that had formed in the carcass of a lion and threw a big wedding banquet, which was mainly a drinking bout. What really got him in trouble, though, was the haircut, courtesy of Delilah, who was working for the Philistines. With all his strength, Samson was no match for the doll. In one of the weirdest and sickest scenes in the Bible (Judg. 16), she asked him repeatedly what the secret of his strength was. He lied at first, and whatever he told her he found done to him—getting tied up with fresh bowstrings or new ropes or having his hair woven with a loom. It was clear that she was trying to make him lose his strength. But he apparently found this little bondage game of chicken thrilling and could not quit. When he finally told her the truth, she had his hair cut while he slept in her lap. The Philistines captured him, blinded him, and put him to work at the mill, bringing him out as entertainment on special occasions. But the Philistines didn't prove to be too bright either. Samson's hair started to grow back, and with it his strength. When they put him on display at a big religious festival in the temple of their god Dagon, he got hold of the pillars supporting the building and pushed on them until he brought down the house, killing himself and everyone else in the place. Clearly his real problem was below the scalp.

Eyes

Curiously, we have not dug up a single description of eye color in our review of Bible files. There are a few descriptions involving eyes, especially relating to blindness. Our old friend Eli was blind because of his advanced age (1 Sam. 4:15), which is why it took the oral report about the loss of the ark and the deaths of his two sons to cause him to topple over and die (vv. 16–18). The prophet Ahijah was also blind in his old age, but it didn't stop him from identifying Jeroboam's wife when she came to see him to inquire whether her son would recover from illness (1 Kings 14:1–6). To make his identification even more impressive, she was also in disguise, although the disguise was probably not intended to fool him but to keep the people of Israel from knowing that their queen was out and about making such an inquiry. The man born blind in John 9 and the blind man from Bethsaida in Mark 8 were both brought to Jesus. He healed them both, although it took him two tries in Mark 8.

The most interesting description of eyes in the Bible is for Leah (Gen. 29:17). Right before the description of Rachel as "beautiful of form and beautiful of appearance" is the statement that Leah's eyes were weak. Since Leah's eyesight seems just fine according to the stories about her, "weak" may not be the best translation here. The word can also mean "soft" or "delicate." There is obviously a contrast being drawn between Rachel and Leah, but it does not necessarily mean that Leah was ugly. Maybe her eyes were her most striking feature and made her attractive. David had beautiful eyes (1 Sam. 16:12), so maybe he and Leah had that in common. It's just that Rachel was drop-dead gorgeous.

Clothes

In criminological investigation we can sometimes make a suspect on the description of clothing when nothing else stands out. In the Bible, too, clothes can make the man. The most distinctively dressed person in the Bible has to have been Joseph. His father, Jacob, gave him a special robe with sleeves (formerly known as the "coat of many colors" or, in high school musicals, as the amazing technicolor dream coat). It was a show of favoritism for Rachel's older son. Joseph wore this garment around his brothers every chance he got. He made sure to rub their faces in it even more by telling them about his dreams where everybody and everything bowed down to him (Gen. 37:5–10). No wonder they hated him. They figured out a way to get rid of him, selling him as a slave to a group of merchants on their way to Egypt. They dipped the special robe in blood and took it to Jacob and let him draw the conclusion that his son had been killed by a wild animal. When Potiphar's wife tried to seduce him and grabbed hold of his clothes, Joseph literally ran out of them to get away, leaving them for her to use as evidence against him in support of her charge of attempted rape (Gen. 39:12–18). Then, when he was brought out of prison to see the pharaoh, Joseph changed clothes again to make himself presentable (Gen. 41:14). In a final example of how clothes helped to make this man, Pharaoh gives Joseph a new wardrobe, complete with jewelry, when he assumes the position of second-in-command in Egypt (Gen. 41:42).

We have already seen how clothes, specifically armor, played a role in the story of David and Goliath. Clothes are also very important in the story that follows directly after David's victory over Goliath. Jonathan, Saul's son and heir, loved David. He took off his clothes and gave them to David along with his armor and weapons (1 Sam. 18:4). The clothes were representative of Jonathan's position as crown prince. So, by giving them to David, Jonathan was basically handing over his kingdom. It was an act of monumental political significance, even if it did leave Jonathan in just his royal Skivvies. When you're prince, you don't have to worry about getting hauled in on an indecent exposure beef.

Another Bible figure who was identified by his clothes was Elijah. The description of him as a hairy man goes on to say that he wore a leather belt (really a waistcloth or loincloth) (2 Kings 1:8). It is also possible to take the designation "man of hair" as a reference to his clothes. Zechariah 13:4 identifies a hairy cloak or mantle as the typical dress of a prophet. That's exactly the way John the Baptist dressed according to Matthew 3:4 and Mark 1:6, which is part of the reason he becomes known as a new Elijah (Matt. 11:14; 16:14; 17:12; Mark 6:15; 8:28; 9:13; Luke 1:17; 9:8). John's mode of dress and of living made people sit up and listen to what he had to say.

Distinguishing features

The problem with clothes for ID purposes is that they can be changed. Not so with distinguishing features like a scar or a limp or a tattoo. Bible characters have such features too. As with other physical traits, they come up in the Bible according to the needs of the narrative.

A whole category of distinguishing features in the Bible falls under the label TMI—too much information. These are descriptions of people's reproductive cycles or organs. The women in Genesis—Sarah, Rebekah, Rachel, and others—dealt with the problem of "barrenness," the inability to conceive children. In Sarah's case, barrenness was compounded by her being postmenopausal, or as Genesis phrases it, "it had ceased to be with Sarah *after the manner of women*" (Gen. 18:11). So Sarah was barren from the time she and Abraham were married (Gen. 11:30), and then her periods stopped. There was no way she was having kids . . . except for divine intervention, which is the point of the story (you can read more about this in the chapter on the Clue of the Echo).

There is a hint of God's intervention already in the second of the so-called wife/sister stories in Genesis 20. Abraham and Sarah lied about their relationship, claiming they were brother and sister, because Abraham was afraid the foreigners they were living among would kill him in order to take Sarah if they knew she was his wife. In this version of the story, God revealed the truth to King Abimelech, who then gave Abraham riches to get him to leave and ordered his people not to molest Abraham or Sarah. Abraham had to pray for Abimelech and his people, the women in particular, because God had closed their wombs (Gen. 20:17-18). Control over human reproduction belonged to God. But that is pretty subtle, and Abraham and Sarah did not get the message until it happened to them. God gave them a son, Isaac (Gen. 21:1-3).

It becomes clear when you compare Sarah's case with Rebekah's that barrenness is being used as a literary theme. The whole Abraham-Sarah story is focused on Sarah's barrenness and their efforts to overcome it or work around it chapter after chapter from the end of Genesis 11 through Genesis 22. Then along come Isaac and Rebekah with the same problem, and it's dealt with in a single verse: "Isaac prayed to the LORD for his wife, *because she was barren*; and the LORD granted his prayer, and his wife Rebekah conceived" (Gen. 25:21). Problem solved. Why didn't Abraham think of that? He did, of course. But in one instance the story was built around the theme of barrenness; in the other it was just a hiccup at the start for continuity.

We've already explored how the theme of barrenness was used in the story of the competition of Rachel and Leah and their handmaids leading to the twelve tribes of Israel. It comes up again outside of Genesis as a problem common to Samson's mother (Judg. 13:2–3) and to Samuel's mother, Hannah (1 Sam. 1:2). In both cases the point is not only God's control of fertility but also the specialness of their sons. The same holds for Zechariah and Elizabeth and their son John (the Baptist) in the New Testament. Like Samson and Samuel, he is also a special dispensation overcoming Elizabeth's barrenness. As a literary theme, it's plain that barrenness displays the domination of males in shaping and telling Israel's traditions, since it's always the women who are barren, never the men. Mary's unwanted pregnancy is a variation on this theme, since God intervenes without any warning to the reader or prompting from a character (Luke 1:26–38).

The TMI complement to barrenness for men (sort of) is eunuchs. These were males who had been castrated. They were part of a political strategy developed by ancient Near Eastern rulers. They were usually boys from upper-class families who were captured in war. They were castrated as boys or infants and trained to serve in the king's court often as guardians or officials in the harem. The thinking was that because they had no families, their loyalties would be first and foremost to the king. They are easy to pick out in ancient reliefs and depictions of kings because they are the men without beards. They were so common that the Hebrew word for eunuch also came to mean "official" in general. So it's not always clear in Bible cases whether the "officials" had a pair or not.

The Bible file that has the most mentions of eunuchs is Esther. That makes sense, because the case of Esther (also called Hadassah) is all about the harem. She was chosen to replace the queen and spent a year undergoing cosmetic treatments and training to please the king, all under the direction of eunuchs. The eunuchs in Esther convey messages from the king to the harem (Esther 1:12, 15), are in charge of the harem (2:3, 14, 15), guard the entrance to the harem (2:21; 6:2), and attend the queen personally (4:4–5). These guys were sackless, but they were everywhere.

The eunuchs in the case of Jezebel's murder (2 Kings 9:32) may also have been *sin cojones*; that would fit well with the likelihood that the building or floor she was in and where she had put on her makeup (v. 30) was the harem. But it could also be that Jezebel was tossed out of the audience window of the palace and that the "eunuchs" were just officials. This goes to the question of why she got all dolled up. Was she making an official appearance, trying to seduce King Jehu, or what? The Bible leaves it up to your interpretation and imagination.

An even more interesting case is the one where Joseph was accused, convicted, and sent away for the attempted rape of Potiphar's wife. Potiphar is described as an official of Pharaoh (Gen. 37:36; 39:1). You guessed it. The word in the report may mean eunuch. You might think castration is ruled out by the fact that he was married. On the other hand, it could explain why she was so hot to trot. Maybe she wasn't getting any at home and decided to seek some attention elsewhere, and good-looking Joseph was close at hand.

Another case where being a eunuch may have had more poignant consequences was the Ethiopian in Acts 8:26–39. It's one of those tantalizing cases where you have more questions than answers about the parties involved after you read the file. This man got shortchanged, and not just because he was 0 for 2 in the balls department; he has also gotten short-shrifted by the press. He probably deserves a shout-out for being the first gentile convert to Christianity. In the book of Acts, Cornelius gets all the attention for that, because he was a Roman centurion and Luke, the author of Acts, is interested in showing that Christianity is compatible with Roman rule. But the Ethiopian beats him by two chapters. Not that the Ethiopian was suffering much. He was a high treasury official of the queen of Ethiopia (the Greek text calls him both an official and a eunuch, leaving no doubt about the state of his nether region). He was riding in a chauffeur-driven chariot. The guy was high-class all the way. He was also a very religious man. He was reading the Bible when Philip met up with him, and not just any Bible. It was his own scroll of Isaiah, which would have been very expensive in the days before the printing press. He had ridden all the way from Ethiopia to Jerusalem to worship, a distance of around fifteen hundred miles and a couple of weeks by chariot. After all that distance, he would not have been allowed to enter the temple, since Deuteronomy 23:1 states, "No one whose *testicles are crushed* or whose *penis is cut off* shall be admitted to the assembly of the LORD." When he asked Philip, "What is to prevent me from being baptized?" (Acts 8:37), that's probably what he was worried about. The notes that he was a eunuch and a black man are much more than incidentals for the story.

Other descriptions of biblical characters that deal with less private matters are no less crucial for analyzing their criminal files. Take Ehud, for example. He's the guy who assassinated the fat Moabite king, Eglon (Judg. 3:12–30). He was left-handed (v. 15). The expression used in this description means "bound/restricted in the right hand," which may mean that he was not born a southpaw but was specially trained to use his left hand. This allowed him to sneak his sword past the guards and to walk right up to King Eglon without anybody suspecting a thing. The Moabite security slogan was apparently "No sword on the left thigh, no worries." So the description of Ehud as "left-handed" is an important plot note and has the added bonus (for Israelites) of making the Moabites look stupid.

WHY THIS CLUE MATTERS

The Clue of the Physical Description is important because full physical descriptions are rare in the Bible. In fact, there isn't a single instance of one. The Bible is just not interested in what people looked like for the sake of creating an image. But it is concerned with the way specific physical features or overall good looks contribute to the plots of the stories it relates. These kinds of descriptions are often essential for understanding why characters behave as they do and why events turn out the way they do.

THE CLUE OF THE PHYSICAL DESCRIPTION CAN HELP US . . .

1. Be aware of and look for physical descriptions of biblical characters.
2. Recognize that physical descriptions are included for a specific reason.
3. Consider the role that a character's particular feature plays in a given story.
4. Look for themes in a group of stories that are built around physical features.
5. Think about the understanding of certain concepts like beauty or race in the Bible as a whole.

THE CASEBOOK

1. The beginning of Song of Songs 1:5 can be translated "I am black and beautiful" or "I am black but beautiful." What difference does the translation make? Are there hints in the context as to which is preferable? What about for the context of the reader?

2. Song of Songs contains several passages (4:1–5; 5:10–16; 6:5–7) where the lovers describe each other. Do these descriptions help you imagine what the characters looked like? How do you understand their function in the book? Just for fun, try to draw what the lovers look like based on what they say about each other. For one person's rendering, do a Google search for "drawing of Song of Solomon woman."

3. How do the contrasting descriptions of Elijah as hairy (2 Kings 1:8) and Elisha as bald (2 Kings 2:23–24) inform these two stories where the descriptions occur? Are the stories related to each other?

4. Bible narratives often point out that a young woman is a virgin (Gen. 24:16; Judg. 19:24; 2 Sam. 13:2; 1 Kings 1:2; Matt. 1:23; Luke 1:27). What role does this feature play in these stories? What does its inclusion say about concepts of gender and sexuality in ancient Israel?

3

The Clue of the

ETIOLOGY

Do you know what desynchronosis is? How about circadian dysrhythmia? (Here's a hint: they mean the same thing.) Unless you're a trained medical person or a world-class crossword puzzle solver, chances are you don't know that both terms refer to a condition that afflicts countless travelers every day. They refer to jet lag. Why is it that familiar aspects of common human experience are sometimes repackaged in such unfamiliar ways? That's a mystery we are not going to try to solve here, but we bring it up because it may have crossed your mind when you read the title of this chapter.

The word "etiology" refers to a story or a tradition that attempts to explain the origin of something. For example, the story that Peter Parker got superpowers and was transformed into Spider-Man when he was bitten by a radioactive spider is an etiology. So is the story that Harry Potter received the lightning bolt scar on his forehead from Lord Voldemort when he was fifteen months old. Etiologies try to explain why things are the way they are. That's a question people have been asking since the dawn of time, so it's not surprising that a text as old as the Bible contains more than a few of them. In fact, some parts of the Bible are etiological treasure troves that offer explanations for all sorts of things, and we'll be spending a lot of time in one of them. In this chapter we'll explore the Clue of the Etiology in order to see how origin stories function in the biblical literature and what they might tell us about its authors and audiences.

But not all etiologies are created equal. On the most basic level, they can be divided into two types: (1) those that matter and (2) those that don't. We can grasp the difference by considering a couple of examples. Here's an etiology from the book of Acts that describes the fate of Judas, the disciple of Jesus who betrayed him. "Now this man acquired a field with the reward of his wickedness; and falling headlong, he burst open in the middle and all his bowels gushed out. This became known to all the residents of Jerusalem, *so that the field was called in their language Hakeldama, that is, Field of Blood*" (Acts 1:18–19). Now read this etiological passage from the Tower of Babel episode in Genesis, which we pick up after the tower has been built.

> THE CLUE OF THE ETIOLOGY:
> a story or a tradition
> attempting to explain
> the origin of something

> The LORD came down to see the city and the tower, which mortals had built. And the LORD said, "Look, they are one people, and they have all one language; and this is only the beginning of what they will do; nothing that they propose to do will now be impossible for them. Come, let us go down, and confuse their language there, so that they will not understand one another's speech." So the LORD scattered them abroad from there over the face of all the earth, and they left off building the city. Therefore it was called Babel, because there *the LORD confused the language of all the earth; and from there the LORD scattered them abroad over the face of all the earth*. (Gen. 11:5–9)

It should be clear which etiology matters more. The first one is without doubt an etiology because it explains how the field called Hakeldama got its name. This might be an interesting tidbit to know, but in the wider scheme of things it's fairly insignificant. The etiological dimension of the Tower of Babel story, on the other hand, conveys information of more consequence that would be of greater interest to a wider audience. It too tells why a particular place got its name, but it also explains why we don't all speak the same language and why we don't all live in the same place. Those are meaty questions that matter. So both stories share a genre in that they are etiological, but they part ways when it comes to their relevance and significance.

When sussing out and examining the Clue of the Etiology, we think it is absolutely essential that you keep this distinction in mind. To make the difference as sharp as possible, we will draw upon forensic terminology to label them "first-degree etiology" and "second-degree etiology." A first-degree etiology is the type found in the Tower of Babel story, one that matters and has greater importance. Those like the one that describes the origin of the name Hakeldama are of less significance and are therefore second-degree etiologies. It is often fairly easy to determine how an etiology should be labeled, but it can sometimes take a bit of thought and elbow grease to determine the degree that it represents.

Etiologies, like crimes, have consequences, and it is those consequences that you should consider when determining which category of etiology you are dealing with. This method is precisely the opposite from that taken in many criminal investigations, in which an important determining factor is often the motivation for the crime rather than its outcome. Take murder, for example. The outcome of every murder is the same, so the degree of the charge against the guilty party is determined by motive rather than by the consequences of the action. A first-degree murder charge implies intent to kill with premeditation and deliberation, while a second-degree murder is a non-premeditated killing.

It's the reverse with etiologies. Every etiology is premeditated and has the same motive—to explain the origin of something—but the outcome varies. Continuing with the crime metaphor, the reader is the "victim" of an etiology, and the main thing to keep in mind is the impact or effect the etiology has on the victim. In a second-degree etiology, the impact is relatively inconsequential since the information might be useful to the reader in some sense but can also be simply entertaining, trivial, or even silly. First-degree etiologies, on the other hand, have the potential to be transformative since they can affect the reader's ideas and beliefs and could have consequences with long-term implications. A second-degree etiology tells you something about the world, like that the name Hakeldama is connected to the death of Judas. But a first-degree etiology can reorient your understanding of the world by explaining why people don't all live in the same place or speak the same language. With this distinction in mind, a useful rule of thumb is the following: When confronted with an etiology, determine its possible consequences; that will tell you if it's a first-degree or second-degree type.

The Clue of the Etiology has much in common with the Clue of the Intrusive Narrator. Many of the intrusive narrator's comments are in fact etiologies, as his voice suddenly appears to inform the reader about the origin of a name, place, or practice. In addition, etiologies make their presence known the same way the intrusive narrator does, by breaking the frame of the narrative to provide information that does not add to the plot of the story. What this means is that the same passage can sometimes be examined through the lens of different clues. This is not unlike your usual crime scene, where evidence of different types like blood, DNA, and fingerprints can all be studied as the investigator tries to determine exactly what happened. At the same time, there is a significant difference between this clue and all the other clues discussed in this book—the Clue of the Etiology is limited almost exclusively to the Hebrew Bible. In fact, the passage in Acts that explains the origin of the name Hakeldama and its parallel tradition in Matthew's Gospel are rare examples of etiologies in the New Testament.

Okay, let's take it from the top again

Not only are etiologies virtually limited to the Hebrew Bible, they also pop up in only certain sections of it. Because they are typically present in stories, they're found primarily in the narrative portions of the text. And even then, groups of etiologies tend to congregate in a limited number of narratives in the Hebrew Bible. In this chapter we limit our investigation to Genesis, the Bible's first book, because it is a hotbed of etiological activity. This shouldn't be too surprising, because Genesis is all about origins—of humanity at large, and of the people who would go on to become the Israelites—and etiologies are the perfect means by which to create and establish an identity. Just ask Spider-Man.

Let there be etiologies, and let them be fruitful and multiply

The first three chapters of Genesis are commonly referred to as the creation stories. Beginning in the seventeenth century, some early European Bible cops did some pretty impressive detective work of their own to make a strong case for the presence of two separate stories in those opening chapters. While some aspects of their work have been

44

challenged in the intervening years, their basic premise has held up to scrutiny, and it is generally agreed that there are indeed two stories in Genesis 1–3.

The first story is found in Genesis 1:1–2:4a, and it recounts how God created everything in six days and then rested on the seventh. It is an extremely orderly account that follows a clear pattern, as all the elements of creation are brought into being one by one—day, night, sky, earth, vegetation, sun, moon, fish, birds, animals, and finally human beings. Given the nature of God's work, there's no doubt that this story is etiological, but is it a first-degree or a second-degree etiology? To answer that question we need to consider the outcome and the effect the story has on the reader/victim. Does it simply inform the reader by imparting information, or does it have the potential to transform the reader's way of thinking?

At first glance, the story seems simply to provide information to the reader about how the world came about, as it describes a series of creative acts by God that brought the various parts of creation into existence. It is therefore a second-degree etiology that merely informs. Case closed. But closer examination reveals that the story is doing more than just informing, because it is also making the claim that God is the one responsible for all that exists. That theological message is a crucial element of the text because it causes the reader to reflect on the nature of the world and the reasons for its existence, and that aspect of the story moves it into the first-degree category.

Implicating yourself

Before we go any further, we need to address the critical difference between "the reader" as an abstract notion and the reality of you as an actual flesh-and-blood reader. This is an important distinction in the field of literary studies, where the former is sometimes referred to as the "implied reader." This is a hypothetical figure the author has in mind when writing a story, a figure who will accept certain things that the real reader would normally never accept. Let's take the tale of "Little Red Riding Hood" as an example. The implied reader of that story is at home in a world in which wolves can talk, little girls don't recognize their own grandmothers, and people can survive inside the belly of an animal that has eaten them. These are things that are accepted by the implied reader but are usually rejected as absurd by real readers. Nonetheless, real readers often put aside their true beliefs and temporarily embrace the beliefs of the implied reader in order to enter into the world of the story.

When investigating an etiology, it is vitally important that you keep in mind the distinction between the implied reader and yourself as a reader. You have to consider the text from the perspective of the implied reader, not your own perspective. The reason will become apparent if we return to the first creation story. We saw that it should be considered a first-degree etiology because of its theological point that God created the world. This is an idea that you, as an actual reader, might be unable to accept for any number of reasons—maybe you don't read the Bible literally, or it doesn't reflect your understanding of God and the world, or you don't believe in God. Those are all perfectly valid views, but they shouldn't influence how you categorize an etiology. That decision is about the implied reader, not about you. The question you need to ask is this: "Is this etiology trying to transform, rather than simply inform, the implied reader?" If the answer to that question is yes, then it's a first-degree etiology, even if it endorses the wackiest idea you've ever heard. In detective work, we sometimes have to put our own views aside and go wherever the clues take us.

A couple of sections of the first creation story really underscore its first-degree status. This can be seen in the way humanity's role in the world is described by God. "Then God said, 'Let us make humankind in our image, according to our likeness; and *let them have dominion* over the fish of the sea, and over the birds of the air, and over the cattle, and over all the wild animals of the earth, and over every creeping thing that creeps upon the earth'" (1:26). The italicized words function as an etiology to explain why humanity has a special status vis-à-vis other creatures. According to this text, people have a certain authority or responsibility in relation to their fellow beings.

The end of the first story has also been influential in shaping beliefs and practices, particularly within the Jewish community. After six whirlwind days of nonstop action, God decides to take a breather, and the seventh day is then given special status in much the same way that humanity was singled out earlier. "And on the seventh day God finished the work that he had done, and he rested on the seventh day from all the work that he had done. *So God blessed the seventh day and hallowed it*, because on it God rested from all the work that he had done in creation"

(2:2-3). This passage is an etiology that explains why the Sabbath should be a day of rest. Notice what a powerful rhetorical role this text plays in legitimizing the practice of observing the Sabbath. According to the story, the Sabbath observance is something that God wove into the fabric of creation at the beginning of time that should be recognized and celebrated in perpetuity.

The second creation account is in Genesis 2:4b-3:24, and it relates the famous garden of Eden story. For the etiology hunter, the passage is a gold mine, because it's overflowing with samples of both the first-degree and the second-degree varieties. We'll begin with the latter. While questioning the first one we come across, we finally get the answer to a question that has kept us up at night—why are there creatures known as the "spiny lumpsucker," the "mustached puffbird," and the "screaming hairy armadillo"? Such animal names do exist, and you can blame Adam. "So out of the ground the LORD God formed every animal of the field and every bird of the air, and brought them to the man to see what he would call them; and *whatever the man called every living creature, that was its name*" (Gen. 2:19). The garden story also provides us with two reasons why we wear clothes. The first couple initially take matters into their own hands to insure their private parts stay that way. "Then the eyes of both were opened, and they knew that they were naked; and *they sewed fig leaves together and made loincloths for themselves*" (3:7). A little later on God deems a wardrobe upgrade to be in order. "And *the LORD God made garments of skins for the man and for his wife*, and clothed them" (3:21). An additional second-degree etiology can be seen one verse earlier, with the naming of the first woman. "The man named his wife Eve, *because she was the mother of all living*" (3:20). While each of these origin stories is informative and entertaining in its own way, the stories do not rise to the level of first-degree etiologies because they don't explain things of significance that might have an impact on how one views the world. Of course, the star-nosed mole and the fried egg jellyfish might beg to differ.

One of the first-degree etiologies also explains how Adam refers to Eve. This time, though, he identifies her in a different way.

Then the man said,
    "This at last is bone of my bones
      and flesh of my flesh;

47

this one shall be called Woman,
for out of Man this one was taken." (2:23)

The two passages naming Eve have the same purpose: each offers an explanation for why the first woman is referred to in a certain way. The reason why they're the same but different has to do with the words "Eve" and "woman." The former is a personal name, and so when it's used in relation to Adam's mate, it refers to a particular individual. But the term "woman" describes a category that comprises more than half the human beings on the planet (in the world of the story, it's exactly one-half). When she is defined by that word, she is no longer just Adam's mate but she personifies and represents all women. This is what moves the etiology into first-degree status, particularly when we note the basis for the designation—she is called woman because she was taken from man. The issue of gender relations is now front and center because it isn't the relationship between Adam and Eve that is being highlighted but that between men and women. This etiology therefore has the potential to influence the reader's attitudes and views regarding issues like how men and women should relate with one another, the power dynamics between them, hierarchy, and patriarchy.

The passage in which Adam refers to Eve as "woman" is interesting for another reason—it is followed immediately by another etiology that, as its first word indicates, is based upon it. "*Therefore* a man leaves his father and his mother and clings to his wife, *and they become one flesh*" (2:24). This type of causal relationship is quite rare among etiologies, and as far as we can tell, this is the only occurrence of it in the Bible. The italicized "therefore" underscores the connection between the two, and the second (but not second-degree) etiology goes on to explain the origin of cohabitation. It is likely as well that the reference to their becoming one flesh is an etiology for why people engage in sexual relations.

As the garden story winds down, God confronts the first couple with the serpent nearby and gives a punishment to each of them that will affect their lives moving forward. These sanctions are all presented in etiological form, but the string of etiologies actually extends beyond them, because immediately after this are found the passages in which Adam names Eve (3:20) and God clothes the couple (3:21). That's a remarkable run of five consecutive origin stories.

The three punishments directed at the serpent, Eve, and Adam are sometimes referred to as curses, but that's really a misnomer since God uses the word "curse" only when speaking to the serpent (although it is used in reference to the ground when God speaks to the man). The deity addresses the serpent first and gives him a double punishment that includes eating dust while he crawls on his belly and being an enemy of the woman and her offspring (3:14–15). The first of these is an obvious etiology meant to solve the mystery of why snakes do not have legs. Eve (called "the woman" here) is punished with *labor pains during childbirth* (3:16). It is unclear if Adam and Eve were originally created to procreate or if giving birth becomes part of humanity only at this point, but this verse explains why it will be a painful experience. Finally, Adam ("the man") is told that he will *earn his keep by working the land, but it will be difficult and painful for him* (3:17–19).

Are these first-degree or second-degree etiologies? We think the answer is both. For the most part, they fall into the second-degree category because they mainly offer explanations for the common everyday occurrences of snakes crawling, women giving birth in pain, and men sweating as they work. Those are facts of life about which there isn't much to puzzle over. But if we look more closely at God's words to the woman, things become more complicated.

> "*I will greatly increase your pangs in childbearing;*
>   in pain you shall bring forth children,
> yet *your desire shall be for your husband,*
>   *and he shall rule over you.*"

The first half of the verse regarding childbirth looks like a standard second-degree etiology, but the second half has a first-degree feel to it. The references to the woman desiring her husband and his ruling over her are open to interpretation, and their meaning is not as clear as the universal experience of labor pains. They give us pause and cause us to reflect on their significance, and so they have the potential to change how we view the world and ourselves. That is precisely what a first-degree etiology does, and so that's why this triple etiology has double degrees.

Riding out the storm

When on the lookout for an etiology, you have to be willing to play the waiting game and not force things. That's a lesson learned from the story of Noah and the flood. You spend a lot of time twiddling your thumbs through much of it, but when his ship finally comes in, the payoff is worth it.

The rain begins to fall in chapter 6 of Genesis, but the etiologies don't start flowing until the end of the story in chapter 9. By that time, you've spent the better part of four chapters and who knows how many days stuck on a boat that's 300 cubits long, 50 cubits wide, and 30 cubits high. (For you landlubbers, that's about 450 feet by 75 feet by 45 feet.)

You have come aboard as a stowaway because you were teased with an etiology just before the first raindrop fell, and you think there might be more where that came from. The prelude to the flood story in Genesis 6:1-3 is an odd little episode that describes how the sons of God were attracted to human women and began to take them as their wives. God is not pleased with this development and issues an edict that is actually an etiology in disguise meant to explain why our days on this earth are numbered, even if the figure quoted is somewhat inflated. "Then the LORD said, 'My spirit shall not abide in mortals forever, for they are flesh; *their days shall be one hundred twenty years*'" (Gen. 6:3). This story is probably meant to be an example of the wickedness of humanity that is the cause of the flood that will destroy most of it.

The etiologies keep on coming after Noah is back on dry land. After Noah leaves the ark, God delivers a lengthy speech, the most significant etiological aspect of which is the establishment of a covenant between the deity and all creatures. "Then God said to Noah and to his sons with him, 'As for me, *I am establishing my covenant* with you and your descendants after you, and with every living creature that is with you, the birds, the domestic animals, and every animal of the earth with you, as many as came out of the ark'" (Gen. 9:8-10). This is a first-degree etiology that explains the origin of the concept of covenant and redefines the relationship that God has with humanity and the rest of creation. This is followed by another etiology, a second-degree one, clarifying how one of nature's more pleasant celestial phenomena came to be. "God said, 'This is the sign of the covenant that I make between me and you and every living creature that is with you, for all future generations: *I have set my bow in the clouds*, and it shall be a sign of the covenant between me and the earth'" (9:12-13).

Noah's three sons play supporting roles in some of the etiologies in this chapter, in ways both good and bad. They are identified as the progenitors responsible for repopulating the earth after the flood, and lengthy lists of their descendants can be found in the tenth chapter of Genesis. "The sons of Noah who went out of the ark were Shem, Ham, and Japheth. Ham was the father of Canaan. These three were the sons of Noah; and *from these the whole earth was peopled*" (9:18–19). The singling out of Ham and his son Canaan is a curious feature of this passage, but it is actually setting the stage for an additional etiology of some importance that is itself dependent upon yet another etiology, this one of the second degree. That latter origin story is a favorite Bible passage of oenophiles everywhere. "Noah, a man of the soil, was *the first to plant a vineyard*" (9:20). There is more than a little irony in describing someone who spends almost his entire biblical career on the water as "a man of the soil."

That tradition explaining the origin of wine sets up another etiology of a more serious nature that has had a profound impact in the history of biblical interpretation and therefore well deserves its first-degree status. The world's first vineyard leads, perhaps predictably, to the world's first hangover, and while Noah is sleeping off the effects of the alcohol, his son Ham sees him lying naked in his tent. When he tells his two brothers about what he has seen, they show respect by averting their eyes and covering their father's nakedness. When Noah awakes, he says this to his sons:

> "Cursed be Canaan;
> *lowest of slaves shall he be to his brothers.*"

He also says,

> "Blessed by the LORD my God be Shem;
> *and let Canaan be his slave.*
> May God make space for Japheth,
> and let him live in the tents of Shem;
> *and let Canaan be his slave.*"

These are Noah's only words in the story, making him the one character in the Bible who speaks only in etiologies. Each name in this passage actually refers to a particular set of people. The descendant/group that bears the brunt of Noah's anger is Ham's son Canaan, who is cursed and will be a slave to the groups associated with the other two brothers. Canaan is also the name of the area that, according to the biblical story, contained the land that was promised to the Israelites by God, and the book of Joshua describes how they entered that land and defeated the Canaanites living there. Noah's words serve as an etiology meant to explain why the Israelites, who were of the line of Shem, were able to dominate the inhabitants of Canaan and, in the language of the text, "enslave" them.

This etiology, commonly called "the curse of Ham," has sometimes been interpreted in deeply troubling ways. Noah's son Ham is typically identified as the ancestor of black-skinned people, and his father's words against his offspring have been cited on occasion to justify racist views. Such interpretations should be denounced as a complete misrepresentation of what the text means. This is an important reminder about the power of biblical etiologies and the need to be ever mindful of the ways that some of them can be misused to harm people.

Pillars of the community

Among the other etiologies in Genesis are explanations of place-names, like this one associated with Abraham: "Therefore that place was called Beer-sheba; *because there both of them swore an oath*" (Gen. 21:31), and another that is part of the Jacob story: "But Jacob journeyed to Succoth, and built himself a house, and made booths for his cattle; *therefore the place is called Succoth*" (33:17). An additional one associated with Jacob explains why his twin brother Esau was also known by another name. "Once when Jacob was cooking a stew, Esau came in from the field, and he was famished. Esau said to Jacob, 'Let me eat some of that red stuff, for I am famished!' *(Therefore he was called Edom.)*" (25:29-30).

These are all by-the-book etiologies that are easy to spot, but rookie biblical sleuths sometimes have a little trouble sniffing out a few others in this part of Genesis that are more subtle. One case that often stumps newbies describes the tragic demise of Lot's wife. Lot and his family flee the area as the cities of Sodom and Gomorrah are being destroyed, but his wife pays the ultimate price for not heeding an angelic order to gaze only straight ahead. "But Lot's wife, behind him, looked back, and *she became a pillar of salt*" (Gen. 19:26). Nothing in this verse suggests it's an etiology unless you know that the area was full of unusual salt formations due to its proximity to the Dead Sea. It is an origin story that explains why one of them had the shape of a person, and to this day there's a sign that says "Lot's wife" on the side of the road along the Dead Sea near a human-shaped rock.

Immediately after this, Lot and his daughters head to the hills to escape the conflagration. Thinking they are the only people left alive, the two daughters devise a plan to continue the human race by getting their father drunk and having sexual relations with him. On the surface level, the story closes in a way that suggests it's a standard etiology meant to explain the origins of two groups of people. "The firstborn bore a son, and named him Moab; *he is the ancestor of the Moabites to this day*. The younger also bore a son and named him Ben-ammi; *he is the ancestor of the Ammonites to this day*" (Gen. 19:37-38). The Moabites and Ammonites were neighboring peoples with whom the Israelites regularly found themselves at odds, and this story is obviously a put-down meant to call attention to their questionable (i.e., incestuous) beginnings. But there's more going on here than meets the eye. These names are loaded with meaning—"Moab" is very close to a Hebrew phrase that means "from father," and "Ben-ammi" translates as "son of my people." So the insult on the neighbors is compounded by giving them names that are constant reminders of their embarrassing origins.

In Jacob's story readers have one of the Bible's great etiologies staring them right in the face, and many don't even realize it, so it's a fitting one to close this investigation on. Like Noah's sons, Jacob represents a large group of people. The fact that he goes by an alias says it all. Twice Jacob is told that he will now be known as "Israel" (Gen. 32:28; 35:10), and his name is often used in the Hebrew Bible to refer to the Israelite people. Just as in the Bible as a whole, where a high concentration of etiologies is found in its first book of Genesis, so too in the Jacob story (Gen. 25-35) the etiological dimension is most evident in its early chapters. This can be seen in the story involving Jacob's brother, Esau, a.k.a. Edom. Edom was also a place-name for the region just south of the Dead Sea that shared a border with Israel. At times the Israelites and the Edomites had a rocky relationship, and Jacob/Israel and Esau/Edom are presented in the Bible as twins who don't get along and are rivals.

The die is cast even before the brothers arrive on the scene. They fight with one another while *in utero*, and during her pregnancy their mother receives a message from God informing her about the etiological significance of her future offspring.

And the LORD said to her,

> "*Two nations are in your womb,*
> *and two peoples born of you shall be divided;*
> *the one shall be stronger than the other,*
> *the elder shall serve the younger.*" (Gen. 25:23)

Esau/Edom is that older son, and the story goes on to explain how the oracle comes to pass as foolish Esau sells his birthright to Jacob for a mere bowl of stew (25:29-34) and then clever Jacob (with the help of his mother, Rebekah) tricks their father and receives the blessing that was rightfully Esau's (27:1-40). Although the story is ostensibly about the troubled relationship between two brothers, it is actually a first-degree etiology meant to explain how the Israelites were able to overcome the obstacles in their way to assume a position of authority over their neighbors.

WHY THIS CLUE MATTERS

We have studied this clue from one angle throughout the entire chapter with our division of etiologies into two groups based on their content—those that matter (first-degree ones) and those that don't (second-degree ones). Quite honestly, some of those in the second-degree category really don't matter much at all because what they inform us about really isn't that significant. But here we should also consider things from a completely different angle, because the question isn't only "Does an *etiology* matter?" but also "Does the *clue* matter?" In other words, does the fact that there are etiologies in the Bible matter? Our answer is a clear affirmative, because etiologies open up and expose important aspects of the text that would otherwise be easily missed or ignored.

THE CLUE OF THE ETIOLOGY CAN HELP US . . .

1. Remember that the Bible is a book concerned with origins.
2. See the Bible as something other than a historical account of events.
3. Be attentive to the presence of wordplay in the Bible.

4. Think about how people in the ancient world saw things and tried to explain them.
5. Recognize that the Bible gives legitimacy to certain views, beliefs, and practices.
6. Know that the Bible is sometimes misinterpreted to give legitimacy to certain views, beliefs, and practices.

THE CASEBOOK

Find the Clue of the Etiology in the following chapters, and determine whether each is first-degree or second-degree:

Genesis 4
Genesis 16
Genesis 17
Genesis 35
Exodus 12
Exodus 13
Exodus 17
Exodus 27
Exodus 28
Deuteronomy 10
Joshua 5
Joshua 6
Joshua 7
Joshua 9
Joshua 10
Judges 15

4

The Clue of the

WEIRD SOCIAL CUSTOM

You never know what you'll learn in the detective business, especially in a city like this one with lots of ethnic neighborhoods. Just last week a call came in about domestic abuse. A woman said she saw her neighbor on the other side of the train tracks beating his wife with a tree branch. It turned out to be an old Czech custom that shows up around Easter. Men lightly spank women with braided willow branches in order to ensure fertility. This was a new one on us, but we've seen plenty of others. Every neighborhood, every group of people has its own special customs and taboos revolving around greetings, eye contact, dress, meals, and special occasions like weddings and holidays:

> The French kiss each other instead of shaking hands.
> Venezuelans never arrive anywhere on time—it's considered rude.
> Egyptians think it offensive to salt food in someone else's home. (The captain's wife likes that one; she's always telling him to watch his blood pressure.)
> Arabs won't use their left hands or show you the bottoms of their shoes unless they really dislike you.
> Malaysians point with their thumbs or their lips but not their index fingers.
> People from Thailand don't cross their legs in public places.
> Scots hold a "blackening" ceremony for prospective brides where they pelt them with rotten fruit and vegetables, eggs and milk,

etc., as a way of getting rid of all of life's problems up front so they'll have smooth sailing in the marriage.

If you don't get married in Denmark by the time you're twenty-five, there's a good chance that your friends will shower you with cinnamon.

Greeks throw children's baby teeth from balconies for luck instead of putting them under a pillow.

A social custom is only weird if you're not used to it. None of these customs is any stranger than letting a rodent forecast the weather. But no one tries to arrest the people in Punxsutawney, PA, or have them committed. There's a reason for every custom, even if it's been long forgotten by the people who observe it and only gets remembered during trivia night at Applebee's, which, come to think of it, is a weird custom in itself.

Social customs are nothing new to those of us who work the Bible Division. We love them, because they are great clues to what is going on in the text. And they are usually easily deduced from the circumstances of a story. The Clue of the Weird Social Custom describes an action or practice that a modern reader would find bizarre or very unusual. Let's crack open some case files about social customs in the Bible and see what we can learn. For convenience, we're dividing them into three categories: customs that are generally recognized as such, customs that are less well known, and supposed customs that did not actually exist and are false leads.

THE CLUE OF THE WEIRD SOCIAL CUSTOM: an action or practice that a modern reader would find bizarre or unusual

What's so weird about that?

Readers have become so familiar with some social customs in the Bible that they barely recognize that anything out of the ordinary is being perpetrated. It's like deciding to have a piñata at your kid's birthday party. You might know it's originally a Mexican custom, but you get one because the neighbor kid two doors down had one at his party last month and it seemed like a cheap and easy way to keep a bunch of ten-year-olds entertained for an hour.

Fit for a king

An example of a run-of-the-mill social custom in the Bible is anointing. Nobody we know practices it today, but everyone knows what it is—a way of designating an individual for a leadership role, usually as king or priest. It was performed by pouring or smearing a special mixture of olive oil and spices on the head of the chosen person. It was usually a prophet who did the honors, at least for kings:

> Samuel anointed Saul (1 Sam. 10:1).
> Samuel anointed David (1 Sam. 16:1–13).
> Nathan anointed Solomon (1 Kings 1:32–40).
> A nameless prophet was sent by Elisha to anoint Jehu (2 Kings 9:1–6).

When we elected Lt. La Rosa captain of the precinct softball team, we poured beer over his head. That was a kind of anointing, so maybe we do still practice it, even if we're not prophets and La Rosa is no king, or even much of a shortstop for that matter.

The whole institution of monarchy is a social custom. Most of us in the US of A have never been subjects of a king, unless you're a huge Elvis fan. We have presidents, governors, and mayors instead. They may think they're kings and act like kings, but our system of government is different. Even so, the language of religious institutions is chock-full of kingly terminology. Jews, Christians, and Muslims talk about God as king and lord and themselves as subjects, about the King of kings, the kingdom of God, and the kingdom of heaven. God is envisioned sitting on a throne, issuing edicts and surrounded by messengers (also translated as "angels") to carry the proclamations to humans.

The king can be known by certain titles—the crown, the throne, the palace. In the Bible, one such title is "anointed." It's not hard to guess why. That title is especially common for Saul and David (1 Sam. 2:10, 35; 12:3, 5; 16:6; 24:6, 10; 26:9, 11, 16, 23; 2 Sam. 1:14, 16; 19:21; 22:51; 23:1). The Hebrew word for "anointed" is *messiah* (pronounced *mesh-she-ach*, where the final *h* is like clearing your throat). The word was translated into Greek as *christos*, which is where we get the English word "Christ."

Jesus of Nazareth was and is called the Messiah or Christ by his followers, who understand him to be David's descendant who, like David, would establish God's kingdom on earth. Not bad for an investigation that started with the humdrum clue of a little oil dabbed on to someone's head.

From head to toe

Another social custom that is quite well known to Bible beat cops is feet washing. For instance, their daily reports mention four cases of feet washing in Genesis:

Abraham greets strangers, who turn out to be God and two angels (Gen. 18:4).
Lot invites the two angels to his house for the night (Gen. 19:2).
Laban hosts Abraham's servant, who has come in search of a wife for Isaac (Gen. 24:32).
Joseph, as the second in command of Egypt, brings his unsuspecting brothers into his house (Gen. 43:24).

In each case the visitors are invited to take a load off and get the Bible equivalent of a pedicure. It's pretty easy to guess from these examples how this custom got started and why it continued. Giving people water to wash their feet was a way of welcoming them into your home. It was a courtesy that provided refreshment from the dust of the road when travel was by foot and people wore sandals.

In the notorious Case of the Hostile Host (also known as the Case of the Contrite Concubine and the Case of the Spurned Savior) in Luke 7:44, Jesus points out the rudeness of his host, a Pharisee named Simon, in not offering him water to wash his feet. A woman off the street who is called a "sinner" steps in and takes care of this by washing Jesus's feet herself. She illustrates another dimension of this custom—it's a task that could be relegated to a slave. Back in 1 Samuel 25:41, Abigail accepts David's marriage proposal by bowing down before him and calling herself a slave to wash his servants' feet, in other words the least of his servants. (Before any of you single boys in blue gets the idea that this is how married life works, you should know that Abigail was a very smart cookie who had just talked David out of whacking a whole gang of people because he was mad at their boss. Managing David was a piece of cake for her.)

In the Gospel of John Jesus washes his disciples' feet. He tells them, "Do you know what I have done to you? You call me Teacher and Lord—and you are right, for that is what I am. So if I, your Lord and Teacher, have washed your feet, you also ought to wash one another's feet. For I have set you an example, that you also should do as I have done to you" (John 13:12-15). Jesus switches social roles with his followers and performs a custom that normally fell to those on the lowest rung of the social ladder, all to teach them the importance of serving one another.

(Super sleuths' warning: Don't confuse the clue of feet washing with the Clue of the Hidden Meaning, the one about the euphemism that involves "feet." That could lead to all kinds of wild goose chases. Remember Freud's wise words [even if he didn't actually write them]: "Sometimes a cigar is just a cigar.")

And in-between

More than a few of the city's finest are Jews, and we've all been invited to bar mitzvahs and bat mitzvahs and even a bris or two, so everyone on the force knows what circumcision is. There's an ongoing debate between two of our colleagues about how it began and what it represents. Both of them are women and both are Jewish. Carey on the New Testament desk claims it's a religious symbol of the Jews as God's chosen people that they practice because it's commanded of them. But Diane, the department sketch artist, calls it a rite of passage and says that lots of societies and cultures practice it. We did a little investigating on our own time to get to the bottom of this mystery. Turns out they may both be right.

First off, in Genesis God tells Abraham, "This is my covenant, which you shall keep, between me and you and your offspring after you: Every male among you shall be *circumcised*. You shall circumcise the flesh of your foreskins, and it shall be a sign of the covenant between me and you. Throughout your generations every male among you shall be circumcised when he is eight days old, including the slave born in your house and the one bought with your money from any foreigner who is not of your offspring" (Gen. 17:10-12). So there is a command from God that Abraham's descendants should follow the ritual of circumcision as a sign of God's promise. Score one for Carey's team.

But that may not be all there is to the story. We dug up a strange little cold case in Exodus that adds an interesting wrinkle. It's an attempted murder beef that was dismissed for lack of evidence. Zipporah, Moses's wife—or one of them anyway, the guy's record is sketchy—accused God of trying to kill either Moses himself or their son. The notes just say "him," so we're not sure who the alleged victim was. According to the witness's testimony—and there's only one witness—Zipporah kept this from happening by circumcising her newborn son. She cut off her son's foreskin and touched "his" feet with it. Here again, it's not certain whose feet get touched. They could be Moses's feet or the baby's. At that point, Zipporah stated, "You are a bridegroom of blood to me. . . . A bridegroom of blood by circumcision" (Exod. 4:25-26). Since she used the word "bridegroom," we think she was talking to Moses.

Here's what we've been able to piece together. It's just a theory, mind you, but we think that the parties involved may be hiding something. What if Diane is correct and circumcision was originally a rite of passage among the ancient Israelites like it is in other cultures. Then, it would have been practiced on adolescents when they became of marriageable age. Later on, the practice came to be applied to infants instead of adolescents as a marker of ethnic and then religious identity, as in God's command to Abraham. At some point, the story told by Zipporah started circulating to explain the change from circumcising adults to circumcising babies. It's a little complicated, and we're usually not into conspiracy theories. But the evidence is pretty tantalizing, even if the bags holding it are few and far between. It's staying in the unsolved file for now, but if you're interested in doing some follow-up, even if it's just to prove us wrong, you can check out the chapter on the Clue of the Hidden Meaning.

Weird family values

The second category in our investigation of social customs concerns some that are a little less known than anointing, feet washing, and circumcision. Maybe that's because some of the main ones in this category have to do with sex and marriage. This is where the intersection of crime fighting and social customs gets freaky and we call in the vice squad.

Heir apparent

A couple of years ago there were rumors about a new group of polygamists who were setting up house(s)keeping downtown. You can peruse
the case file in Genesis 16. The patriarch of the group was a guy named
Abram (a.k.a. Abraham). His first wife's name was Sarai (a.k.a. Sarah).
Word on the street was that Abe had another wife on the side, an Egyptian dish named Hagar (no alias, that's how you could tell she wasn't
from the neighborhood). This was not your usual affair. You may be
a low-down dirty dog to have an affair, but you can't get tossed in the
slammer for it.

Allegedly, these two women knew about each other; Hagar even had
a kid with the guy. We notified Vice; they checked it out. There were two
women, all right, and by the time Vice got involved there were two families, because Sarai had had a kid of her own. They arrested the whole
kit and caboodle of them and were ready to throw the book at Abe. But
the case got dismissed on a technicality. The defense argued that it was
all a big misunderstanding. Abe and Sarai had been married for quite
a while without having any kids. Having children was very, very, very
important to Abe, who had been given some promise about being the
father of a nation, like George Washington on steroids. Abe was going
to have innumerable descendants, even more than the stars in the sky.
Problem was, Sarai was having trouble getting knocked up, and neither
of them was getting any younger. Get this—*she* came up with the idea
of getting Abe to sleep with her maid Hagar and to father a child with
her. The child would have been considered Abe and Sarai's.

The key pieces of evidence trotted out by the defense were marriage treaties from ancient Mesopotamia. These treaties specified that it
was the bride's responsibility to provide an heir for her husband. If she
couldn't get the job done herself, she was obligated to provide a surrogate in the form of her maid. Hagar was like a servant or employee, but
she was also supposed to serve as a surrogate mother if need be. Abe and
Hagar were never officially married in the same way Abe and Sarai were.
The judge ruled in favor of the defense and said that the police had failed
to take into account a different social custom. The members of Vice were
not too pleased; they had put a lot of time into the case, and it gave them a
black eye. The multiple-mom family didn't last long. Since Sarai had her
own son now, she didn't need Hagar or her kid any longer. She convinced
Abe to get rid of them. He wasn't supposed to be able to do that according

to those same documents from Mesopotamia. Vice followed up with a report to Family Services, but they didn't want to touch the case after all the bad publicity. Besides, Hagar and son were long gone by that time.

Lev-her-what?

The Case of the Presumed Polygamist (called the Case of the Handmaid's Tail in some dark corners of the precinct), the Abram-Sarai-Hagar file, taught Vice an important lesson—always consider social customs when you're investigating a Bible mystery. It's a good thing, too, because not long after that one they ran into another case of purported polygamists that really set their nightsticks to twirling. Even long-term Vice dicks were amazed at the kinkiness of this one. They were suspicious from their first briefing when they learned that the target of the investigation was a guy named Judah, who was Abe's great-grandson. We'll let the report in the case file take it from there:

> Subject: Judah ben-Jacob. Wife: Bat-Shua. Three sons: Er, Onan, Shelah. Er married Tamar. Er deceased. (Principals report, "The Lord considered Er wicked and the Lord killed Er.") Judah ordered Onan to have sex with Tamar and produce a child to be raised as if it were Er's. Onan pretended to go along, but actually "spilled his semen on the ground" and refused to complete the act with his sister-in-law. Onan deceased. (Principals: "So the Lord killed him too.") On Judah's orders, Tamar returned to her father's house to live. She was supposed to marry son #3, Shelah, when he grew up. But Judah did not follow through. Subject reports he was afraid of losing Shelah like he lost Er and Onan. Bat-Shua deceased. Judah took a business trip. Tamar found out about the trip. Tamar dressed up in disguise as a hooker. Tamar located and seduced Judah. Tamar turned up pregnant. Judah wanted her burned alive. Tamar claimed Judah was the father and produced personal effects of his as proof. Judah canceled burning. Judah admitted he was in the wrong. Tamar had twin boys. (Based on Gen. 38)

This time Vice didn't jump to any conclusions, in spite of the weirdness of the situation. They discovered that this was another instance where a social custom was involved. It didn't take much digging to come to that conclusion, because it's spelled out in Deuteronomy: "When brothers reside together, and one of them dies and has no son, the wife of the deceased shall not be married outside the family to a stranger. Her husband's brother shall go in to her, taking her in marriage, and performing the duty of a husband's brother to her, and the firstborn whom she bears shall succeed to the name of the deceased brother, so that his name may not be blotted out of Israel" (Deut. 25:5–6).

The social custom even has a name. It's called "levirate marriage" (from Latin *levir*, for brother-in-law). Forensics thinks it got started as a kind of ancient welfare program, a way to take care of widows when there weren't opportunities for them to go out and get jobs, like today. It may also have been a way of keeping property within a family or clan or tribe. And it may also have been a means of preserving the memory of the dead guy, so he could be memorialized with food offerings in the underworld.

The text in Deuteronomy continues:

> But if the man has no desire to marry his brother's widow, then his brother's widow shall go up to the elders at the gate and say, "My husband's brother refuses to perpetuate his brother's name in Israel; he will not perform the duty of a husband's brother to me." Then the elders of his town shall summon him and speak to him. If he persists, saying, "I have no desire to marry her," then his brother's wife shall go up to him in the presence of the elders, pull his sandal off his foot, spit in his face, and declare, "This is what is done to the man who does not build up his brother's house." Throughout Israel his family shall be known as "the house of him whose sandal was pulled off." (Deut. 25:7–10)

So when you consider the case of Judah and Tamar from the perspective of the social custom of levirate marriage, you get a different view of the actions of the parties involved. Onan was expected to try to father a child with Tamar. He had an out, according to Deuteronomy: he could have refused, but then he would have suffered shaming and social ostracizing—having his face spat on by Tamar and getting a bad reputation as someone who was unreliable in Israel. Instead, he opted to be dishonest about it, pretending to go through with his obligation but withdrawing at the last second. That way he made everyone think it was Tamar's fault that she did not get pregnant. Plus, it had the added benefit of getting him off—until he was permanently offed. What a perv! Judah wasn't much better. He copped out of his responsibility to marry his remaining son Shelah to Tamar. At least he fessed up at the end, although he didn't really have a choice, since his daughter-in-law had him by the short hairs. It's hard to blame Tamar for what she did. It was a little extreme maybe, transforming herself from the grieving widow to the happy hooker, but she was driven to it by Onan and Judah. She was trying to hold on to her rights, not to mention her sense of dignity and self-worth. What other choice did she have? Vice let this case go without filing charges.

Another levirate marriage case . . . sort of

When the vice squad was reading up on levirate marriage, they came across another Bible case where the procedures were a little different than in Deuteronomy 25. It grabbed their attention initially because of an allegation of soliciting against this woman named Ruth. She was from Moab and lived with her mother-in-law, whose name was Naomi, and their story is told in the Bible file titled "Ruth."

At first, Vice thought they might be trying to set up a prostitution ring, but it turned out that the two women were just after one man, a rich guy named Boaz. That's where levirate marriage comes in—sort of.

Naomi and Ruth were both widows. Their husbands had both died while the family was living across the river in Moab, which was the ancient equivalent of New Jersey. Boaz was related to Naomi's deceased husband, and Naomi was determined to get Boaz to act like the brother-in-law in Deuteronomy and marry Ruth. She concocted a plan for Ruth to sneak in on Boaz while he was sleeping off a night of partying at harvest time and to "uncover his feet" (Ruth 3:4, 7). The boys at the station always wink and nod at this point when they tell the story, as if it means something dirty. Maybe it does; all we know is it wasn't illegal; they were both consenting adults, so what they did is none of our business. Whatever it was, it worked, because Boaz agreed to marry Ruth. But there was an obstacle that had to be cleared first. While Boaz was a close relative, there was another man who was closer and had first right of refusal. Boaz arranged a meeting with him and with some city elders the next day at the city gate. The man was interested in some land holdings Naomi had but not in marrying Ruth, so he turned the deal down. He sealed his refusal by pulling off his sandal and giving it to Boaz (Ruth 4:7-8).

That's the way the story is told by the members of the vice squad down at the station. You may have noticed that there are several differences between it and the details about levirate marriage in Deuteronomy and in the story of Judah and Tamar. For one thing, Boaz wasn't Ruth's brother-in-law—or Naomi's either, as far as we can tell. He's always just called the "next of kin" or "redeemer." Also, when the closest relative declined to marry Ruth, she didn't spit in his face. She wasn't even present at the sit-down in the city gate. He did lose his sandal, but the file explains that this was the custom for sealing a deal at the time and was not shameful: "Now this was the custom in former times in Israel concerning redeeming and exchanging: to confirm a transaction, the one took off a sandal and gave it to the other; this was the manner of attesting in Israel" (Ruth 4:7).

The strangest difference is that if you check the records down at City Hall (or in Ruth 4:17-22), you will find that the family genealogy is traced through Boaz and not through Naomi's husband (Elimelech, for the record) or Ruth's (Chilion). There's corroborating evidence in the genealogy of Jesus in Matthew 1:5. Yet that was supposed to be the whole point of the custom of levirate marriage in the first place according to Deuteronomy 25:5-6. So what gives? Short answer: We're not sure. It could be that the practices changed over time and expanded from brother to next of kin. Or maybe the practices associated with the custom were different in different parts of ancient Israel. Our preferred explanation is that the tradition is confused, by which we mean that the bozos in Vice got the story mixed up and imported details from other cases like Judah and Tamar.

Paul's advice

Not to overlook the obvious, but marriage is a social custom, and it was the subject of a revealing mini-essay by Paul in 1 Corinthians 7. Paul was dealing with questions and issues that had been brought to his attention by oral reports and also by a letter from the church in Corinth. Up until chapter 7, he was addressing the reports he had received. In 7:1 he turned to the letter, as you can tell from his statement, "Now concerning the matters about which you wrote." It's not clear if the sentence that follows, "It is well for a man not to touch a woman," was Paul's own advice or whether he was quoting from their letter to him. It doesn't really matter, because the rest of the chapter explains his position.

Basically, Paul thought marriage was a sort of necessary evil for people who couldn't control their sexual urges. "It is better to marry than to be aflame with passion" (1 Cor. 7:9). He wished everyone could be like him in that regard. We don't know exactly what Paul's history was—widowed? divorced? never married? But he was apparently single. He advised unmarried people not to get married unless they just could not help themselves. He also advised married people not to divorce. This might have been a burning question for people who had converted to Christianity but whose spouses had not. The key concept for Paul was status quo. He made it clear that this was his opinion rather than a command from God: "This I say by way of concession, not of command" (1 Cor. 7:6); "To the rest I say—I and not the Lord . . ." (v. 12).

The reason Paul gave for his antimatrimonial sentiments was what he called "the impending crisis" (v. 26), or as he says in verse 29, "the appointed time has grown short." He explains that people without families will have an easier time in this imminent "crisis" and will be able to concentrate on their duties to God without worrying about their families. The New Testament squad is virtually unanimous in interpreting this as Paul's belief that Jesus was about to return and bring an end to the world. He seems to have believed that a period of persecution for Christians would precede the world's end, and maybe even that this period was beginning as he wrote. Since none of that happened, we wonder what Paul would say about marriage today. Unfortunately, he's not around to fill in the blanks. Our guess is that he would still adopt the "necessary evil" position. We'd put him to work in Vice for a couple of days; he'd learn fast that marriage does not scratch the itch of all sexual urges.

Red herrings

We don't want to give the wrong impression about marriage customs. Don't think that if you're arrested on a vice charge you can scream "social custom" and waltz right out of lockup. That's why we investigate. The Big House is full of lowlifes who tried to put one over on us. We are detectives, and we're good at detecting all sorts of fake social customs, fake alibis, and so on. We've even sniffed out a few questionable instances in the Bible.

The perp in one case was Laban. He's the guy who welcomed Abraham's servant by offering him water to wash his feet (Gen. 24). He played the charming host on that occasion because of the treasures brought by the servant (Gen. 24:30-31), who had been charged to find a wife for Isaac and was impressed by Laban's sister, Rebekah. Laban was happy to pawn her off for the right price, which is why we had him under surveillance. When Rebekah had some trouble with her twin sons and sent Jacob to live with Laban (Gen. 27:42-45), we suspected Laban could not resist the chance to try and pull a fast one. Sure enough, Laban played host again for a while (Gen. 29:13-14), but Jacob had come empty-handed, without the riches displayed by Abraham's servant. Laban wasn't about to have anyone—relative or not—sponging off him, so he quickly turned Jacob out to earn. They made a deal for Jacob to work for seven years in exchange for Laban's daughter Rachel, who had become Jacob's love interest (Gen. 29:15-20). Jacob proved to be a good worker, and Laban threw a big wedding seven years later. He also got Jacob a little snockered at the reception and pulled the old switcheroo on the wedding night, replacing Rachel with her older sister, Leah. He claimed that he did this because of a social custom that required the older daughter to be married before the younger (Gen. 29:26). But we checked it out and could find no corroborating evidence for the existence of such a custom. We're convinced that Laban was making it up to double the amount of free labor he got from Jacob (Gen. 29:27). It was extortion, pure and simple. It fits the creep's m.o.—using women to benefit himself.

Laban's daughters inherited his criminal mind. They also proved adept at falsifying a social custom to get what they wanted. Well, not actually falsifying. The custom was real enough; they just misappropriated it. Laban was responsible for creating the circumstances. In married life, Jacob favored his one true love, Rachel. But Leah took advantage of the little attention she got and started producing babies. She had four kids in a row, all boys—Reuben, Simeon, Levi, and Judah (Gen. 29:31-35). Rachel couldn't get pregnant. She became frantic and borrowed a page from Sarai's playbook. She sent her handmaid, Bilhah, to Jacob as a surrogate. Bilhah popped out a couple boys—Dan and Naphtali (Gen. 30:1-8). Leah figured two could play this game. She wasn't conceiving anymore, so she sent in her maid, Zilpah, who also had two sons, Gad and Asher (Gen. 30:9–13). Leah started experimenting with an aphrodisiac/fertility drug called "mandrakes" that was on the market at the time, and as a result she had two more pregnancies, resulting in Issachar and Zebulun (Gen. 30:14–20). Rachel eventually did have a couple of sons herself—Joseph and Benjamin—but it was a struggle for her. She died in childbirth with Benjamin (Gen. 30:22–24; 35:17–20).

But we're getting off track. The point is that both Rachel and Leah were fudging with the handmaid custom. If you recall the Case of the Presumed Polygamist, the reason for that marriage custom was to produce an heir for the husband when the wife was not able to do so. But in Jacob's case, Leah produced four heirs right off the bat. Rachel was desperate to get a kid into the mix; the handmaid custom was just a pretense to give her a way of getting involved. Leah just followed her lead. Neither of them was really trying to steal like their father did. At least their motives were more noble than just making a living off of someone else. Actually, we think that the misuse of the custom in this case probably doesn't go back to Rachel and Leah anyway, but to the writer of the story. The Clue of the Weird Social Custom, or the lack thereof, gives way to the Clue of the Etiology. The story explains the origin of the twelve tribes of Israel.

The crime gene was passed on to Rachel's and Leah's sons. When they had grown up, their sister Dinah was attacked, raped, and kidnapped by a spoiled lowlife named Shechem (Gen. 34:1–2, 26). In a weird twist that rarely happens in rape cases, the assailant fell in love with the victim and wanted to marry her (Gen. 34:3–4). He got his old man to contact Jacob and see about arranging a marriage. His old man was a big shot in Canaan. Jacob, on the other hand, was a resident alien. He was outnumbered by the natives and afraid that he could be wiped out if he failed to comply.

But Jacob's sons were having nothing of it. They were plenty steamed at the way their sister had been treated and decided to retaliate. They took over negotiations and bent a social custom in order to neutralize the superior numbers of their enemy. And we do mean *bent*. They told Shechem's pop that they could only intermarry with them if their men went through the rite of circumcision. You might think that would be a tough sell, but Shechem and his dad pulled it off. They convinced the men of the city to undergo circumcision, arguing that intermarriage would benefit them because they would be able to take over the great wealth of Jacob and his family. Their case was no doubt made easier by the fact that the city was named Shechem. It was hard to go against the city's main benefactor. Jacob's sons waited for a couple of days after the mass circumcision. Then, Simeon and Levi entered the city and killed them all. The men were incapacitated by pain from their recent operation and couldn't fight back. The other brothers followed them and pillaged the city, taking all the property and the women and children as slaves (Gen. 34:25-29).

Obviously, the key to their victory and to the story was their distortion of the custom of circumcision. It is true that the command of circumcision to Abraham included slaves and foreigners living in his household (Gen. 17:12-13). Also, slaves and resident aliens in Israel who had undergone circumcision were permitted to eat the Passover, while foreigners were not (Exod. 12:43-49). But Jacob's sons were not interested in converting Shechemites or bringing them into the family, so to speak. The circumcision requirement was a ruse so they could weaken them and murder them. Maybe they had a good reason considering how Dinah was treated, but legally it was still the perpetration of a deception in the form of a social custom to aid in the commission of homicide.

WHY THIS CLUE MATTERS

The Clue of the Weird Social Custom matters because the events that the Bible narrates took place within specific cultures and societies, namely, those of ancient Israel and the ancient Near East and of ancient Greece and Rome. Those societies were in a very different time and place from our own, and they had customs that were very different from ours. The biblical writers do not pause to explain social customs most of the time. Rather, they simply assume that the reader is familiar with them. So having an awareness of the custom(s) presupposed in a given passage of the Bible is essential for understanding it. In some cases, the social custom is at the very center of the plot. In others, a custom determines how the characters act and what they say.

THE CLUE OF THE WEIRD SOCIAL CUSTOM CAN HELP US . . .

1. Be sensitive to the different cultures from which the Bible emerged.
2. Focus on specific details of a text or story that we might otherwise gloss over.

3. Understand the reasons behind the deeds and words of biblical figures.
4. Gain an understanding of the origin and meaning of common terms in the Bible.
5. Appreciate the real-life concepts that lie behind Bible words and ideas that have influenced our culture and way of life.

THE CASEBOOK

The exercises for this chapter are borrowed from the section of the Bible detective's manual that deals with cultural sensitivity training.

1. Consider how the funerary and burial practices reflected in the following passages differ from our own and from those of other societies:

    2 Kings 13:20-21
    John 11:1-44
    Matthew 27:58-66; Mark 15:43-16:8; Luke 23:50-24:12; John 19:38-20:15

2. Some Christian denominations practice foot washing as a religious ritual because of Jesus's command to his disciples in John 13:14. What is the difference between a social custom and a religious ritual? Are there any clues in the text that allow us to tell them apart?
3. In the book of Ruth, Boaz met with the elders and the closer next of kin at the city gate (Ruth 4:1). Amos 5:15 talks about establishing justice in the gate. What clues do these verses give as to the cultural function of the city gate in ancient Israel? These additional verses from passages we have considered may furnish further clues: Genesis 34:20; Deuteronomy 25:7; Amos 5:10, 12.
4. One of the most difficult passages in the New Testament is 1 Corinthians 11:1-16, which deals with a custom (v. 16). What clues are in the text as to the nature of this custom? What seems to have been the controversy? Was it a clash of social or religious customs?

5

The Clue of the

INCONSISTENCY

It's high time we exercise our pedagogical authority and give you a pop quiz. Choose the correct answer to the following question:

> According to the New Testament, what were Jesus's last words?
> (a) "My God, my God, why have you forsaken me?"
> (b) "Father, into your hands I commend my spirit."
> (c) "It is finished."
> (d) All of the above.
> (e) None of the above.

If you answered (d) (for detective), you got it right. All three of the options are correct, depending on which gospel you read. In Matthew and Mark Jesus asks the question in (a) just before he dies, in Luke he says the second sentence, and in John's Gospel he utters the third one. That's a little peculiar, to say the least. And things aren't any less murky if we go back to the beginning of the gospels to see how Jesus's family history is presented. Only Matthew and Luke give Jesus's genealogy, and here are the names that appear in each of those books:

Matthew (1:2–16): <u>Abraham</u>, <u>Isaac</u>, <u>Jacob</u>, <u>Judah</u>, <u>Perez</u>, <u>Hezron</u>, Aram, <u>Aminadab</u>, <u>Nahshon</u>, <u>Salmon</u>, <u>Boaz</u>, <u>Obed</u>, <u>Jesse</u>, <u>David</u>, Solomon, Rehoboam, Abijah, Asaph, Jehoshaphat, Joram, Uzziah, Jotham, Ahaz, Hezekiah, Manasseh, <u>Amos</u>, Josiah,

Jechoniah, Salathiel, Zerubbabel, Abiud, Eliakim, Azor, Zadok, Achim, Eliud, Eleazar, Matthan, Jacob, Joseph, Jesus

Luke (3:23-38): Jesus, Joseph, Heli, Matthat, Levi, Melchi, Jannai, Joseph, Mattathias, Amos, Nahum, Esli, Naggai, Maath, Mattathias, Semein, Josech, Joda, Joanan, Rhesa, Zerubbabel, Shealtiel, Neri, Melchi, Addi, Cosam, Elmadam, Er, Joshua, Eliezer, Jorim, Matthat, Levi, Simeon, Judah, Joseph, Jonam, Eliakim, Melea, Menna, Mattatha, Nathan, David, Jesse, Obed, Boaz, Sala, Nahshon, Amminadab, Admin, Arni, Hezron, Perez, Judah, Jacob, Isaac, Abraham, Terah, Nahor, Serug, Reu, Peleg, Eber, Shelah, Cainan, Arphaxad, Shem, Noah, Lamech, Methuselah, Enoch, Jared, Mahalaleel, Cainan, Enos, Seth, Adam

To make things easier for you, we've underlined all the names that the two lists have in common. (We also underlined all the words that Jesus's three final statements, above, have in common—a grand total of none.) For the time period in which the two lists overlap between Abraham and Jesus, a span of about 1,800 years according to the generally accepted biblical chronology, a total of eighteen names are found in both. Sometimes a name, like Salmon/Sala, is written in two slightly different forms that will be noticed only by a super-attentive reader (like our proofreader, who really should consider a career in Bible detecting). During that same period, Matthew has twenty-two names that are not in Luke's list, and Luke has thirty-nine that are not in Matthew's. That adds up to three sets of last words and two different family trees, while the rest of us get only one of each.

THE CLUE OF THE INCONSISTENCY: differences that occur within a story or between two or more versions of a story

You've just met the Clue of the Inconsistency, one of the most common clues in the Bible. Biblical inconsistencies come in many shapes and sizes. They can be internal, as when you find conflicting information within the same story, and they can be external if something in one book of the Bible disagrees with something said in another one. In some cases they are obvious—competing family histories and last words for the same person tend to get noticed—and elsewhere they can be very hard to detect. We'll be encountering examples of all these types of inconsistencies in this chapter.

Note, however, that an inconsistency is sometimes more than just a mistake. That's not to say that an inconsistency can't only be a mistake, as the following example will illustrate. There's a scene in the movie *The Wizard of Oz* in which a talking tree is throwing apples at the Scarecrow and Dorothy, and for a brief moment you can see that she is wearing black shoes instead of her famous ruby slippers. (Check out the YouTube video clip at this link: https://www.youtube.com/watch?v=VxC2iVt2aE. The slipup occurs at around the 45-second point, and right after that she's back in her usual dazzling footwear.) We doubt it cost the film the Academy Award for best picture that year (*Gone with the Wind* took home the hardware in 1940), but somebody sure screwed up royally on that one.

We advise you to avoid that reaction when you come face-to-face with a biblical inconsistency because it will likely prevent you from recognizing it for what it might be—an opportunity rather than just a mistake. Even though there's something "wrong" about an inconsistency, it can still provide us with important information about a text or its author. In fact, that information usually becomes available to us only *because* it's wrapped up in an inconsistency. Without the tension between it and what's said in another text, we might very well pass it by and not give it a second thought.

Let's see how this plays out in the genealogies of Jesus in Matthew and Luke. If we had only one of them and not the other, we'd be tempted to consider it to be accurate and similar to the list of his forebears that Jesus would have received from Ancestry.com had it been around two thousand years ago. But because the two lists do exist and are so different from one another, they practically demand that we ask, "What in Jesus's name is going on here?" Quite a bit, it turns out. We can't conduct a full inquiry and get into all the differences between the two lists, so we'll just mention a couple of them to illustrate our point. Did you notice that they move in opposite directions? (Good detectives always pay attention to which way the wind is blowing.) Matthew's ends with Jesus, while Luke's starts with him. They also have different beginning points, as Matthew traces Jesus's line to Abraham while Luke goes back to Adam.

These differences are due to the unique view of Jesus, or Christology, that each gospel writer has. Matthew highlights Jesus's Jewishness in his gospel, and so he chooses to begin the family line with Abraham, the person with whom God first established the covenant and circumcision as the sign of that covenant. The Christology of Luke's Gospel sees Jesus as a more universal figure, and therefore it does not stress his Jewishness as much as Matthew's does. Consequently, Luke extends the family line back to Adam, the first person, and so views Jesus within a broader scope. Matthew has the genealogy end with Jesus because he's the culmination of Jewish history as the Messiah, while Luke closes with Adam in order to present Jesus within the framework of human history in its totality. So which one gets it right? We'll never know if one or neither one hits the nail on the head, but from a certain perspective it doesn't really matter. In a sense, despite their discrepancies, both genealogies are correct because they each support the understanding of Jesus that their authors wished to convey. Understanding the differences as opportunities and not just mistakes helps us make that claim, and so a useful rule for the Clue of the Inconsistency is the following: When you find an inconsistency in the Bible, determine if it provides you with an opportunity to learn something about the text and/or its author.

So you want to be a Bible detective?

Before we proceed further, we feel obligated to come clean about a matter of some urgency. This clue will force you to confront an aspect of biblical detective work that many trainees find unsettling and has led to the undoing of more than a few of them, and it is this—the job involves a tremendous amount of uncertainty, and we're not just talking about the hours and career advancement opportunities. The more you study and wrestle with the Clue of the Inconsistency, the more you question the historical accuracy and reliability of what you read in the Bible. This is an occupational hazard that stems mostly from two factors: (1) the presence of contradictions in the text, and (2) the fact that virtually none of the events described in the Bible can be verified by other sources. The combination of those two things means one big thing—when we read the Bible, we can never know for sure what, if anything, really happened.

That's another way of saying that we biblical detectives aren't like the regular detectives you see on TV and in movies. Unlike their cases, most of ours remain unsolved. They're able to make use of eyewitnesses, camera surveillance, DNA, and other means at their disposal to often establish exactly what happened and who did what to whom. That's not the way biblical detectives earn their keep. Our examination of the evidence (i.e., the Bible, as well as other ancient texts and artifacts) allows us to offer theories, present hypotheses, and float ideas, but we're hardly ever able to prove something beyond the shadow of a doubt. The result is that there are often disagreements among us, some of them quite contentious, and so you rarely see groups of us hanging out together in bars like those other detectives do. Here's the bottom line—if you're the kind of person who can tolerate a high level of uncertainty on a constant basis and you're comfortable staking your reputation on things that many of your coworkers will disagree with, then biblical detective work just might be your calling.

The New Testament Gospels are particularly fertile ground for tracking and uncovering the Clue of the Inconsistency. Those four texts offer accounts of the life of Jesus, but each one does so in its own way, so there are inconsistencies galore. To take advantage of the riches they offer, we will begin each section of this chapter with a consideration of how the Gospels of Matthew and Luke recount the birth story of Jesus (they are the only two gospels that mention Jesus's birth). After that, examples of inconsistencies from the Hebrew Bible and other New Testament passages will be considered in each section. We've dusted off and consulted our old training manual from our days as students at the academy to help us organize this chapter. Back then we were taught to keep the "five Ws" in mind when working a case: who, what, when, where, and why. This strikes us as still being a solid foundation on which to conduct an investigation, so why reinvent the wheel? We've modified it slightly by dropping the final W since we ask the "Why?" question in other chapters of this book, so we now turn to the who, what, when, and where of the Clue of the Inconsistency.

Who?

(Read Matt. 1:18–2:23; Luke 1:5–2:52.)

The first two chapters of the Gospels of Matthew and Luke are often referred to as the "infancy narratives," even though they mostly describe events that took place prior to Jesus's birth, so there isn't always an infant around. In addition to Jesus, his mother Mary, and her husband Joseph, other characters play roles in these texts, and here's a listing of them (in order of appearance):

Matthew
King Herod (2:1)
Wise men (2:1)
Chief priests and scribes (2:4)
<u>An angel</u> (2:13, 19)
Murdered children (2:16)

Luke
Zechariah (1:5)
Elizabeth (1:5)
People (1:10)
Angel Gabriel (1:11, 19, 26)
God (1:26)
John the Baptist (1:41)
Shepherds (2:8)
<u>An angel</u> and group of angels (2:9, 13)
Simeon (2:25)
Anna (2:36)
Teachers (2:46)

The Clue of the Inconsistency can be seen in two ways here. The first is the disparity in the lengths of the lists, with Matthew's being the more streamlined production with a smaller cast. Of more importance for our purposes is the lack of agreement between the two lists, with only an angel appearing in both. The angels have relatively small parts in the stories, which means Matthew and Luke do not agree on the key players in the birth story of Jesus beyond its three main characters.

If Matthew and Luke disagree so strongly on who was involved in the birth story of Jesus, how can we know for sure what really happened? Well, we can't, and we believe that's the wrong question to be asking. (That statement, more than any other we make in this book, illustrates the difference between a biblical detective and the other kind.) The gospel writers were not recording events, they were interpreting events. They were writing *about* history, not writing history. It's the same thing we saw with the conflicting genealogies for Jesus in the same two gospels. Each goes its own way because of its Christology as it tries to present a particular portrait of Jesus, and that's exactly what's happening here. So as we interrogate the infancy narratives (or any other biblical text), the question we should pose is not "Did these events actually happen?" but rather "What do these events as described mean?"

Both gospels report that a group of people comes to see Jesus soon after his birth, the wise men in Matthew and the shepherds in Luke. Although the two groups are quite different in many ways, they share a key trait—each supports the Christology of its gospel. We have noted that Luke presents Jesus as a universal figure, and throughout his gospel he shows that Jesus has come for all people, especially those who have been oppressed or are on the margins of society. This is likely a reason why women figure so prominently in Luke's Gospel. The shepherds are Luke's first example of this inclusivity because they were among the lowliest of people and yet they are the first to be told of Jesus's birth and are the ones through whom others hear of the news (Luke 2:8-20). Matthew's wise men, on the other hand, reinforce his Christology by keeping Jesus's Jewishness front and center. This is made clear in their first and only line of dialogue in the story: "Where is the child who has been born *king of the Jews*?" (Matt. 2:2). They're two distinct sets of visitors to the newborn Jesus with two different purposes. In an analysis of the inconsistency, it's essential to focus on what each visit means, not if it happened.

The Clue of the Inconsistency can sometimes be seen in a sudden shift in the way a character is referred to or described. A good example can be seen with Moses's father-in-law, who goes by three different names in the Bible. In Exodus 2:18 he is identified as Reuel, in the next chapter he is called Jethro (Exod. 3:1), and then in the book of Judges his name is Hobab (Judg. 1:16; 4:11). A similar change is present in several passages in the second half of the Acts of the Apostles in the New Testament. Throughout the first fifteen chapters of the book the events are described from a third-person perspective, but then out of the blue that changes, as a first-person plural narrator begins to tell the story. "So, passing by Mysia, *they* went down to Troas. During the night Paul had a vision: there stood a man of Macedonia pleading with him and saying, 'Come over to Macedonia and help us.' When he had seen the vision, *we* immediately tried to cross over to Macedonia, being convinced that God had called *us* to proclaim the good news to them" (Acts 16:8-10; cf. 20:5-15; 21:1-18; 27:1-28:16).

These inconsistencies are clues that point to the editing process that created the text, and they are most easily explained as evidence of the sources the author or editor drew upon to compose the story. There were probably multiple traditions about the name of Moses's father-in-law floating around, and more than one of them found their way into the biblical text. In the case of the "we passages" in Acts, it has been suggested that they might point to the existence of a travel diary or similar document that the author might have used in writing the account of Paul's voyages.

A second type of *who* clue can be seen in those passages in which a character acts out of character. It can be a little tricky to detect because characters, like people, often change, but sometimes the change is much too dramatic and the characters are exhibiting all the symptoms of the Clue of the Inconsistency. Job is one biblical figure most certainly afflicted with this clue, along with his many other ailments. It's like there are two Jobs—the one of the prose portions of the book in chapters 1-2 and 42:7-17, and the one of the poetry that's found in the long section between them. The prose Job is quite accepting of the lousy hand he's been dealt in the card game of life, while his poetry counterpart wants to check the deck and is demanding a reshuffle. Compare his last words in the prose section with his first words of the poetry: "Shall we receive the good at the hand of God, and not receive the bad?" (2:10) is immediately followed up with

> "Let the day perish in which I was born,
>   and the night that said,
>   'A man child is conceived.'" (3:3)

The most reasonable explanation for his mood swing is that the prose and poetry sections were composed separately and were later joined together to form the book we now have.

An additional Hebrew Bible character who is not a model of consistency is Daniel, who is best known for spending an entire night in a lions' den and emerging the next day unharmed (Dan. 6:10-28). His book can be neatly divided into two six-chapter halves, with the first half composed of court tales that recount Daniel's adventures as a servant for the king of Babylon and the second describing a series of apocalyptic visions Daniel has. As those two different genres of writing suggest, the two halves were originally independent of one another and were brought together by an editor. This explanation of the book's origin is supported by the two Daniels described within it and, at its midway point, the sudden loss of a power he possesses. In chapters 1-6 Daniel has the ability to interpret the visions other people have, but when he starts to have his own visions in the seventh chapter, he no longer has that talent.

A final example of a character who acts out of character is Jesus in John's Gospel. Actually, John's Jesus is remarkably consistent within the confines of the Fourth Gospel, but when we compare him to his alter egos in the other three gospels, he begins to look like a New Testament version of Job. One of the most common forms of discourse Jesus uses to instruct his followers in the Synoptic Gospels is the parable, a usually short saying in the form of a story or image that is meant to teach a lesson through a comparison. The Gospels of Matthew and Luke each contain around two dozen parables, while in Mark's Gospel Jesus speaks in parables eight times. In John's Gospel, on the other hand, Jesus seems to be all parabled-out, because he doesn't utter a single one. But something Jesus does not tire of doing in John is talk about himself. This type of self-referential language is sometimes called an "I am" saying, and each of the three Synoptic Gospels has Jesus use that phrase fewer than five times. In John's Gospel there are forty-five "I am" sayings on the lips of Jesus. That's the Clue of the Inconsistency writ large. As with other discrepancies we've considered in the Gospels, this one is best explained by Christology. One of the main themes of the Fourth Gospel is the identity of Jesus, and so John goes to great lengths to have him speak about himself as often as possible.

One last type of clue in the *who* category causes the reader to ask, "Where did they go?" It refers to a situation in which a character completely drops out of a story or somehow isn't all there. We see this in the case of Samuel, who is the central figure in the book that's named after him even before he's born. The first through third chapters of 1 Samuel describe his conception, birth, and call to be a prophet, and then— *poof!*—he's nowhere to be found. We hear about him in the first verse of chapter 4, and then not a peep until the beginning of the seventh chapter. As odd as Samuel's disappearance is, there's no need for us to file a missing person report because there's a perfectly good reason for his absence. The intervening three chapters describe how the ark of the covenant was captured by the Philistines and spent seven months in their territory, and it's likely that this section originally circulated as an independent tradition until it was inserted into Samuel's story.

A different type of disappearing act can be seen in the case of King Solomon. Probably the most famous story involving him is where he solves a dispute between two women who claim to be the mother of the same child by threatening to cut the baby in half. Take a moment now and read the story in 1 Kings 3:16–28 with this clue in mind. Did you catch the anomaly? In that story, Solomon isn't mentioned by name a single time. That's really odd, especially when we extend our perimeter and discover that his name appears seven times in the fifteen verses of the same chapter prior to this story and fourteen times in the thirty-four verses of the following chapter. Only in this story's thirteen verses is Solomon's name missing. A plausible explanation for Solomon's sudden departure is that this story wasn't originally about him. As with Samuel's extended holiday, this may be a later addition to the text. It may have been a tradition about some anonymous king that the author or editor added to the Solomon story as a demonstration of the king's great wisdom. It would have been a wise move on his part if he had also added a mention or two of Solomon's name to cover his tracks.

What?

The *what* of a story refers to the events that take place within it, which can be listed in outline form. When the infancy accounts of Matthew and Luke are presented in this way, here's how they compare:

Matthew
1. Mary becomes pregnant (1:18).
2. Joseph wants to divorce her (1:19).
3. An angel reassures Joseph (1:20-24).
4. Jesus is born (1:25).
5. The wise men visit Herod (2:1-8).
6. The wise men visit Jesus (2:9-11).
7. The wise men return to their country (2:12).
8. An angel warns Joseph to flee to Egypt, and he does so (2:13-15).
9. Innocent children are put to death by Herod (2:16-18).
10. Herod dies (2:19a).
11. An angel tells Joseph to return from Egypt (2:19b-20).
12. Joseph and the family settle in Nazareth (2:21-23).

Luke
1. Zachariah is told by an angel that Elizabeth will have a son (1:5-23).
2. Elizabeth becomes pregnant (1:24-25).
3. Mary is told by an angel that she will have a son (1:26-38).
4. Mary visits Elizabeth (1:39-45).

5. Mary praises God (1:46–55).
6. Mary returns home (1:56).
7. Elizabeth gives birth to John (1:57–66).
8. Zachariah speaks a prophecy (1:67–79).
9. Joseph and Mary go to Bethlehem (2:1–5).
10. Mary give birth to Jesus (2:6–7).
11. Shepherds learn of Jesus's birth from angels and go to visit him (2:8–20).
12. Jesus is circumcised and named (2:21).
13. Jesus is presented to the Lord in the temple (2:22–24).
14. Simeon praises God and speaks to Mary (2:25–35).
15. Anna praises God and speaks about Jesus (2:36–38).
16. Family returns to Nazareth (2:39–40).
17. Twelve-year-old Jesus is left at the temple (2:41–51).

These two outlines contain a number of inconsistencies. Five of the seventeen events in Luke's version concern the birth of John the Baptist, something not even mentioned in Matthew. Of the other twelve events described by Luke, only Mary's pregnancy and the birth of Jesus are also found in Matthew. In addition, significant differences exist after the visits of the wise men and the shepherds, with Matthew describing the family's flight to Egypt while Luke has them stay put in Palestine as they spend time at the temple and interact with other characters there.

We hate to sound like a broken record, but many of these differences can be attributed to the distinct Christologies of the two gospels. That's because of one of the basic principles of New Testament detective work. When you are examining an instance of the Clue of the Inconsistency in the gospels, a good rule of thumb is to approach it first from the Christology angle because that's where you'll probably end up anyway. The differences among the gospels are often the result of each author's attempt to present a unique take on Jesus, and paying careful attention to the distinctive elements can tell us a great deal about a particular writer's agenda.

You don't have to be the most careful reader in the world to notice that the two texts disagree on who the lead character is in the story. In Matthew it is Joseph—he's the one who gets visited by angels, makes the key decision to not divorce Mary, and leads the family into and out of Egypt. Meanwhile in Luke, Mary gets top billing, as she speaks with an angelic visitor, takes a trip to visit Elizabeth, breaks out in song, and is the focal point. But if you're an eagle-eyed reader who's in full detective mode, you may have also noticed an additional task Joseph is charged with in Matthew that he doesn't have in Luke. In his first encounter with an angel he's told to give the child the name Jesus (Matt. 1:21), and that's precisely what he does. "When Joseph awoke from sleep, he did as the angel of the Lord commanded him; he took her as his wife, but had no marital relations with her until she had borne a son; *and he named him Jesus*" (Matt. 1:24–25). Luke's account is less clear on who does the naming because the angel tells Mary she will name him Jesus (Luke 1:31), but when the time actually comes the passive voice is used and the text says, "*And he was called Jesus*, the name given by the angel before he was conceived in the womb" (Luke 2:21b).

We've seen that Matthew's Jesus is the Jewish Messiah who comes from the line of David, and the way he is named in the gospel reinforces that identity. The Davidic connection is made even before the naming because the angel addresses Joseph as "Joseph, *son of David*" (Matt. 1:20). So far so good, but there's a glitch, and it's a big one. The genealogy in Matthew (and the one in Luke as well) identifies David as one of Joseph's ancestors, but Jesus isn't Joseph's biological offspring according to Matthew's Gospel since he was virginally conceived. So Matthew solves that problem by having Joseph name Jesus, which was a form of adoption in the ancient world that now put him in the family line. That shows how subtly significant the Clue of the Inconsistency can be—seemingly minor differences are sometimes rich with meaning.

From here to the end of this section we're going to look at two stories as we ask the *what* question. They serve as case studies that let us explore some of the nuances and details of this aspect of the Clue of the Inconsistency. In addition, they show the clue in two different guises, since the first is an example of inconsistency within a single story and the second is a case of inconsistency between two different versions of the same event. The first text is the flood story featuring Noah (which is also discussed under the Clue of the Doublet), so read Genesis 6:5–9:1 and list all the inconsistencies you can find in it.

The flood story was one of the parts of the Bible on which the earliest biblical detectives cut their teeth as they debated the significance of the many inconsistencies in the narrative. A prominent one that established the basis for many modern views on sources behind the Pentateuch is the presence of different names for God in the story. In the Hebrew text the deity is sometimes referred to as *Elohim* (usually translated "God") but in other places is called *Yahweh* ("the LORD"). We're so used to seeing both of those terms in reference to the deity, that it's easy to miss all the switching back and forth, but this is a nice example of the Clue of the Inconsistency.

Other details of the narrative are equally inconsistent and often easier to spot. Just about every depiction of the loading of the ark in children's Bible books shows the animals in orderly lines patiently waiting to march in two by two, but that's only part of the story. It accurately depicts what's said about bringing aboard a pair of each species (Gen. 6:19-20; 7:8-9, 15), but Noah is also told to load seven pairs of clean animals and one pair of the unclean ones (7:2-3). So how many animals were with him on the ark? A similar issue exists regarding where the floodwaters came from, because sometimes rain falling from the sky is mentioned (7:4, 11-12; 8:2) and other times the water is described as bubbling up from below (7:11; 8:2). And then there is the matter of how long the flood lasted. Depending on which part of the story you consult, it continued for either 40 days (7:4, 12; 8:6) or 150 days (7:24; 8:3). Finally, what kind of bird did Noah release when he wanted to see if the water was subsiding, a raven (8:7) or a dove (8:8)? It might seem like we're piling on here, but a detective has to gather as much evidence as possible in order to establish an airtight case. The accumulated weight of the evidence points in only one direction—the flood story is actually two stories that have been joined together. That's the simplest way to explain why it contains so many inconsistencies from beginning to end.

For an example of an external inconsistency, we'll now consider how the Gospels of Mark and Matthew relate the same tradition describing a miracle Jesus performed on the Sea of Galilee. Read Mark 4:35-41 and Matthew 8:23-27 and write down any inconsistencies you find between them. When analyzing two versions of a story, a good first step is to outline their main events in general terms. After comparing the outlines, you can dig deeper and start poking around in the details. Here's how we break down Mark's account of what happens:

1. Jesus gets in a boat with his disciples.
2. A storm arises as Jesus sleeps.
3. The disciples awaken Jesus.
4. Jesus calms the storm.
5. Jesus questions his disciples about their lack of faith.
6. The disciples are amazed.

This outline shows the standard three-part structure of many miracle stories: (1) the setup, (2) the miracle, and (3) the response. Compared to the outline of Matthew's version of the story, it matches up perfectly, except for one thing—items 4 and 5 have been reversed by Matthew. Hmmm . . . now that's an interesting little switch, especially when we extend our perimeter to bring in another witness for questioning and notice that Luke follows Mark's order in his version (Luke 8:22–25). What's Matthew up to?

It looks to us like Matthew has tampered with the evidence in order to throw us off the trail that Mark and Luke want us to follow and to prompt us to open up a new line of inquiry. In those other two gospels the focus is on the miracle, as Jesus wows the disciples with a demonstration of his power over the forces of nature. The way Mark and Luke tell the story, Jesus's rebuke of his disciples for their lack of faith is almost an afterthought. But Matthew foregrounds that part of the story by having Jesus chastise the disciples before he turns his attention to the storm. This changes the whole point of the story—for Mark and Luke the spotlight is on Jesus the miracle worker, but in Matthew's retelling our attention is directed to the disciples.

That shift in emphasis can also be seen in some other clues Matthew leaves on the scene, hoping they'll be discovered by some sharp-eyed biblical detective. Mark opens the story by saying the disciples took Jesus with them into the boat "just as he was," suggesting that they were the ones calling the shots. In his account Matthew turns things around and says when Jesus got into the boat, "his disciples followed him." Here Jesus takes the lead, and with his use of the verb "to follow" Matthew lets the reader know that a main theme of the story is discipleship. The same can be said about the words he puts in the disciples' mouths to arouse Jesus from his slumber. Mark has them address him as "teacher" and ask if he cares that they are dying, but in Matthew they utter a panicked command that is loaded with theological significance—"Lord, save us!" Jesus takes their plea as an opportunity to teach them a lesson about what it means to be a faithful follower, and so he opts to calm the storm within them before taking care of the one raging around them. Flipping the order of two events might not seem like much of an inconsistency, but this time it completely transforms the point of a story.

When?

Neither Matthew nor Luke provides a specific date for any of the events described in their infancy narratives, and so they don't give us information about when Jesus was born. Although they're short on specifics, both gospels mention certain historical details that might allow us to date things in relative terms. Whether or not those details are accurate and can be trusted is another matter, but in both cases they reveal the presence of the Clue of the Inconsistency.

The Gospel of Matthew refers several times to King Herod (sometimes called "the Great") as the ruler in power when Jesus was born. The visit of the wise men took place "in the time of King Herod" (Matt. 2:1), and Joseph and his family remained in Egypt until Herod's death (Matt. 2:15, 19–20). Matthew also states that Joseph settled in Nazareth because he was afraid of Herod's son Archelaus, who had taken over as ruler in Judea after his father's death (Matt. 2:22). The reigns of both Herod and Archelaus are well documented outside the Bible, so these are not figures Matthew created on his own, and what we know about Herod's time on the throne is significant because it exposes an example of the Clue of the Inconsistency. It is well established that Herod died in 4 BCE, which means that if we accept Matthew's claim that Jesus was alive at the time of the king's death, he was born at least a half decade or so prior to the BCE/CE (or BC/AD if you prefer) divide. It's a bit odd to think of the first Christmas as occurring in the BCE era, but that's where Matthew's Gospel definitely places it.

As does Luke's, because he also locates Jesus's birth during Herod's reign (Luke 1:5). He then outdoes Matthew by mentioning two other political leaders who might be of assistance in dating the events. Luke explains that Jesus was born in Bethlehem because Mary and Joseph happened to be there to take part in a census. "In those days a decree went out from *Emperor Augustus* that all the world should be registered. This was the first *registration* and was taken while *Quirinius* was governor of Syria. All went to their own towns to be registered" (Luke 2:1–3). Augustus ruled as Roman emperor from 27 BCE to 14 CE, so that doesn't help at all, because Jesus was certainly born sometime in that range of years. But the reference to a census during Quirinius's time looks really promising. If there's a record of when Quirinius's census was taken, that would go a long way toward pinning down when Jesus was born. Well, we do know the exact year of Quirinius's big head count, and it leads to one big headache because it took place in 6 CE—ten whole years after the death of the same Herod who Luke himself says was king when Jesus was born. So with his double reference to the "days of King Herod" and the census of Quirinius just one chapter apart from each other, Luke is guilty of a whopper of a historical inconsistency.

How to work your informants

Even if Quirinius's census had been a decade or so earlier and right in the sweet spot that would allow us to date Jesus's birth, we'd still have to be really cautious and think twice about its usefulness. That's because of something we in the trade call "the criterion of multiple attestation," which is just Bible detective lingo for "the more, the merrier." The CMA's basic premise is the following: the likelihood that something mentioned in the New Testament actually occurred rises with the number of sources that refer to it. In other words, if two or more gospels mention an event, this increases the probability that it may have really happened. This is standard operating procedure in investigative work—if all your sources and informants agree on who was the last guy to be seen with the missing person, it's probably time to bring him in for a talk. But there's a caveat. Because we know that some writers were dependent on others for their information, the identities of those sources matter. If only Matthew and Mark refer to an event, that isn't very significant because the general consensus is that Matthew used Mark's Gospel to write his own. But if that same event is also related in the Gospel of John, who doesn't appear to have relied on the other gospels, then that's a point in favor of it having occurred. If the letters of Paul also refer to it, that increases the likelihood even further. At the other end of the spectrum, because Luke's Gospel is the only one to mention Quirinius, it would be best to avoid using his census for dating purposes, even if it had taken place during the ideal Goldilocks Zone time period.

Counting time

The book of Judges contains an interesting example of the Clue of the Inconsistency on a matter of chronology, but it escapes the notice of almost all its readers. It's a clue that builds up, literally over time, and the best way to discover it would be to have a calculator close at hand as you read the entire book. The work describes the careers of twelve individuals called judges who served as leaders of the Israelite people from the time they entered the land until the rise of the kingship. More attention is devoted to some judges than to others in the book, but in almost every case the number of years the person served as judge is specified, as well as the amount of time that sometimes passed between judges. According to the text, there was only one judge at a time, as each replaced the previous one. The problem becomes apparent when we add up the number of years mentioned in the book and discover that the era of the judges lasted a bit over four centuries. That is more than twice the amount of time that the generally agreed-upon biblical chronology allots for the period between the entry into the land and the rise of the monarchy (approximately 1200 BCE to 1000 BCE). This indicates that the book of Judges was not written as a historical account but is rather a theological document that describes the ongoing lack of faith of the Israelites.

The Clue of the Inconsistency can sometimes identify the different time periods in which portions of a text were written. This is especially useful for those sleuths interested in piecing together how a biblical book took shape. In the book of Isaiah, for example, paying attention to the peoples and political entities that are mentioned can help to isolate its various stages of composition. This can be seen through a comparison of these three passages:

> Ah, *Assyria*, the rod of my anger—
>   the club in their hands is my fury! (Isa. 10:5)

> And *Babylon*, the glory of kingdoms,
>   the splendor and pride of the Chaldeans,
> will be like Sodom and Gomorrah
>   when God overthrew them. (Isa. 13:19)

> [God] says of *Cyrus*, "He is my shepherd,
>   and he shall carry out all my purpose." (Isa. 44:28)

Each verse refers to an empire of the ancient Near East that exercised control over Israel for a period of time. The Assyrians were the dominant force for about three hundred years until the seventh century

BCE, when they were defeated by the Babylonians, who controlled the area until the middle part of the sixth century BCE. The Babylonian Empire was replaced by the Persian Empire, which was headed by Cyrus the Great (590-530 BCE), who is mentioned in the third passage above.

It stands to reason that the passages that mention them would have been written only when the empires were at the height of their powers and would have posed a potential threat to Israel. Consequently, those sections of the book that refer to a particular empire can be dated in relative terms with a high degree of confidence. This shows how the Clue of the Inconsistency—in this case, one regarding foreign peoples—can sometimes be a helpful aid in efforts to reconstruct how a biblical book developed.

One final temporal Clue of the Inconsistency is a very interesting case from the New Testament. All four Gospels agree that on the night before he was put to death Jesus met with his closest followers for a final meal known as the Last Supper. What they don't agree on is when that gathering took place. The three Synoptic Gospels all identify it as a Passover meal (Matt. 26:17-19; Mark 14:12-16; Luke 22:7-13), but John doesn't follow suit. His account of the Last Supper begins with the words "Now *before the festival of the Passover* . . ." (John 13:1), and he remarks that during Jesus's trial the Passover had not yet begun. Similarly, John points out that Jesus's death took place the day before Passover (John 19:14a).

John doesn't change the day of the Last Supper just to be a contrarian, but because it better fits his Christology. For him Jesus is the Lamb of God, a title bestowed on him in the very first chapter of the gospel (John 1:29). It isn't the timing of Jesus's last meal with his disciples that John is interested in but the timing of his death. He realizes that if the Last Supper was the night before Passover, then Jesus died the next day just as the Jewish people were slaughtering the lambs that they would eat during the feast that started at sundown. John highlights Jesus's role as the Lamb of God by including an episode that's only in his gospel. Soldiers charged with breaking the legs of the crucified to hasten their deaths do not break Jesus's legs because he is already dead, which leads John to comment, "These things occurred so that the scripture might be fulfilled, 'None of his bones shall be broken'" (John 19:36). That citation is an allusion to two Hebrew Bible passages that forbid the breaking of the bones of the Passover lambs (Exod. 12:46; Num. 9:12). As in so many other cases, this inconsistency is not a mistake but an opportunity to discover something profound about a text.

Where?

It is perhaps the most iconic image in all of world literature, one that has been reproduced literally thousands of times by artists, sculptors, filmmakers, and grammar school kids everywhere. We're talking about the nativity scene that depicts the birth of Jesus. Even if you haven't set foot in a church in decades, you can conjure it in your mind—the baby in the manger, his mother and Joseph nearby, the wise men with their gifts, a group of shepherds and their flock, angels floating in the air, the star twinkling above it all.

That world-famous scene doesn't exist anywhere in the pages of the New Testament. It's a potpourri of items taken from two of the gospels that blend together to form a memorable and heartwarming picture that isn't depicted *in toto* in Sacred Writ. The angels, shepherds, and manger are from Luke, while the wise men and the star appear courtesy of Matthew. That discovery got us thinking that it would be a good idea to broaden our investigation to see what other place-related inconsistencies we might be able to uncover in the infancy narratives.

The results were eye-opening, to say the least. About the only thing the two stories have in common place-wise is that Jesus was born in Bethlehem. Beyond that, it's one big Clue of the Inconsistency. In Matthew, it looks like it was a home birth because that's where the wise men head when they pay their visit. *"On entering the house*, they saw the child with Mary his mother; and they knelt down and paid him homage" (Matt. 2:11a). There's not a manger in sight, and as far as we can tell, the family was living in Bethlehem when Jesus was born. The visitors are hardly out the door when Joseph is told by an angel to get out of town because King Herod is on the warpath and the child is in danger. So he and the family head to the land of the pharaohs, where they have to lie low because of the demands of a crazed politician. Once Herod gives up the ghost, they're able to return, but things still aren't safe in Bethlehem, so they settle in the northern town of Nazareth in Galilee.

The family's trek is in the exact opposite direction in Luke, minus the side trip to Egypt, as they begin in Nazareth and end up in Bethlehem. As in Matthew, Joseph and Mary will soon be on the move because of a politician's proclamation, but this time it's the notice of Quirinius's census that has them packing their bags. Because they were far from home and there was no room for them where travelers usually stayed, Mary had to place Jesus in a manger after he was born. The inconsistency is impossible to miss—in Matthew they're from Bethlehem and Jesus is born at home, but in Luke Nazareth is their hometown and Jesus is born on the road.

With those two different starting points, each gospel writer has a problem to solve—Matthew has to explain how the family moves from Bethlehem to Nazareth, while Luke must figure out a way of getting Mary to Bethlehem from Nazareth so Jesus can be born there. Luckily, the politicians come to the rescue (we never thought we'd write that sentence). Even though Herod is no longer alive, things are still dangerous for the family in Bethlehem, so Matthew has them settle in Nazareth to avoid Herod's son Archelaus. Similarly, the census called by Quirinius provides Luke with the perfect excuse to point Joseph and Mary toward Bethlehem.

There's one more thing, though. At the risk of sounding like Lt. Columbo wannabes (readers under a certain age will need to consult YouTube), we have a final question to ask before we put this case to bed. Why the interest in both Bethlehem *and* Nazareth? Matthew and Luke agree that Jesus was born in Bethlehem, so if they had just left things at that there would be no need to complicate the story by bringing Nazareth into the picture. Here's where it gets really interesting and, perhaps for some, a bit disturbing. For Luke and Matthew the reason why Jesus must be born in Bethlehem is a no-brainer—he was the Messiah, the Messiah would come from the line of David, and Bethlehem was the city of David.

But there's a curious fact about the Jesus/Bethlehem connection that we can't ignore—the only places it's made in the entire New Testament are in the first two chapters of Matthew and Luke. Outside the infancy narratives, Bethlehem is never identified as the birthplace of Jesus. Whenever he's connected with a location elsewhere, that place is Nazareth. He's consistently "Jesus of Nazareth," not "Jesus of Bethlehem." He's associated with Nazareth in twenty-two passages in the New Testament, and they're found in all four Gospels and the Acts of the Apostles. That's a pretty broad distribution—do you recall the criterion of multiple attestation? Matthew and Luke *had* to mention Nazareth because everyone knew that's where Jesus hailed from.

We're sorry to break the news to you so soon after you learned the truth about the nativity scene, but in all likelihood Jesus was born in Nazareth and not in Bethlehem. We've said all along that detectives have to go where the evidence takes them, and that appears to be our destination in this case. It was its connection to David and therefore the messianic line that tipped the scale in Bethlehem's favor for Matthew and Luke. Nonetheless, that christological reasoning aside, all the evidence suggests Nazareth was Jesus's birthplace, and Luke and Matthew say as much later on in their gospels.

Another famous biblical scene that has been reproduced countless times by artists and others is God giving the Ten Commandments and the rest of the law to Moses. If you ask people where that event took place, almost every one of them would say Mount Sinai, but they'd be only half right because in quite a few places in the Bible it also goes by the name Mount Horeb. We know these are names for the same spot and not two different locations because they're both identified as the place where Moses received the law, and that was a onetime event. Here's how it's described in the book of Exodus just before Moses gets the Ten Commandments from God: "Now *Mount Sinai* was wrapped in smoke, because the LORD had descended upon it in fire; the smoke went up like the smoke of a kiln, while the whole mountain shook violently" (Exod. 19:18). In another biblical book the same scene is mentioned, but there the mountain is referred to by its other name. "There was nothing in the ark except the two tablets of stone that Moses had placed there at *Horeb*, where the LORD made a covenant with the Israelites, when they came out of the land of Egypt" (1 Kings 8:9). As with Moses's father-in-law and his three names, this Clue of the Inconsistency indicates that the mountain of the law was called two different things, suggesting that there were probably multiple sources behind the biblical text.

Over in the New Testament, a passage in the Gospel of Mark suggests that its author might have been directionally challenged. One indication of this is found in a verse that describes the initial encounter Jesus has with a man he will go on to heal. "They came to the other side of the sea, to the country of the Gerasenes. And when he had stepped out of the boat, *immediately* a man out of the tombs with an unclean spirit met him" (Mark 5:1-2). One of Mark's favorite words is "immediately," and in fact he uses it more times in his gospel than it's found in the rest of the New Testament combined (a good detective is always aware of a person's tendencies). This is one time too many, though, because the town of Gerasa (Jerash in modern-day Jordan) is located about thirty miles south of the Sea of Galilee, and so there is no way the man would have been able to greet Jesus as soon as he left the boat.

But it gets worse. Mark goes on to dig a bigger hole for himself when he describes how Jesus cures the man. "Now there on the hillside a great herd of swine was feeding; and the unclean spirits begged him, 'Send us into the swine; let us enter them.' So he gave them permission. And the unclean spirits came out and entered the swine; and the herd, numbering about two thousand, rushed down the steep bank into the sea, and were drowned in the sea" (Mark 5:11–13). We've had lots of fun trying to imagine that scene, given the water's thirty-mile distance from Gerasa. As far as we know, this is the only biblical passage related to the expression "When pigs fly." Matthew is obviously aware of Mark's problem because in his version he changes the location of the story to Gadara. Nice try, but that's still six miles from the Sea of Galilee.

WHY THIS CLUE MATTERS

The Clue of the Inconsistency forces us to do something that is vitally important—it demands that we ask questions of the biblical text. The questions vary depending on the type of inconsistency, but they're all the same in that they make us think carefully about what we are reading. Many people are encouraged to be passive readers of the Bible, and they're often taught from a very young age to accept what it says, no questions asked. That approach is challenged by the Clue of the Inconsistency because it reminds us that the questions are already there in the text, whether we ask them or not, just waiting for an active and engaged reader who is willing to try to answer them. This clue can help you become that type of reader. Never forget—inconsistencies are sometimes opportunities and not just mistakes.

THE CLUE OF THE INCONSISTENCY CAN HELP US . . .

1. Learn to ask questions of the Bible.
2. Consider issues related to the sources of the biblical writings.
3. Discover the agenda and concerns of an author.
4. Appreciate the complexity of the biblical literature.
5. Read more carefully and critically.
6. Realize that inconsistencies can be opportunities.

THE CASEBOOK

Your assignment for this chapter continues the comparative study of the Gospels of Matthew and Luke that was undertaken in each section with regard to their infancy narratives. Now you will read their passion narratives of Jesus's arrest and death that are found in Matthew 26:36–27:66 and Luke 22:39–23:56 and put together a case file that identifies those places where the Clue of the Inconsistency is present in the stories. Do this with reference to the same four Ws that were discussed throughout the chapter—who, what, when, and where. Bonus points will be given to those whose case files also include the passion narratives of the other two gospels in Mark 14:32–15:47 and John 18:1–19:42.

6

The Clue of the

DOUBLET

Every time a new murder mystery hits the big screen, we see a bump in whatever crimes it depicts. The reason? Copycats—sickos who act out for the publicity. Who knows when the first copycat crawled out from under a rock, but the term was coined with Jack the Ripper clones. The sensational London newspaper reports brought them out of the woodwork, and they haven't stopped since. As late as 2008, some whacko named Derek Brown was still following the Ripper's footsteps in Whitechapel 120 years after the fact. Jack's case may be the most famous, but it's sure not the only one to spawn copycats. There was the creepy Zodiac killer in San Francisco in the 1960s, who was also never caught. And thirty years later, Heriberto ("Eddie") Seda was trying to copy him in New York. Sadly, the most prominent copycat cases these days are school shooters who copycat Eric Harris and Dylan Klebold's rampage at Columbine High School in Littleton, Colorado, in 1999. Harris and Klebold may have been copycats themselves, borrowing from a couple of school shootings three years earlier.

There have been movies about copycats, like *Copycat* in 1995, starring Sigourney Weaver and Harry Connick Jr. (the perfect choice to play the lead in a film with that title since he's made a fortune channeling crooners like Frank Sinatra over the years). There have been enough cases of actual copycats to spawn a reality show, *Copycat Killers* (REELZ channel, 2016-). Ironically, a lot of the cases they present were copying fictional murders from TV or the movies. The most notorious case of copycatting fiction is probably John Hinckley Jr.'s near assassination of President Ronald Reagan in 1981. Hinckley got a little carried away with the characters in *Taxi Driver* and was trying to impress Jodie Foster. There are lots of other instances, too, involving copies of scenes from *Dexter*, *The Matrix*, and *Scream*. One of our favorite shows of all time, *Breaking Bad*, has been copycatted repeatedly, and not just for its murders. Blue meth inspired by the series turned up in Kansas City, Missouri, in 2010; an Alabama drug dealer adopted the name Walter White, like the alias of the lead character in the show; and there was at least one case, in 2013, of a schoolteacher who got cancer and started dealing drugs to pay for his treatments, pausing along the way to shave his head, just like W.W. did.

THE CLUE OF THE DOUBLET: repetition in the text in which the same or similar information is given two (or more) times

There is plenty of the sincerest form of flattery in the Good Book. Pioneering Bible sleuths called such cases doublets, and the name stuck. (According to IMDb, there haven't been any movies titled *Doublet* yet, but maybe this chapter will help to spawn one.) With all due respect, the term doesn't quite cut it, because there are sometimes multiple imitations—triplets and quadruplets. We like "copycats," but we're no G-men or anything, just a couple of local Bible dicks, so we're not looking to rock any boats.

The Clue of the Doublet is a type of repetition in the text in which the same or similar information is given two (or more) times. Doublets can take different forms. They can be alternate versions of the same story. They may repeat a particular element that stands out in two different stories. Sometimes a doublet is the repetition of an element within a single story. If the doublet consists of alternate versions of the same story, they can be woven together into a single narrative. The differences between the versions of a doublet often provide valuable information about the text or the author's intentions, such as different sources behind the biblical text, editorial work, or the theology/ideology of a text. They can also indicate dependence of one text or story upon another.

The forests around the trees

There are major cases of doublets in the Bible files. We're talking whole books. These are so well known that people often miss the fact that they're repeats. We may as well start with the best known and biggest of them all—namely, the New Testament Gospels.

Double doublet

There are four New Testament Gospels, so that makes them a double doublet or a quadruplet, which is pretty rare, biblically speaking. They are a foursome because they all tell the story of the life of Jesus. When you start looking at them closely, there's not a whole lot that all four of them have in common. For instance, the only miracle they all recount is the feeding of the five thousand (Matt. 14:15-21; Mark 6:35-44; Luke 9:12-17; John 6:5-13). That's mainly because John is the outlier, the lone wolf copycat, you might say. Matthew, Mark, and Luke form a triplet that even bears a name: the Synoptic Gospels (or Synoptics for short). They all follow the same basic outline and have lots of stories in common. The theory that explains this relationship is textbook—literally. It's in the training manuals for New Testament detectives in most forces across the country. It's called the "two-source theory," and it looks like this:

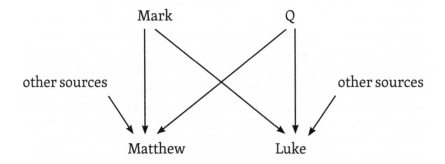

Its basic line of reasoning is that Mark was the oldest gospel written and Matthew and Luke both used Mark as one of their main sources. That explains the material they all three have in common. But there are chunks—mostly sayings of Jesus—that Matthew and Luke have but are absent from Mark. That's where the presumed second source comes in. They call it Q. That's short for *Quelle*, which means "source" in German. The eggheads who came up with the theory were Germans and not very imaginative where names were concerned. Matthew and Luke also had their own individual sources (Luke copped to this in Luke 1:1-4, but Matthew never came clean about it), which is why they each have things that none of the other gospels have. Plus they each have their own takes on the whole Jesus story.

John's take is way different from the takes of the other three. It follows a different outline for Jesus's life. While the Synoptics have Jesus spending all his ministry in Galilee and coming to Jerusalem only for the last week of his life, when he is arrested, tried, and crucified, John has Jesus going back and forth constantly between Galilee and Jerusalem. That's why in John Jesus drives the merchants out of the temple at the beginning of his gospel in chapter 2, whereas according to Matthew, Mark, and Luke, he did that near the end, shortly before he was arrested. It might be hard to piece together a timeline because of the diversity of testimony, but the four Gospels are still a quadruplet because all four tell the story of Jesus's life on earth. As is often the case with copycats and doublets, we learn more from the differences than from the similarities.

Law-full

The first five books of the Bible (Genesis, Exodus, Leviticus, Numbers, Deuteronomy) go together. They are called the Pentateuch (the prefix "penta-," as in Pentagon, is a dead giveaway). Don't worry; they're not going to one-up the gospels by forming a quintuplet, and there's no such word as "pentuplet." As Jewish scripture, they are referred to collectively as the *Torah*, which means "law" or "instruction." Here's why: in Exodus 20 Moses comes down from Mount Sinai to deliver to the people of Israel the message from God that he received on the mountain. From that point on, it's pretty much all law (with notable exceptions like the golden calf episode in Exodus 32) for the rest of Exodus (which has a total of forty chapters), all of Leviticus (twenty-seven chapters), and the first nine chapters of Numbers.

Not only that, but the book of Deuteronomy is also mostly law, which is what its name means: "Deuteronomy" = "second law." The word "second" is a strong clue that we're looking at a doublet. The setting of Deuteronomy is a location near the promised land, as Moses reviews the law for the people right before they cross over the Jordan River to enter it. There are laws in Deuteronomy that are new or different, like the one about levirate marriage that we explore in the Clue of the Weird Social Custom. But there are also laws that are similar to those presented earlier. Again, though, even with the similar laws, it is the differences that are most telling. A prime example is the Ten Commandments. There's a version of them in Exodus 20 and another in Deuteronomy 5, but they don't add up to twenty commandments. They are virtually identical, with a couple of exceptions.

One of those exceptions is in the Sabbath law. Actually, the law is the same; the rationale for it is where the difference comes in. Exodus 20:11 says, "For in six days the LORD made heaven and earth, the sea, and all that is in them, but rested the seventh day; therefore the LORD blessed the sabbath day and consecrated it," while Deuteronomy 5:15 reads, "Remember that you were a slave in the land of Egypt, and the LORD your God brought you out from there with a mighty hand and an outstretched arm; therefore the LORD your God commanded you to keep the sabbath day." Not close at all. Exodus harks back to creation and says that God rested on the seventh day when he created the world and made the Sabbath day holy, so you need to do the same. Deuteronomy takes the exodus as the reason: You know what it's like to be a slave. You were blessed because God rescued you, so you need to give your own slaves, as well as your animals, a break from work on the Sabbath. The authors or editors of the two books who incorporated the Ten Commandments had different orientations about theology and society. Maybe the people they were writing for did too.

Pair of kings

The books of Samuel and Kings tell the story of the Israelite monarchies. Monarchies—plural—because Israel split into two countries, Israel in the north and Judah in the south, and each had its own set of kings. First Samuel is mostly about Saul, the first king of Israel, and David; 2 Samuel is all about David, mostly about his reign. First Kings 1–11 is about

Solomon. Then, after his reign, the division takes place, and 1 Kings 12–2 Kings 17 toggle back and forth between the two countries until the destruction of Israel by the Assyrians (722 BCE). The rest of 2 Kings is all about Judah, until its destruction by the Babylonians (586 BCE).

A lot of civilians who never walked a beat aren't aware that there's another version of this history in the Bible—in 1-2 Chronicles, a biblical neighborhood that most folks avoid at all costs. That's understandable; 1 Chronicles begins with nine chapters of genealogies that are hard to slog through. Then, when you get to the David story in chapter 10, all the good stuff is left out. There's no Bathsheba story and nothing about Absalom's revolt (check out 2 Sam. 11-20). It's like a history of the Clinton presidency with no mention of Monica Lewinsky or the Whitewater controversy. The Chronicler also left out the story of the Northern Kingdom, except where it happened to intersect with Judah. He tossed in plenty of religious stuff about the temple and priests, but you can still see how he was able to condense four books into two. It's *Reader's Digest* without "Laughter, the Best Medicine." At least that's what most Bible detectives think happened. There are one or two inspectors in Scotland Yard who hold a more complicated theory that both the author of Samuel-Kings and the author of Chronicles had access to an independent history that they each tweaked according to their individual proclivities. We don't buy it, but this shows the kinds of disagreements you can have with a doublet as large as six whole books encompassing the entire national histories of two separate countries. On the other hand, what can you expect from cops called bobbies who live on an island and still have a queen (or king, depending on how long it takes this book to come out)?

Tell me why, why, why

Now that we've seen how big doublets can be, we turn to the much trickier question of why they occur. Unfortunately, there's no one-size-fits-all for them, any more than there is for murders. They run the gamut from Cain to Jack the Ripper to OJ. Money, jealousy, notoriety, mental illness, video games—people kill for all kinds of nutty reasons. Sometimes the reason is obvious, and other times you never find it out. We don't claim to be shrinks or anything like that, but we do have lots of experience with doublets. So we're going to propose half a box of donuts worth of categories behind why doublets occur. We're not saying these are the only reasons, just that they're ones we have observed. And, we're watching our waistlines these days, so we're cutting down on the donuts.

Dominos

Let's start simple. One category of doublet is the repetition of the end of one book at the beginning of another book as a way of linking them, kind of like "previously on [insert the name of your favorite cop show]." The best example is the first two and a half verses of the book of Ezra, which basically repeat the last two verses of 2 Chronicles:

> 2 Chronicles 36:22-23: In the first year of King Cyrus of Persia, in fulfillment of the word of the Lord spoken by Jeremiah, the Lord stirred up the spirit of King Cyrus of Persia so that he sent a herald throughout all his kingdom and also declared in a written edict: "Thus says King Cyrus of Persia: The Lord, the God of heaven, has given me all the kingdoms of the earth, and he has charged me to build him a house at Jerusalem, which is in Judah. Whoever is among you of all his people, may the Lord his God be with him! Let him go up."

> Ezra 1:1-3a: In the first year of King Cyrus of Persia, in order that the word of the Lord by the mouth of Jeremiah might be accomplished, the Lord stirred up the spirit of King Cyrus of Persia so that he sent a herald throughout all his kingdom, and also in a written edict declared: "Thus says King Cyrus of Persia: The Lord, the God of heaven, has given me all the kingdoms of the earth, and he has charged me to build him a house at Jerusalem in Judah. Any of those among you who are of his people—may their God be with them!—are now permitted to go up to Jerusalem in Judah, and rebuild the house of the Lord. . . ."

The repetition signals an affiliation between the two books, even if it's not clear what that affiliation was. Maybe Chronicles and Ezra were written by the same person, at least at some stage in their development. That's what most of the old-timers thought. But the common wisdom in Bible enforcement these days is that they were written by different authors and that Chronicles was a prequel to Ezra-Nehemiah. The Greek Septuagint translation has repetitions like this at the end of 1 Samuel and beginning of 2 Samuel, the end of 2 Samuel and start of 1 Kings, the end of 1 Kings and start of 2 Kings, and the end of 1 Chronicles and beginning of 2 Chronicles. The first chapter of Exodus is like this in its list of those who came to Egypt with Jacob, which recaps the end of the Joseph story from Genesis, especially Genesis 46:26-27.

Over in the New Testament we have a similar thing, but the rookie investigator can be easily tripped up and not sniff out the presence of the doublet. The first chapter of the book of Acts opens up with a reference to Jesus's ascension into heaven, which is exactly how the Gospel of Luke ends. This is one of many reasons why, in a rare show of unity, it's agreed by Bible detectives in forces around the world that the same author wrote both works. The only problem is, we have a clear case of breaking and entering that makes the connection between them less obvious because the Gospel of John comes between Luke and Acts. This creates a twenty-one-chapter-long gap between the two references to Jesus's ascension that reminds us to keep our noses to the ground and always stay alert for doublets no matter how cold the trail may seem.

Copycats

We don't mean to create our own doublet here, but another straightforward case of this sort is when one biblical book lifts a text from another. Isaiah and Jeremiah have both been brought up on charges of copycatting and have been convicted in more than one court. Isaiah 36-39 is virtually identical to the bulk of 2 Kings 18-20, and Jeremiah 52 effectively repeats the last three verses of 2 Kings 24 and all of 2 Kings 25. The long narrative sections from Kings stand out from the biographical and prophetic materials in Isaiah and Jeremiah like a showing of *Mary Poppins* at a film noir festival. Isaiah 36-39 interrupt the transition from chapter 35 to chapter 40, and Jeremiah 52 looks like it was tacked on at the end. Unfortunately, it's not always so easy to tell who the copycat was. Psalm 18 is essentially the same as 2 Samuel 22, but it's not clear who was looking over whose shoulder or whether both writers committed the infraction by peeking at a third party's paper. Sometimes the hints are there and you've just got to be tenacious, like a basset hound on the scent of an escapee. Here's what we mean: in 1 Kings 17:17-24 and 2 Kings 4:32-37 there are two stories about a prophet (Elijah, Elisha) raising a boy from the dead. (We talk about this lucky lad in the chapter on the Clue of the Echo, which is a distant cousin of the Clue of the Doublet.) As always, when you get a bunch of detectives together, there are different theories about how the doublet was committed. They boil down to three options: the Elijah version ripped off the Elisha one, or vice versa, or they both swiped the story from someone else.

We're going to go out on a limb here and argue that the evidence is pretty clear on this one even if the details need to get ironed out. The Elisha rendition is part of a longer story about a rich woman who befriends the prophet and adds an upper room on her house for him to stay in when he drops by for a visit (we've checked, and she filed all the necessary paperwork for a zoning variance). The Elijah one is also a sequel to a story in which he saves a widow and her son who are about to starve to death. Sometime after, the kid gets sick and bites the big one. In 1 Kings 17:17 this widow is called "the mistress of the house." It's weird that a destitute widow would have a house, and even stranger that she would be called the mistress or lady of the house, which is a title for an upper-class woman. Those terms fit the situation of the rich woman in the Elisha account and begin to make you suspect that that's where they come from. To seal the deal, in 1 Kings 17:19, Elijah takes the dead kid up to his room and lays him on his (the prophet's) bed. The upper room and the bed are straight out of the Elisha story in 2 Kings 4, but they're out of place for Elijah and the poor widow. Maybe it's not absolute proof that Elijah was the copycat, but it's strong enough for us to borrow our friend E. A. Poe's word and call it "telltale."

One and one make a whole

The old-timers who coined terms like "doublet" cut their teeth on cases in the neighborhood of Genesis 1–11 where there's a doublet on every block. The classic case from the beginning (literally) was Genesis 1-2, which contains two originally independent creation stories. They both begin the same way with a temporal clause + a parenthesis describing what the world was like when God started creating + the first thing God created. (We're going to use our own translations here to make the point, but we'll spare you the technical mumbo jumbo that lies behind them; just take our word for it that this is the way the testimony of forensic experts comes out):

Genesis 1:1–3: When God began to create the heavens and the earth (the earth was formless and empty, darkness was on the surface of the deep, and God's wind/spirit swept over the surface of the waters), God said, "Let there be light." And there was light.

Genesis 2:4b–7: When ("in the day that") YHWH God made the earth and heavens (there was no wild plant on the earth yet, nor had any wild grass sprouted because Yhwh God had not caused it to rain on the earth and there was no human to work the ground, but a mist came up from the earth and watered the whole surface of the ground), YHWH God formed the human from the dust of the ground and breathed into his nostrils the breath of life so that the human became a living being.

Already you can see that both accounts deal with the same thing—creation of the world—but in very different terms. They use different language, such as "create" versus "make" and "heavens and earth" versus "earth and heavens." Even their names for God are different: "God" versus "the Lord God" (or Yahweh, YHWH God). Their description of the earth at the moment of creation is also different: in the first one the earth is basically all wet, in the second it is basically all dry. The differences become more pronounced as the testimonies continue. In Genesis 1, creation takes place over a six-day period with God resting on the seventh day, or Sabbath. People are the last thing created, and the order goes like this:

Day 1—light	Day 4—sun, moon, stars
Day 2—sky (dome)	Day 5—birds, fish
Day 3—seas & dry land + vegetation	Day 6—land animals + humans
Day 7—Sabbath	

In Genesis 2 there is no timetable, and the order is completely different:

the man
the garden
the animals
the woman

The old-timers weren't much interested in figuring out how and why these doublets fit together. They assumed that source documents had been pieced together by the cut-and-paste method and were only concerned with pointing out the doublets. Things have changed, though, and there's more interest these days in the whole *megillah* and how it got that way. If you look at the facts of the case from that angle, there's a certain logic to putting the two accounts together one right after the other, whether it was done by an author or an editor. If you don't get too picky about the details, you can read the second one as a more focused version of the creation of humans from the first account. You can take "in the day" in 2:4b as referring specifically to day 6 from Genesis 1 rather than as a general time expression for "when." So in Genesis 1–2 the two texts that form the doublet have been placed together to convey a single, continuing picture of creation.

Interweaving the elements

This category has some twists and turns, so you may need your magnifying glass, not to mention your rain slicker. Sometimes the elements of a doublet aren't placed side-by-side or back-to-back or end-to-end but are woven together like a fabric. There's strong evidence for this kind of doublet in the Noah story in Genesis 6–8. This guy started off so righteous and blameless he didn't even have a parking ticket or a record to put it on. Next thing you know, he absconds with a whole boatload of animals. The righteous and blameless assessment (Gen. 6:9) is part of a doublet. It goes on to say, "Noah walked with God." Right before that, Genesis 6:8 reads, "Noah found favor in the sight of the LORD." The two statements make the same point and constitute a doublet. What's more, each of them describes Noah in contrast to the rest of the population, which God had decided to destroy. Genesis 6:5–7 goes with the "found favor" version and puts it this way: "The LORD saw that the wickedness of humankind was great in the earth, and that every inclination of the thoughts of their hearts was only evil continually. And the LORD was sorry that he had made humankind on the earth, and it grieved him to his heart. So the LORD said, 'I will blot out from the earth the human beings I have created—people together with animals and creeping things and birds of the air, for I am sorry that I have made them.'" Genesis 6:11–13, from the "walked with God" version, says the same thing in somewhat different terms, "The earth was corrupt in God's sight, and the earth was filled with violence. And God saw that the earth was corrupt; for all flesh had corrupted its ways upon the earth. And God said to Noah, 'I have determined to make an end of all flesh, for the earth is filled with violence because of them; now I am going to destroy them along with the earth.'"

God tells Noah to build an ark (Gen. 6:14–18), and then there's another doublet. Everybody knows the two-by-two version of the story where God tells Noah to bring one pair of every kind of animal aboard the ark (Gen. 6:19–21), but that's only half the story. There's a whole other version in Genesis 7:2–3 where Noah is supposed to bring seven pairs of clean animals (those that can be sacrificed and eaten) and only one pair of unclean animals. This can be a shocking revelation to people who began life under a crib mobile with pairs of animals on it, so if you need a moment, we understand. Lt. La Rosa was so bummed he had to take the afternoon off. To soften the blow a little, we'll just point out that there are doublets about where the floodwater came from (fountains of the great deep and windows of the heavens in 7:11 versus rain in 7:12) and how long it lasted (40 days and nights in 7:12 versus 150 days in 7:24), not to mention the two different birds to test the water's recession—a raven in 8:7 versus a dove three times in 8:8–12—and two separate promises not to destroy the world again by flood (8:21; 9:11–17). The second one is called a covenant and is sealed by the rainbow.

What these variants show is that in contrast to the other categories we've surveyed so far (except for just plain copycatting) where the two versions of a story were placed together, in the flood story they were interlaced. The result is the same as the one-and-one category—the doublets were combined to form a single story—but the modus operandi of the doers was different. This case is a good illustration of the close connection between the Clue of the Doublet and the Clue of the Inconsistency, where Noah's animal heist is also discussed.

Separate projects

Doublets don't have to be together at all. The doublets involving whole books that we looked at earlier represent separate projects. They tell much the same story as another book, but with key differences. Maybe those differences are due to other information available to the authors.

Maybe they're due to a different take on the story. In either case, they want to do something different, or at least one of them does. They may even borrow from the other. If the "two-source theory" is right, Matthew and Luke were both aware of Mark and used it, but they wanted to tweak the story of Jesus differently. Ditto for Chronicles with regard to Samuel-Kings; the Chronicler wanted to present a more sanitized version of David, in part by leaving out some things that might have tarnished the ruler's reputation.

On a more limited scale, there are two versions of Paul's conversion in the New Testament that together constitute a doublet. One is Paul's own account in Galatians 1:15–17; the other is in Acts 9:1–19, which has duplicates of its own in Acts 22 and 26, making the story in effect a triplet or rare quadruplet. The Acts versions, being from the same author, are pretty similar to each other, but Galatians 1 is different enough that you have to look at them together to recognize that they're talking about the same set of events. Acts is the more exciting of the two. Saul (Paul's former name) is on his way to Damascus to arrest Christians when he sees a bright light that blinds him and hears Jesus speaking to him. He continues into the city, where he remains blind for three days until a man named Ananias comes to him, heals him, and baptizes him. He stays in Damascus until he learns of a plot against him. He escapes by being let down through an opening in the city wall. Then he goes to Jerusalem, where he is eventually accepted after Barnabas vouches for him.

Paul himself in Galatians doesn't mention anything about the bright light or being blind. He also says he did not confer with anyone but went away to Arabia and only later returned to Damascus, but still did not go to Jerusalem for three years. The reason for these differences is that Paul and Luke, the author of Acts, are writing two different kinds of documents with two different objectives. Paul is making the argument that he received his revelation about the gospel directly from Jesus without any human intervention and especially without getting any stamp of approval from the leaders in Jerusalem. Luke is trying to show the unity of early Christianity under the initial authority of Jerusalem and the growth of the church radiating out from there. Since they have different projects, they emphasize different details. It's still a little odd that Paul doesn't mention any of the miraculous events that Luke does. It may be that he assumes the Galatians already know the basic story, since he doesn't even mention that he was on his way to Damascus to begin with. On the other hand, that basic story may have changed over time. Paul's version was firsthand because he was there. Luke was writing several decades later, and the story may have taken on some legendary features in the meantime. So the versions of the story they each began with were perhaps as different as the projects they used them for.

Building blocks

Our last category is sort of a combination of the "Separate Projects" and "One and One Make a Whole" categories. That's partly because we're not sure—and neither is any other Bible detective—whether these cases involve just one author/editor or more than one. Your guess is as good as ours as to whether we're dealing with a single perp or a gang. That's what makes them mysterious.

The best examples of this category are in the file on Abraham and Sarah we like to call the "Deuce of the Dunes," because their cases pair off quicker than inmates and guests on conjugal-visits day. Right off the bat there's what the old-timers called the "wife/sister stories." The name itself suggests a doublet, although we'll use the official PC terminology: tales about the endangered ancestress. Actually, it's more—a triplet in Genesis 12, 20, and 26:1-11. Like all *ménages à trois*, the relationships are complicated. The old-timers just assigned the cases to two different sources, and some of the younger folks on the force think that's exactly where they belong. Why two instead of three? Because chapter 12 and 26:1-11 work well in tandem, just like Sergeant Joe Friday and Officer Bill Gannon in the old *Dragnet* TV series. The characters in the two stories are all different. Chapter 12 is about Abraham and Sarah (a.k.a. Abram and Sarai) in Egypt with the pharaoh, while 26:1-11 is about Isaac and Rebekah in Gerar with a king named Abimelech. There's no contradiction between the stories if the son used the same trick as his old man to fool people in a different location. Both texts use the same name for God (YHWH), and 26:1 even mentions the famine in chapter 12, so it looks like they're written by the same author as two distinct episodes in the story of Abraham's family. The two still constitute a doublet in a way because their story lines sync up. They show how the same author could create a doublet by retooling and reusing the same building block.

Chapter 20, though, muddies the waters. It uses a different name for God and portrays him as having a definite preference for dreams as a means of communication. Trying to fit chapter 20 with 26:1-11 is especially tricky, because both have the same victim, Abimelech of Gerar, who would be warier the second time around. ("Fool me once, shame on you; fool me twice, shame on me.") That's why the old guys jumped on the different-sources-cut-and-pasted theory. However, some more recent Sherlock types have observed that certain details in chapter 20 seem to explain open questions from chapter 12—namely, Abraham's motive (20:11: Abraham said, "I did it because I thought, There is no fear of God at all in this place, and they will kill me because of my wife"), Abraham's lie (20:12: "Besides, she is indeed my sister, the daughter of my father but not the daughter of my mother; and she became my wife"), how the king/pharaoh put the pieces together (20:3: a dream), and whether the king/pharaoh actually had sex with the ancestress (20:6: "I did not let you touch her"). These overachievers have also pointed out that 20:18 uses the name YHWH ("the LORD").

So everything's up in the air right now about these cases. Was chapter 20 from an older source, the work of the same author as 12 and 26:1-11, or a later writer trying to clear up ambiguities in the older story? Geez, you'd think answers would come easier with more evidence. Instead, more evidence just clouds the issue.

Another story pair in the Abraham and Sarah file is an oldie but goodie: There are two versions of God making a covenant with Abraham. One of them is in Genesis 17, where God says "I will make my covenant between me and you." Easy peasy. There's a promise of the covenant—to make Abraham's descendants numerous—and a requirement for Abraham and those descendants—circumcision. We talk about that practice in the chapter on the Clue of the Weird Social Custom. Fun times! The point for the moment is that Genesis 17 shows how a covenant is supposed to work. There's a little give and take on both sides, so everybody wins. The author of this chapter was well practiced in the art of covenants, which he sprinkled throughout Genesis. Remember the covenant with Noah in 9:11-12? This is one of the telltale signs of his hand. Another is his preferred name for God—El Shaddai—translated "God Almighty" by the NRSV in Genesis 17:1. The old-timers nailed down this author as a priest (P for short), and that identification has stuck in the annals of Bible crime fighting.

But there's another, less obvious covenant in Genesis 15, where God (called YHWH God, "the LORD") tells Abe to cut up some animals and lay the pieces over against one another. Then Abe watches as a smoking firepot and a flaming torch pass between the pieces. While this is going on, the dialogue is all about how God is going to multiply Abe's descendants and give them the land of Canaan to possess. This is a covenant or treaty-making ritual from the ancient Near East that God is using to seal the deal with Abe. Notice that the ritual comes in response to Abe's question in verse 8, "How am I to know that I shall possess it?" The ritual guarantees the promise. The investigative files from the 1960s tend to lump Genesis 15 with Genesis 20 as part of the same source. But modern techniques have raised doubts with a lot of the squad, so that the majority theory now is that Genesis 15 is called non-P. No one doubts it's a doublet, but no one knows where it came from.

The Abraham and Sarah cases, whatever their origin—distinct sources or creation by an author or editor—served as building blocks to form the longer, extended story of Israel's ancestral couple. There's at least one New Testament example of the same thing. In the Gospel of Mark, three times in three chapters in a row there are similar notices about Jesus's efforts to teach his disciples about his upcoming arrest, suffering, crucifixion, and resurrection:

Mark 8:31-33: Then he began to teach them that the Son of Man must undergo great suffering, and be rejected by the elders, the chief priests, and the scribes, and be killed, and after three days rise again. He said all this quite openly. And Peter took him aside and began to rebuke him. But turning and looking at his disciples, he rebuked Peter and said, "Get behind me, Satan! For you are setting your mind not on divine things but on human things."

Mark 9:30-32: They went on from there and passed through Galilee. He did not want anyone to know it; for he was teaching his disciples, saying to them, "The Son of Man is to be betrayed into human hands, and they will kill him, and three days after being killed, he will rise again." But they did not understand what he was saying and were afraid to ask him.

Mark 10:32-34: They were on the road, going up to Jerusalem, and Jesus was walking ahead of them; they were amazed, and those who followed were afraid. He took the twelve aside again and began to tell them what was to happen to him, saying, "See, we are going up to Jerusalem, and the Son of Man will be handed over to the chief priests and the scribes, and they will condemn him to death; then they will hand him over to the Gentiles; they will mock him, and spit upon him, and flog him, and kill him; and after three days he will rise again."

In line with the two-source theory, Matthew and Luke follow suit and have parallels to all three passages (Matt. 16:21–23; 17:22–23; 20:17–19; Luke 9:22, 44–45; 18:31–34), making this one whopper of a doublet—a nonuplet actually—three passages in each of three gospels. In all cases, the disciples are perplexed and don't know how to react. Their bewilderment highlights the importance of these passages in the structure and Christology of the Synoptic Gospels, Christology being the theology of the nature of Jesus as Christ or Messiah. The disciples did not expect Jesus to suffer and die; they believed he was the Messiah who would save Israel from the Romans and set up a new Davidic kingdom. (On the meaning of Messiah as "anointed," see the Clue of the Weird Social Custom.) One of the main reasons for writing the gospels was to explain that Jesus was a different kind of Messiah who brought a different kind of salvation—a spiritual one—than had been expected. His suffering and death as atonement for sin were a big part of the Synoptics' understanding of Jesus's identity and mission.

There you have it, the six explanations that we have uncovered for doublets. Again, we're not saying these are the only ones there are. Maybe someone only ordered a half-dozen donuts to begin with. Then again, maybe the box was full and we've only picked out our favorites, leaving less obvious explanations for others, like the fruit-flavored cake kind that stay in the box and get stale until you're forced to eat them two days later when you forgot to bring a sandwich or money for lunch and didn't want to hit up your partner because you were already into him for twenty bucks because of the lousy way the Packers played on Sunday, which was why your wife was mad and didn't make you a sandwich to begin with. But we digress. Maybe it's time to move on to another clue.

WHY THIS CLUE MATTERS

The Clue of the Doublet matters because it illustrates the diversity of biblical literature and gives insights into the process of composition behind the Bible. Doublets reflect sources used by authors, different perspectives of different authors, and the creativity of individual authors, reusing older material, combining doublets into a cohesive work, and transforming a single story into a doublet for the sake of the larger narrative.

THE CLUE OF THE DOUBLET CAN HELP US . . .

1. Be on the lookout for texts that tell the same story or accomplish the same purpose.
2. Focus on the differences between the elements of a doublet that hint at the reasons for it.
3. Pay attention to the ways in which individual stories contribute to the whole narrative.
4. Distinguish different perspectives and ideologies in similar texts.
5. Be aware that the Bible is not a single book but a library of works from various constituencies of ancient Israel and early Christianity.

THE CASEBOOK

1. A famous doublet long identified by biblical scholars concerns God's introduction to Moses in Exodus 3:4-6, 13-15 and 6:2-3. Why are these two passages considered a doublet? What do they have in common? What are their differences? Can you see a way of reconciling the differences to read these two texts as parts of a unit? Why is the statement in 6:3 that God did not make his name known to Abraham, Isaac, and Jacob surprising?
2. The account of David's origins in 1 Samuel 16-17 contains a doublet or even a triplet. Can you isolate the individual stories? What differences do you find between them that give distinct pictures of where David came from?
3. How would you explain the two versions of Saul's death in 1 Samuel 31 and 2 Samuel 1? Is this a domino doublet linking the two books? Are there indications that the Amalekite in 2 Samuel 1 is lying? If so, could the two versions be working together?

4. Matthew 27:3–10 and Acts 1:18–19 contain a doublet about what Judas did after betraying Jesus. How are the accounts different? What is the same about them? You may find it helpful to consult some of the case files in the chapters on the Clue of the Etiology and the Clue of the Messy Manuscript.

7

The Clue of the

ECHO

One night not too long ago we were working late with the forgery unit making our way through some cold cases (not beer, the other kind). All we were getting for our trouble was a whole lot of nothing, and the only thing that kept us going was the overtime dough we knew would be making an appearance in our next paychecks. We were just about ready to pack it in and call it a day when we came across a file that told us the night was about to get a whole lot longer. It was part of the 2 Kings folder, which has pushed more than a few biblical detectives into early retirement. There were no screaming red flags, but something about it just didn't feel right. It was the write-up of the events described in the fourth chapter of the book that grabbed our attention. The outline of the chapter in the case file looked like this:

1. Subject provides woman with unending supply of oil.
2. Subject brings woman's dead son back to life.
3. Subject improves quality of inedible meal for group of people.
4. Subject feeds large crowd with limited amount of food and has leftovers to spare.

The unnamed "subject" in this case was a prophet known as Elisha (a.k.a. "Baldy"), who had been the right-hand man and eventual successor of a shadowy cult leader with rumored magical powers named Elijah. It seems Elijah took a Jimmy Hoffa stroll one day, never to be heard from again. The last time he was seen he was heading off toward the Jordan River near Jericho in the company of—you guessed it—one Baldy the prophet. They dredged the river but never found a trace of Elijah, so Baldy was able to skate and ended up taking over Elijah's entire operation. The whole ugly affair is laid out in 2 Kings 2.

That brings us back to our case file. It was the second and fourth items in the outline that caught our attention, the ones about Elisha bringing the lady's boy back from the dead and then feeding an enormous crowd with the amount of food each of us consumes during the first two minutes of an NFL game. These were some weird stunts, but they sounded familiar. Where had we seen this m.o. before? When you've worked as many cases and pulled as many late shifts as we have, things can get a little blurry when you're trying to connect the dots. We couldn't quite put our finger on who Baldy reminded us of, and we were just about to turn the page and move on to the description of chapter 5 when—Bingo!—Lady Luck came calling and we hit the jackpot.

Actually, it was our friend Carey who works in the New Testament division and happened to be walking by at that moment. She asked what we were up to, took a look at the write-up, and said she'd be right back. A few minutes later, here she comes with a humongous folder of her own with the name "Luke" on it that she plops down in front of us. She grabs the file labeled "Chapter Seven" and shows us the outline. In the number two spot, right below "Subject heals centurion's servant," we read "Subject brings woman's dead son back to life." Then she pulls out the one for chapter 9, and sitting right there before "Subject comes clean about his identity" is "Subject feeds large crowd with limited amount of food and has leftovers to spare." We put the Baldy file beside the Luke one and eyeballed them carefully just to be sure, but there was no doubt about it—they were a perfect match, except the subject in question in the Luke one was none other than Jesus.

What we've just described is an example of what we're calling the Clue of the Echo. This clue is based on the fact that sometimes a biblical

> THE CLUE OF THE ECHO: a story that reminds the reader of another story (or set of stories) with which it has some things in common

text can remind the reader of another text (or set of texts) with which it has some things in common. That sort of connection is made all the time when you read the Bible, so it's important at the outset that we're clear about what the Clue of the Echo is not. It doesn't refer to passages with enough common vocabulary that each one makes you think of the other(s). For instance, throughout the book of Genesis we often find the expression "These are the descendants of X," followed by a listing of the offspring of a particular person (Gen. 5:1; 6:9; 10:1; 11:10, 27; 25:12, 19; 36:1). These are clear examples of repetition, but they are not echoes as we're defining the term.

To qualify as an echo, a passage has to be a story (or part of a story) that has clearly discernible parts that interact with one another to form a plot. All plots have one thing in common: change. If there's no change there's no story—end of story. The change can take different forms, but it has to be there. It could be a change of status, appearance, location, knowledge, or any combination of the above. Think about your favorite childhood story, and change will be at the heart of it. Every single episode of the most mindless television sitcom to ever air is designed around the notion of change because things are different at the end of the thirty minutes than they were at the beginning.

An echo exists when two or more stories have a similar plot and share the same general journey from point A to point Z. We can see how this works in the two traditions involving Elisha and Jesus that were mentioned previously. Take a moment to read through 2 Kings 4:18-37 and Luke 7:11-17, both of which describe resuscitating a dead person. The details of the stories certainly differ, but the following outline shows that the same overall structure and component parts are found in both:

1. Woman has an only son.
2. Son dies.
3. Subject has compassion on the mother.
4. Subject raises the son from the dead.
5. Subject returns the son to the mother.
6. Subject's power is acknowledged.

Now read 2 Kings 4:42-44 and Luke 9:12-17, which recount how Elisha and Jesus were able to miraculously feed a large crowd of people, and you'll see that they also share a common structure:

1. Subject gives instruction to feed a group of people.
2. Subject's assistant(s) objects that there is not enough food.
3. Subject insists that the crowd be fed.
4. Crowd is fed by the assistant(s).
5. Food remains after all have eaten.

Don't let those nice, neat outlines deceive you. Pursuing this biblical clue can prove almost as challenging as trying to capture an actual echo and wrestle it to the ground. For starters, it requires almost encyclopedic knowledge of the Bible. Computer technology and search engines have made the job a bit easier, but being a biblical detective often demands a panoramic perspective on the literature. You have to be able to focus on the broad outline of a story and not get lost in the details. Look again at the passages from 2 Kings 4 and Luke 7 describing how Elisha and Jesus brought back those two sons. The details in one are so rich and different from those in the other that it's easy to miss the forest for the trees and not realize you're dealing with an echo.

When you're looking for an echo, you want to start with the big picture and not the brushstrokes, so here's a good principle to keep in mind: Echo analysis moves from the general to the specific; first identify the outline the stories have in common, and then explore their differences. The second task is as important as the first. Those differences are crucial because biblical echoes aren't like the ones you produce at the Grand Canyon or someplace else that are perfect duplicates of what you just shouted. Biblical echoes resemble each other but are not spitting images of one another; they're fraternal twins rather than identical ones. As we prepare to enter the Bible's echo chamber, remember to pay attention to both the similarities and the differences.

Echo soundings

We have good news and bad news for you. First the good—you've been such outstanding trainees so far that we've decided to go easy on you and not give you any homework this chapter, so there isn't a casebook section at the end of it. Actually, that's not why there is no casebook section, and hence the bad news—you'll be doing your homework in class. We're going in a different direction this time because of the nature of the Clue of the Echo. Finding it is a needle-in-a-haystack quest because it entails wading through sometimes lengthy sections of text to find what you're looking for, and therefore we'd like you to read the relevant passages on your own so we don't have to include them in the chapter. After you've read through the material related to a particular echo, we want you to jot down the general outline of the story just like we did earlier with the accounts of how Elisha and Jesus raised the sons and fed the crowds. We'll be operating under the honor system, so we ask that you don't cheat and look ahead to see the outlines that we've come up with for each one. Don't think of this as busywork, but as a training exercise that's preparing you for your future investigative career. You'll be getting some valuable experience on how to write up a case report, so this chapter is really a lab or practicum in the grunt work that comes with being a detective.

Well, well, well . . .

Read Genesis 24:1-51, Genesis 29:1-20, and Exodus 2:15-22 and write up the outline of the echoes in them.

While some people today meet their future spouses at a watering hole of a different sort, it appears that the neighborhood well was sometimes a place where biblical couples would get acquainted. Here are our case notes that show how we outline what's going on in these scenes:

1. Subject (or his representative) goes on a journey.
2. Subject stops near a well.
3. Woman arrives at the well.
4. Woman is identified in relation to her father.
5. Subject overcomes an obstacle.
6. Woman returns home to tell family member(s) about the subject.
7. Subject is invited into the home.
8. Subject marries woman.

All three stories have the same general structure, and they map on to this outline quite well. There is some slight variation in the sequence of events, which is not uncommon for the Clue of the Echo, but each is present and accounted for in all three accounts. Now let's meet our happy couples.

The most notable thing about the story of how Isaac and Rebekah get together is that the groom-to-be is nowhere to be found (Gen. 24:1-

51). Abraham's unnamed servant does all the traveling and negotiating, and he's also responsible for another distinctive feature of this story—its length. This text is the longest of the three because beginning in verse 34 the servant repeats virtually everything that has happened so far in the story, and he even quotes extensive sections of earlier dialogue as he explains to Laban the reason for his visit. It is, in a sense, an echo within an echo. This type of repetition is not uncommon in the biblical literature, and perhaps it's being used here as a way of verifying for the reader that the servant has followed Abraham's instructions perfectly. Being the detectives that we are, though, we wonder if the off-the-cuff reference to Abraham's servant being "the oldest of his house" (v. 2) isn't a tip-off that maybe the old-timer was showing his age and starting to repeat himself. The obstacle the subject or his representative has to overcome varies from story to story, and here that obstacle is the servant's doubt (v. 21) about whether or not he has come to the right place (perhaps another sign of creeping senility?), a source of concern that isn't resolved until Laban arrives on the scene and invites him home.

The early courtship of Jacob and Rachel is different because, unlike his father Isaac, Jacob actually shows up and is an active participant (Gen. 29:1-20). Making another appearance is Jacob's uncle Laban, who was present in the previous scene and so is the only character to play a role in more than one of these encounters at a well. The obstacle facing Jacob is the large stone over the opening of the well that prevents access to the water and normally requires several men to move (v. 3), but once he sees Rachel he is undeterred by this impediment and is able to remove the stone on his own.

The third story, the most streamlined of the three, features Moses (Exod. 2:15-22). This time the subject is a fugitive—Moses is fleeing for his life because Pharaoh wants to kill him for his involvement in the death of an Egyptian (v. 15). No interaction between the couple is reported because the future wife is part of a group of seven sisters who have come to the well together, and we don't learn her name until the report of her marriage to Moses (v. 21). This is the only story in which the man and the woman are not members of the same extended family, and in a number of places the fact that she is a foreigner is highlighted (vv. 15, 16, 19, 22). The obstacle is overcome when Moses comes to the assistance of the women, who are being prevented from watering their flock by a group of shepherds (v. 17).

Are these three different stories or one story told three different ways? The details vary wildly, but in each case the hero gets hitched and he or his representative goes through the same stages along the way. This kind of echo is sometimes called a "type scene," which is a literary term that describes scenes in literature that are so common and familiar that when they commence the reader knows exactly where things are headed.

The triple use of the well scene in these stories shows us that the biblical authors were familiar with and used the standard literary conventions of their time, and in all likelihood their audiences would have been clued in to what they were doing. But that's not the only thing writers can do with type scenes—sometimes they play with them and exploit them to achieve certain effects. The differences among the three versions of the biblical scene at the well are likely due to the authors' attempts to put a twist on a well-known story line. But other biblical authors tinkered with the tried and true wedding-at-the-well formula as well. Here's where we need to take that wide-angle approach mentioned earlier and train our magnifying glass on other parts of the biblical canon. It seems that Jesus didn't only look to Baldy as a model.

Read John 4:1–42 and do a write-up of its outline for your file. This looks like a slam-dunk case of an intertestamental echo to us. This episode from the New Testament fits quite comfortably into the outline shared by the other three from the Hebrew Bible. Here's how we draw it up:

1. Subject goes on a journey.
2. Subject stops near a well.
3. Woman arrives at the well.
4. Subject overcomes an obstacle.
5. Woman is identified in relation to her husbands.
6. Woman returns to city to tell others about the subject.
7. Subject is invited into the city.
8. People of the city "marry" the subject.

They're not duplicates, but until you get to the final item, this outline looks a lot like the other one. Certain aspects of the story reflect the thematic concerns and the agenda of John's Gospel, but we can still detect the echo. The author's hand is most obvious in the obstacle that the subject has to overcome, which is the woman's inability to recognize who Jesus is. This is a common theme in the Fourth Gospel, where John sometimes shows how the people who encounter Jesus slowly come to realize his true identity. Another interesting difference is that the woman is identified by her relationships with her husbands rather than that with her father, as in the other three. That wrinkle puts the skids on things, and readers who think they know where the story is headed are suddenly at a loss since it's unlikely that Jesus is about to become husband number six. The eventual outcome is the other significant departure from the pattern that Isaac, Jacob, and Moses have established. The woman follows the script perfectly and heads back home, but now she announces the stranger's arrival to the entire city and not just to her family. This leads to a larger than usual "wedding" when many of its citizens express their belief in Jesus and pledge their commitment to him.

Someone connected to John's Gospel—we don't know if it was the author, the editor, or somebody else—was obviously familiar with this type scene and realized, along with his predecessors, that a well is one of the best places to produce an echo.

You're what?

Find the echoes in the following chapters and write up their common outline: Genesis 21, Genesis 25, Genesis 29, Judges 13, 1 Samuel 1, 2 Kings 4, and Luke 1.

There's a whole forest of family trees in the Bible, and we've climbed into and fallen out of most of them. One thing all those lists of generations hammer home is what a fertile lot the Israelites were. Every once in a while, though, as you read through the family records, you come across a story that reminds you that some folks had trouble keeping up with the Joneses in the baby-making department. Lucky for them, the problem proved to be a temporary one and they were able to add another branch to the tree. These echoes describe a string of wanted pregnancies in the Bible that can all be traced back to the same source, and here's how we outline them:

1. Subject is unable to conceive a child.
2. God intervenes.
3. Subject becomes pregnant.

4. Child is born.
5. Child is named.
6. Child's identity is established.

This is a very easy echo to spot, and the only thing that can sometimes take some work figuring out is the sixth point in the outline, because the child's identity can be established in different ways. Sometimes something about the newborn's identity is tied to his (they're always boys) name, and you usually need to read the text in Hebrew to make the connection. For example, Sarah says that God has brought laughter to her, and her son Isaac's name comes from a Hebrew root that means "to laugh" (Gen. 21:6).

Regarding Samson and John the Baptist, the meanings of their names are not mentioned, but something is said about what each child's future life has in store. In both of these cases divine intervention takes the form of a visit from an angelic being who tells the parent what the child will go on to do. Samson's mother is told that he will live his life as a Nazirite who is dedicated to God (Judg. 13:2-5), while Zechariah is informed that John will also lead an ascetic lifestyle as a precursor to Jesus (Luke 1:15-17).

You may have paused while reading the first chapter of Luke's Gospel to consider whether or not it contains a double echo of the unexpected pregnancy motif. Read Luke 1:26-38 and compare its outline to that of the other pregnancies. Unlike most of the others, this is not a wanted pregnancy, because Mary does not pray to God to request a child. All six parts of the outline are present in this story except the fourth one, because Jesus will not be born until the next chapter. In addition, the reason why Mary is unable to conceive a child is different here. She is the only one of the women in these stories who is not married, and, as she states, she has not had sexual relations with a man, so the news that she'll be a mother is surprising, to say the least. The remarkable nature of Jesus's conception highlights something that it shares with those of the other children, but in a more dramatic way—God's role in causing the pregnancies. The main point of all these stories that echo one another is that God is the source of life.

I'm what?

Outline the echoes in these chapters: Isaiah 6, Jeremiah 1, and Ezekiel 1–3.

There's a set of fifteen files we try to avoid like the plague. Each one contains transcripts of statements that have been made by the person whose name is on it. Names like Amos, Hosea, Zephaniah, and Habakkuk. They call themselves prophets, but here around the office they're known as "the pros." The "Big Three" among the pros are Isaiah, Jeremiah, and Ezekiel, and their files are among the thickest that the folks who work the Bible beat have to lug around.

We'd rather not deal with the pros because they tend to be all talk and no action. Some of the files don't contain the slightest whiff of a story while the pro in question just blabbers on and on. It's both what they say and how they say it that make the pros so unbearable.

The pros have a lot of moxie, but where does it come from and what gives them the right to spout off like they do? The Big Three provide the answers to those questions in the echoes we're about to investigate. Their tough guy status is something that's been bestowed on them, and they claim they're only following orders from the boss they answer to. It turns out they're all made men who went through an initiation that gave them membership in an exclusive fraternity whose sole purpose is to keep people on the straight and narrow. There's no doubt that Isaiah, Jeremiah, and Ezekiel all went through the same secret ceremony, and here's how we outline it:

1. Subject receives an initial word from God (or God's representative).
2. Subject is commissioned.
3. Subject objects to the commission.
4. Subject is reassured.
5. Subject is given a sign.

These scenes are often referred to as prophetic call narratives. Almost all the parts of the outline are found in each one, but there's quite a bit of variety in how they're arranged in the three versions. In Isaiah 6, the initial word is spoken by strange six-winged creatures known as seraphs that proclaim God's holiness (v. 3). But then instead of having the commission come right after that, we get Isaiah's objection and reassurance. He claims he has unclean lips and is unworthy to look upon God, and then one of the seraphs addresses that concern by placing a hot coal on Isaiah's mouth (vv. 6-7). The commission then follows, and it's a curious one—Isaiah is to speak to the people in a way that will prevent them from understanding and being saved (vv. 9-10). The sign that concludes this call narrative will come about in the future because Isaiah is told that he should stop speaking to the people only when they are sent far away from the land for their offenses (vv. 11-13).

In Jeremiah 1 the commission is more spread out and is first mentioned in the initial word (v. 5). The objection and reassurance then follow, and these are similar to their counterparts in Isaiah because they are associated with Jeremiah's mouth and ability to speak (vv. 6-9). God's act of reaching out and touching the prophet's mouth is reminiscent of the seraph touching the coal to Isaiah's lips. The commission is then elaborated upon as Jeremiah is told he has been charged with destroying nations and kingdoms (v. 10). The sign he receives is actually a double one involving an almond tree and a pot in the north that is about to spill its contents (vv. 11-19).

Neither of those scenes prepares us for their echo in Ezekiel, whose call narrative goes on for three chapters. It is preceded by a vision of God's glory that takes up the whole first chapter and includes four-faced creatures that dart about like lightning in vehicles that have wheels covered with eyes. The call narrative commences in chapter 2 and continues through chapter 3. All the elements are there, but they aren't presented in a logical and coherent order. Ezekiel receives a commission to speak to the people that is similar to those in Isaiah and Jeremiah, but it's interspersed throughout the chapters in 2:3-4, 7; 3:4-6, 10-11, 16-21, 27. He is reassured in 2:6, 8-10; 3:1-2, and some of this entails a hand outstretched toward his mouth like the one in Jeremiah. Several signs are given to Ezekiel, including a promise to make his face harder than flint (3:8-9), being transported great distances (3:12-15, 22-23), and becoming mute (3:24-26). There is no objection in Ezekiel's call narrative. In fact, the prophet never utters a single word in the three chapters.

The prophetic call narratives demonstrate that in the Clue of the Echo the individual examples do not have to be perfect replicas of one another. At times the author introduces variation in order to highlight some dimension of the text or to make a point. For example, the lack of an objection by the prophet in Ezekiel's call narrative is likely a way of indicating that he was completely persuaded by the vision he had, and that he was convinced that he was being commissioned by God for a particular task.

Echoes of eternity

Identify and outline the echoes in these chapters: 1 Samuel 4, 2 Samuel 11, and 2 Samuel 18.

Up to this point you might have the impression that the Clue of the Echo is present only in the warm and fuzzy Hallmark moments of life like engagement parties, baby showers, and promotions at work. But that's not the case. The biblical literature also addresses the more tragic aspects of our existence in all their painful messiness, and sometimes its authors draw upon type scenes to describe moments of tremendous pathos and angst.

And what fact of life better captures the downside of the human condition than its temporariness? In this section we consider a couple of examples of death-related scenes in which the Clue of the Echo makes an appearance. The first set includes the chapters listed above, each of which relates an episode we might call "the Messenger of Death." Here's its outline:

1. Someone dies in battle.
2. Messenger goes to the subject to relay the news.
3. Messenger reports on the battle.
4. Subject learns of the death.
5. Subject reacts.
6. Someone mourns the death.

All the elements of the outline can be seen in the first passage (1 Sam. 4:10–22), but as often occurs with the Clue of the Echo, the author tweaks things a bit to call the reader's attention to certain parts of the story. Eli's sons have been killed in battle, but it is clear that he is more concerned with the fate of the ark of the covenant than with what happens to his children. The messenger first reports on the outcome of the battle before mentioning that the Philistines have killed the sons and captured the ark. Eli's reaction is exactly what we might expect from a grieving parent, as he falls to the ground and breaks his neck in the process, but his sons' deaths are not the cause of his own because the text mentions specifically that it was the news about the ark that led to his literal downfall. The focus then shifts to the unnamed pregnant wife of one of the sons, who also loses her life when she hears what has happened. But, like her father-in-law, she is mourning the capture of the ark rather than her late husband, and the name she gives her newborn with her dying breath is an expression of her grief over its loss. The unexpected responses of Eli and his daughter-in-law can be explained by extending our investigation into the previous chapter, where Eli learns from God through Samuel that his sons' days are numbered. He therefore anticipated that they would not return home from battle, but the ark's capture was more than he could bear.

The second passage involves King David and a man named Uriah, whose death is best categorized as collateral damage (2 Samuel 11:17–27). After his dalliance with Uriah's wife, Bathsheba, results in an unwanted pregnancy, David must come up with a way to get her husband out of the picture so everyone will assume the baby is Uriah's. His death on the battlefield is orchestrated by the king, so when the messenger comes to the palace bearing the news, the reader knows that it's what David is expecting and hoping to hear. The envoy first gives a detailed report on what has taken place during the battle, and only at the tail end of it does he refer to Uriah's death. Bathsheba's reaction to her husband's death is what we would expect of a grieving spouse, as she engages in the customary mourning rituals, and it is never clear to the reader if she knows or suspects the truth about Uriah's death.

David is also the protagonist of the third passage, which hits closer to home for him because this time his son Absalom is killed (2 Sam. 18:9–33). This account also follows the outline, and perhaps its most significant departure from it is that two messengers are sent to David instead of one. The author probably doubles the number of messengers in order to increase and prolong the dramatic tension of the episode. The first to arrive gives a report about the progress of the battle, but he is unable to answer the king's question about the condition of his son. The second messenger also begins with a more general statement about the success of the battle, and he then informs David of Absalom's death. The king's reaction to this news combines the fifth and sixth elements of the outline because it is the only time in the three passages when the person notified of the death actually expresses grief and mourns for the deceased one. His words are raw with emotion and anguish, and they are a microcosm of the Clue of the Echo because David repeats himself throughout them. "O my son Absalom, my son, my son Absalom! Would I had died instead of you, O Absalom, my son, my son!"

We close our investigation of the Clue of the Echo with a brief treatment of another death-related scene. This one is not as fully formed as "the Messenger of Death" one, and some might question if we should even call this an echo, but we think there's a likely clue here even if the fingerprints are a bit smudged. Search for the echoes in these chapters: Genesis 27, Genesis 49, and 1 Kings 2. We're going to call this one "the Messenger at Death's Door," and we outline it this way:

1. Subject is near death.
2. Subject's offspring gather around him.
3. Subject mentions his impending death.
4. Subject discusses the future of the offspring.

This time the subject delivers the message, and it is directed to one or more of his offspring about their future. It's a type scene that is commonly set at a deathbed, but in the Bible the person doesn't always die, at least not right away. As usual, there are idiosyncrasies in some of the passages that can mask the presence of the echo.

The rivalry between the twin brothers Jacob and Esau is the background to the story in Genesis 27. Here the deathbed scene is spread out through much of the chapter because the sons come individually to meet with Isaac. The first two verses of the chapter describe the father's feeble state, and Isaac himself suggests that death is near as he calls Esau to his side. The brothers' futures are laid out by their father, but they are explained separately, as Jacob (disguised as Esau) is promised success and prosperity (vv. 27-29) while pain and misery are predicted for Esau (vv. 39-40). Despite his frailty here, Isaac rallied and went on to live a long life. It is reported later that he lived to be 180 years old (Gen. 35:28-29), which makes him the longest-living of the patriarchs.

The outline can be seen in its purest form in Genesis 49. It actually begins at the end of the previous chapter when Jacob, identified as Israel, tells his son Joseph that he is about to die (Gen. 48:21). Jacob gathers all twelve of his sons to his bedside (Gen. 49:1), and then one by one he tells each of them something about what awaits them in the future (vv. 2-27). His words to them are in poetry, something not seen in the other passages, and the chapter concludes with a report of Jacob's death (v. 33). This is the only explicit reference in these passages to the subject being in a bed, although it appears that Isaac is reclining in the previous scene because he is told twice to sit up so that he might eat (Gen. 27:19, 31).

The third passage recounts the final father-son chat between King David and his successor, Solomon (1 Kings 2:1-9). It opens with a double reference to David's imminent death, including one on his own lips, and it is immediately followed by a report of his passing. This time the message about the subject's offspring contains two parts. In the first, David tells his son that as long as he follows the law and obeys God's commandments, he and his own offspring will have long and successful reigns. And then things take a more ominous turn as David proceeds to advise Solomon about how to conduct himself in the immediate future. He identifies a number of people with whom he has had dealings in the past, and with a wink and a nod he lets Solomon know which ones should live and which should die.

Before we call this clue a wrap, we open the New Testament files to see what light they might shed on this investigation. As strange as the idea might seem, we think Jesus is yet another example of "the Messenger at Death's Door." Read John 13 and compare its outline with the one for Genesis 27, Genesis 49, and 1 Kings 2. This chapter is the beginning of a long speech found only in John's Gospel that Jesus makes to his disciples at the Last Supper. He will be arrested that night and executed the next day, and he knows he is near death, as his followers, or "offspring," have gathered around him (vv. 1, 3). He alludes to his impending death when he tells them, "I am with you only a little longer" and "Where I am going, you cannot come" (v. 33). Throughout the chapter Jesus indicates what the future holds for his "offspring" in different ways. He refers to specific individuals when he mentions the one who will betray him (vv. 10-11, 18, 21) and when he tells Peter that he will deny him (vv. 36-38). He also lays out his vision for the future of the group when he explains to them the need to serve one another (vv. 14-15) and to love one another (vv. 34-35). His speech goes on for four more chapters, and throughout it Jesus keeps returning to the two main themes of the outline—his imminent death and what lies ahead for his followers. The similarities between this scene and the others are intriguing, and we think it's yet another instance of "the Messenger at Death's Door."

WHY THIS CLUE MATTERS

Echoes are fleeting phenomena, both in life and in the Bible. The words leave your mouth, you hear them repeated faintly, and then they're gone forever. Perhaps that's where their power resides—the momentary and transitory nature of an echo leaves a mark and makes it memorable.

The same might be said about their biblical counterparts. They are limited in number and there aren't many examples of each, but they make an impression on us. While they're not perfect replicas of one another like spoken echoes, they have enough in common that we can see the connections. In fact, it's precisely their differences that make biblical echoes so notable, and that's why they need to be carefully studied. The subtlest clues are often missed, even by the most experienced observers, but they're sometimes the ones that can tell us the most about who left them behind.

THE CLUE OF THE ECHO CAN HELP US . . .

1. Realize that the biblical authors wrote with certain literary conventions in mind.
2. Notice similar stories in different parts of the Bible.
3. Pay attention to the details in stories that point to the author's interests or agenda.
4. Develop our skills of comparative analysis.
5. Raise questions about the historicity of some passages.

8

The Clue of the

REPEATED PATTERN

We are creatures of habit, so they say. But then you look around and you see just how true it is. What can really bend your badge is when you start noticing the deep rut your partner is in. We're not talking about each other. But we used to have a third wheel, a trainee, named P. Richard Tracy. He liked for people to call him "Dick," as in Dick Tracy, after the comic strip detective. We found out the P stood for Peter and started calling him "Repeat," because he followed the same routine all the time.

We'd walk in every morning to find him reading the sports section. Well, not reading exactly—just checking out scores. God forbid he should actually read the rest of the paper, let alone a book. When he finished he never refolded the sports pages, just tossed the whole thing on our desks like we were the recycle bin. He always had a cup of coffee in his hand, and whenever we were out in the car we had to stop at Starbucks. He kicked off his shoes always seven minutes (!) after sitting at his desk and propped his feet up. He wanted Mexican for lunch every day. Never a burger. Never Thai. His wife called same time every afternoon. Didn't matter where we were going or who we were talking to. He used the same font—Courier New—to fill out reports, even though it takes up more room and looks weird, and the whole time he was here he misspelled the same words. It's burglary, not burgalry. How hard is that?

But the worst thing about Repeat was the way he talked about m.o., modus operandi. First of all, he mispronounced it—*modisoperati*—like it was one word. It took us a while to figure out he wasn't talking about the opera. Repeat thought m.o. was the key to solving every crime ever committed. Forget about fingerprints, motive, or any other aspect of criminology. He always started hunting for the m.o. He was really good at searching for patterns in the computer database; we'll give him that. "Criminals are very predictable," he used to say. "Figure out their *modisoperati* and you can get them for each and every infraction they ever did." That didn't always work so well for catching the bad guys, but once you had them, you could rely on Repeat to pile on the charges by searching online for similar crimes. And we've got to admit, that paid off more than once. We learned a lot from Repeat about criminal patterns of behavior, but we were still glad to see him go to another precinct.

People do get locked into patterns, and literary works are human creations, so they often contain patterns. Repeated patterns can be easy to spot in the Bible, and searching for the reasons behind them is a rewarding enterprise. The Clue of the Repeated Pattern exists when the same structure can be seen in more than one subsection of a text. The key is the similarity of language appearing in such forms as recurring formulas and set phrases. The vocabulary is identical or nearly so in each example of the pattern. Repeated patterns tend to occur close to one another, so they're relatively easy to spot. The repetition suggests intention in the organization of the material in the text. Often it serves a rhetorical purpose, such as highlighting a theme, directing readers' attention, stressing a theological point or ideological perspective, or simply creating suspense. It can have a mnemonic function to make memorization easier. A repeated pattern can also indicate dependence of one text or story upon another.

> THE CLUE OF THE REPEATED PATTERN: recurring formulas and set phrases in more than one subsection of a text

The examples we've culled from our cases are organized according to the length of the passage in which the pattern is repeated—small, medium, and large. Small passages are those consisting of just a few verses. Medium passages are longer, up to a whole chapter or two. Large ones involve a whole book. In honor of Repeat's Starbucks obsession, we're borrowing their categories: Tall, Grande, and Venti. So sit back and enjoy your drink as we compare Bible m.o.'s.

Tall

Let's begin with a beverage that's a couple of swallows shy of the brim. It's only one verse, and it starts out like a sign on your neighbor's fence. But it's got a nice repeated pattern. It's Philippians 3:2, "*Beware* of the dogs, *beware* of the evil workers, *beware* of those who mutilate the flesh!" You can make out the pattern in English translation, but you need to dig into the Greek to get the full effect. The phrase "beware of the" is repeated three times. What you can't tell from the English is that the word that follows in all three cases begins with the Greek letter kappa. The last one is a noun that means mutilation by hacking or cutting. It's used here in a negative sense for circumcision, and especially for those who taught that it was necessary for Christians. How do we know it's negative? Because it's in parallel with "dogs" and "evil workers." Dogs were not viewed in those days as loving and lovable family pets the way they are today, but as disgusting scavengers. The reference to mutilation is a little unusual, and you might ask, "Why didn't Paul just say circumcision or people who teach circumcision, if that's what he meant?" Now you have an answer: the regular word for circumcision would not have fit the "beware of the k . . ." pattern. Just like many of us today, Paul was set in his ways.

While we're at it, here are a couple of other short repeated patterns in Paul's writings. In Romans 8:38-39 we find "For I am convinced that *neither* death, *nor* life, *nor* angels, *nor* rulers, *nor* things present, *nor* things to come, *nor* powers, *nor* height, *nor* depth, *nor* anything else in all creation, will be able to separate us from the love of God in Christ Jesus our Lord." You might consider this just a simple list. But the way it is laid out with the repetition of "neither, nor" (Greek *oute*) ten times in two short verses reinforces the negative side of the statement in a positive way. That is, Paul is affirming that nothing, and he means nothing at all, can separate us from God's love.

In 1 Corinthians 12:8-10 there's a repeated pattern that is more pronounced in English than it is in Greek. "To one is given through the Spirit the utterance of wisdom, and *to another* the utterance of knowledge according to the same Spirit, *to another* faith by the same Spirit, *to another* gifts of healing by the one Spirit, *to another* the working of miracles, *to another* prophecy, *to another* the discernment of spirits, *to another* various kinds of tongues, *to another* the interpretation of tongues." The phrase "to another" occurs eight times in these three verses. It translates two different Greek words: *heterō* twice, and *allō* the other six times. The variation in words breaks up the monotony without disturbing the pattern that much, since the two words mean the same thing. The repetition helps to make Paul's point in the following verses that there is no hierarchy where spiritual gifts are concerned; all gifts are equally important, and what matters most is the unity of the body. He finishes this point off nicely with another repeated pattern: "*Are all* apostles? *Are all* prophets? *Are all* teachers? *Do all* work miracles? *Do all* possess gifts of healing? *Do all* speak in tongues? *Do all* interpret?" (1 Cor. 12:29–30). Here, the same Greek expression (*mē pantes*) is used seven times to introduce seven rhetorical questions, all anticipating the answer no. The point is that no one person can do everything. The church body is intentionally diverse and should work together for the good of all.

As much as Paul likes a good repeated pattern, no book of the Bible shows more affinity for them than Amos. It's the idea of repeating a pattern rather than the repetition itself that Amos loves. The book doesn't stick with any one pattern very long, but lots of patterns get repeated. They are Amos's *modus operandi*. Which brings us back to Det. Tracy, Repeat. He used to sing a song when we were closing in on a suspect—"Oh Sinner Man," made famous by Nina Simone and recorded by a lot of folk groups, including the Seekers and Peter, Paul, and Mary. Here's a sample:

Oh, sinnerman,
Where you gonna run to?
All on that day
Run to the rock
Oh rock won't you hide me
All on that day
But the rock cried out
I can't hide you,
All on that day
So I run to the river
It was bleedin'
All on that day
So I run to the sea
It was boilin',
All on that day.

You can enjoy Ms. Simone's version in the bowler hat scene of the 1999 flick *The Thomas Crown Affair* with Pierce Brosnan, Rene Russo, and Denis Leary. It was Repeat's favorite movie—ironic, since the bad guy gets away with it. The song might have been inspired by Amos 9:2–4, which makes the point that there will be no place to hide on the day of divine reckoning, and it does so with a repeated pattern:

> *Though* they dig into Sheol,
>   *from there* shall my hand take them;
> *though* they climb up to heaven,
>   *from there* I will bring them down.
> *Though* they hide themselves on the top of Carmel,
>   *from there* I will search out and take them;
> *and though* they hide from my sight at the bottom of the sea,
>   *there* I will command the sea-serpent, and it shall bite them.
> *And though* they go into captivity in front of their enemies,
>   *there* I will command the sword, and it shall kill them;
> and I will fix my eyes on them
>   for harm and not for good.

The pattern consists of the repetition of the words "though" or "and though" combined with "from there" five times in these verses to pose a series of hypothetical hiding places that will prove useless.

Grande

Feel the need for a little more caffeine? Stick with Amos. There is a nice Grande cup in the first two chapters. They contain a collection of oracles/prophecies against the nations—Aram/Syria (1:3–5), Gaza/Philistia (1:6–8), Tyre/Phoenicia (1:9–10), Edom (1:11–12), Ammon (1:13–15), Moab (2:1–3), Judah (2:4–5), and Israel (2:6–16). They use a repeated formula: "*For three* transgressions of X and *for four* I will not revoke the punishment." The numbers are not to be taken literally. It's like when we say "three or four," we're not trying to be specific. The point is that YHWH ("the LORD") is going after the nation for however many crimes it has committed. The pattern continues by naming one or two of these offenses, which fall in the categories of what we might call treaty violations and war crimes. Then there's an announcement of punishment—

what YHWH is going to do to each guilty nation. The oracles begin and end the same way with a "Thus says the LORD" at the start and a "says the LORD" at the end. The repeated pattern shows that however the oracles originated—whether they were delivered separately by Amos or all on one occasion, for instance—they have gone through literary crafting. The sameness of the form and repeated elements also focus attention on the crime and punishment portions of the oracles. What did each nation do wrong? How do their crimes and their judgments compare to each other? The reader is led to consider each case separately and at the same time to see them all together as a whole in a single, literary entity.

Sing-along

Thanks to Nina Simone, we have music on the mind. Songs are both a good reason and a source for repeated patterns. They are basically poems put to music, and music helps with learning. Not a big fan of soul or folk music? How about a little classic rock? It's an oldie and a goodie. And by oldie we mean really ancient. See if the words ring any bells:

> For everything there is a season, and a time for every matter under heaven:
>> a time to be born, and a time to die;
>> a time to plant, and a time to pluck up what is planted;
>> a time to kill, and a time to heal;
>> a time to break down, and a time to build up;
>> a time to weep, and a time to laugh;
>> a time to mourn, and a time to dance;
>> a time to throw away stones, and a time to gather stones together;
>> a time to embrace, and a time to refrain from embracing;
>> a time to seek, and a time to lose;
>> a time to keep, and a time to throw away;
>> a time to tear, and a time to sew;
>> a time to keep silence, and a time to speak;
>> a time to love, and a time to hate;
>> a time for war, and a time for peace. (Eccles. 3:1–8)

It's a song for the birds. Well, actually, by the Byrds, featuring David Crosby, who addressed the topic of repeated patterns in his own song "Déjà Vu." Pete Seeger wrote "Turn, Turn, Turn" in the late 1950s as a protest song against war, but he lifted the words pretty much straight out of the Bible. You can see the repeated pattern. The phrase "a time to (or for)" occurs an astounding twenty-nine times. (That's more than the number of "I knows" Bill Withers sings in his '70s hit "Ain't No Sunshine.") That, plus the pairs of contrasting verbs ("be born"/"die," "plant"/"pluck up," "kill"/"heal," etc.), makes it easy to sing along with the Byrds. It may have been a well-known poem even before the author of Ecclesiastes/Qoheleth used it to convey the repetitiveness and futility of life. We don't know whether it had a tune to go with it way back then, but it sure could have.

We're pretty sure that the psalms in the book of that name had tunes. We just don't know what they were. Some of the headings have musical instructions, but we don't know what they mean. And even we aren't old enough to know what ancient Israelite music sounded like. That mystery will likely still be unsolved long after we've earned our wings in the precinct in the sky. Still, you don't need the notes on paper to have a good idea of how some of the psalms might have worked. A good example is Psalm 136, where the clause "for his steadfast love endures forever" is repeated at the end of every verse. Twenty-six verses, twenty-six repetitions. (That's *exactly* the number of "I knows" Withers sings in "Ain't No Sunshine.") Once you learn that clause, you've got half the psalm down. It's a good guess that the psalm functioned antiphonally, where a priest chanted the first half of each verse and a group of priests or maybe even the people responded with the chorus. Like the police union choir when you have one good soloist (here's to you, Officer Bryant), so everyone else sings backup.

A *is for alphabet*

Maybe you're not into rock either. How about country? Like Eddy Arnold's "M-O-T-H-E-R" (feel free to hum as you read):

M is for the million things she gave me.
O means only that she's growing old.
T is for the tears she shed to save me.

H is for her heart of purest gold.
E is for her eyes with love lights shining.
R means right and right she'll always be.

Pass the Kleenex and repeat after us: Acrostic. That's a kind of poem where a letter in each line—usually the first one—combines with the others to spell out something. It can be one of the easiest clues to detect, at least in Hebrew. Unfortunately, you can't see it in English translations unless someone has taken the trouble to reproduce the effect, and that usually means committing crimes of a different sort. Psalms 25, 34, 37, 111, 112, 119, and 145 are all acrostics on the alphabet. Psalm 119 is unique in that each of the twenty-two letters in the Hebrew alphabet has eight lines devoted to it, each of which begins with that same letter. This is why it's the longest chapter in the Bible, 176 verses (22 x 8). If it seems strange that the longest chapter in the Bible is a Grande instead of a Venti, just think of it as a Grande with eight shots. If that doesn't satisfy you, you won't like where we've put Lamentations either. While not in the book of Psalms, Lamentations is a psalm in a way, actually a collection of psalms, and most of them are acrostics—four of the five chapters in the book are in that format. Think of those chapters as cup carriers holding four Grandes. That's why chapters 1, 2, and 4 have twenty-two verses. Chapter 5 breaks the pattern with twenty-two verses and no acrostic, but broken patterns are a topic for a later time (like the next chapter). If your caffeine intake is keeping you alert, you can probably guess that chapter 3 has sixty-six verses because it's a triple shot that starts each set of three verses with a new letter of the alphabet. A final famous acrostic in the Bible is the poem about the worthy woman in Proverbs 31:10–31, which gets us back to Mom. She'd like you to think about how that pattern might have influenced the set of qualities that make up the woman described in the poem.

Memory work

Not every repeated pattern is meant to be sung. Music or not, repeated patterns make memorization and recitation easier, and often that seems to be the purpose for them. Take the Ten Commandments, for instance. Jews and Christians number them differently, but they agree that there are ten and that they're mostly composed of "Thou shalt nots." The "Thou shalt nots" don't match up exactly with the ten in either way of counting, but they do facilitate memorizing the whole thing:

> I am the LORD your God, who brought you out of the land of Egypt, out of the house of slavery; *you shall have no* other gods before me.
>
> *You shall not* make for yourself an idol, whether in the form of anything that is in heaven above, or that is on the earth beneath, or that is in the water under the earth. *You shall not* bow down to them or worship them; for I the LORD your God am a jealous God, punishing children for the iniquity of parents, to the third and the fourth generation of those who reject me, but showing steadfast love to the thousandth generation of those who love me and keep my commandments.
>
> *You shall not* make wrongful use of the name of the LORD your God, for the LORD will not acquit anyone who misuses his name.
>
> Remember the sabbath day, and keep it holy. Six days you shall labor and do all your work. But the seventh day is a sabbath to the LORD your God; you shall not do any work—you, your son or your daughter, your male or female slave, your livestock, or the alien resident in your towns. For in six days the LORD made heaven and earth, the sea, and all that is in them, but rested the seventh day; therefore the LORD blessed the sabbath day and consecrated it.
>
> Honor your father and your mother, so that your days may be long in the land that the LORD your God is giving you.
>
> *You shall not* murder.
>
> *You shall not* commit adultery.
>
> *You shall not* steal.
>
> *You shall not* bear false witness against your neighbor.
>
> *You shall not* covet. (Exod. 20:2-17)

The same principle lies behind Matthew's presentation of the Beatitudes in Matthew 5:3-11, and it may not be a coincidence that there are nine of them:

> "*Blessed are* the poor in spirit, *for* theirs is the kingdom of heaven.
> "*Blessed are* those who mourn, *for* they will be comforted.

"*Blessed are* the meek, *for* they will inherit the earth.
"*Blessed are* those who hunger and thirst for righteousness,
    for they will be filled.
"*Blessed are* the merciful, *for* they will receive mercy.
"*Blessed are* the pure in heart, *for* they will see God.
"*Blessed are* the peacemakers, *for* they will be called children of God.
"*Blessed are* those who are persecuted for righteousness' sake, *for*
    theirs is the kingdom of heaven.
"*Blessed are* you when people revile you and persecute you and utter
    all kinds of evil against you falsely on my account."

Matthew presents Jesus as a new Moses delivering a new (actually "renewed") law. In Matthew's version, Jesus goes up on a mountain to deliver the Beatitudes (hence, the "Sermon on the Mount"), while Luke has Jesus on a plain (Luke 6:17). The Beatitudes in Matthew correspond to the Ten Commandments, and their repeated pattern was an aid to memory in the early church and up to the present. It's not just the beginning "Blessed are" but the regular pattern of blessing a category of people and then explaining the reason: because theirs is the kingdom of heaven, because they will be comforted, because they will inherit the earth, etc. This kind of list with a repeated pattern had precedent in the Hebrew Bible, and not just in the Ten Commandments. Take another look at Luke's version:

"*Blessed are you* who are hungry now,
    for you will be filled.
"*Blessed are you* who weep now,
    for you will laugh.

"*Blessed are you* when people hate you, and when they exclude you, revile you, and defame you on account of the Son of Man. Rejoice in that day and leap for joy, for surely your reward is great in heaven; *for that is what their ancestors did to the prophets.*

"But *woe to you* who are rich,
    for you have received your consolation.
"*Woe to you* who are full now,
    for you will be hungry.

139

"Woe to you who are laughing now,
 for you will mourn and weep.

"Woe to you when all speak well of you, *for that is what their ancestors did to the false prophets."* (Luke 6:21–26)

Luke has a set of "Blesseds" followed by a set of "Woes," and each is tied up neatly with a reference to the prophets. Both features would lend themselves to memorization and recitation in early church communities.

Venti

You're going to need a break soon to get rid of all the coffee you've been drinking. So let us quickly introduce you to some repeated patterns that run through whole books and are clues for understanding how those books were written and organized.

Finished product

If the New Testament gospel writers were police cadets, Matthew would get stellar grades for his written reports. The Gospel of Matthew is perfectly organized. There's an introduction (chapters 1–4), a body (chapters 5–25), and a conclusion (chapters 26–28). The body is divided into five great discourses with some miracles thrown in. You can tell where one discourse ends and another begins by a pattern that Matthew repeats:

When Jesus had finished saying these things, the crowds were astounded at his teaching. (Matt. 7:28)

When Jesus had finished instructing his twelve disciples, he went on from there to teach and proclaim his message in their cities. (Matt. 11:1)

When Jesus had finished these parables, he left that place. (Matt. 13:53)

When Jesus had finished saying these things, he left Galilee and went to the region of Judea beyond the Jordan. (Matt. 19:1)

When Jesus had finished saying all these things, he said to his disciples . . . (Matt. 26:1)

The first words in each of these sentences are the same in Greek (Καὶ ἐγένετο ὅτε ἐτέλεσεν ὁ Ἰησοῦς—we threw in the Greek just for Sgt. Kokolopoulos, who's usually stuck at the front desk and is always looking for something to read). This clause and the verb "finished" do not occur anywhere else in the gospel outside of these five verses. Very neat. The reason there are five sections in the body instead of, say, three probably has to do with Matthew's objective in writing. Just as the Beatitudes, which begin the first section, present Jesus in the likeness of Moses articulating the Ten Commandments, as we saw earlier, so the five sections of the gospel correspond to the five books of Moses, otherwise known as the Torah or the Pentateuch. Jesus is portrayed by Matthew as the continuation or fulfillment (in the sense of bringing to full purpose) of Mosaic revelation.

Return post

We don't know anything about Paul's singing voice, but it's clear in the book of 1 Corinthians that he adopted his own brand of antiphonal response. He uses the expression "Now concerning" six times in 1 Corinthians to introduce diverse topics:

7:1—*"Now concerning* the matters about which you wrote . . ."
7:25—*"Now concerning* virgins . . ."
8:1—*"Now concerning* food sacrificed to idols . . ."
12:1—*"Now concerning* spiritual gifts . . ."
16:1—*"Now concerning* the collection for the saints . . ."
16:12—*"Now concerning* our brother Apollos . . ."

Either Paul was really bad at segues or he had some kind of checklist of topics that he wanted to cover. Is there any way to tell which it was? Yes. The key is 7:1, "Now concerning the matters about which you wrote." Paul is responding to a letter from them. In 5:9, he also refers to a previous letter that he wrote, so they were keeping the post office busy. If that wasn't enough, Paul was also getting oral reports. He mentions a report from "Chloe's people," whoever they were, in 1:11, and he responds to what he heard from them in the first six chapters. It must have been a juicy report, because the issues in those chapters are divisions in the Corinthian church, how to deal with a case of sexual immorality, and lawsuits between Christians. In 7:1 he takes up the matters raised in their letter and addresses them one by one. Paul has a tendency to go off on tangents, so there's sometimes a lengthy stretch between the "Now concernings." Still, the letter from the Corinthian church provided the organizational scheme for Paul's letter to them. It's a handy way to see what their concerns were and for getting a glimpse at some of the earliest church problems.

WHY THIS CLUE MATTERS

The Clue of the Repeated Pattern is important because of the flexibility and usefulness of patterns for both authors and readers. Authors use patterns to form the structures of passages and documents, and to display artistry. Patterns can indicate major themes and ideological interests of the author and therefore point to a work's purpose. They can also help to determine the boundaries of distinct literary units. They can display an author's preferred vocabulary and sometimes highlight unusual terms or phrases that have been adopted to fit a pattern. Readers find the repetition of patterns to be helpful for memorization and recitation.

THE CLUE OF THE REPEATED PATTERN CAN HELP US . . .

1. Look for repetitions in vocabulary and expressions within a given text.
2. Appreciate how repetition can contribute to the beauty of a piece of literature.
3. Pick out the structure of a passage or document as conveyed by one or more repeated patterns.
4. Look to repeated patterns for major themes and preferred vocabulary.

5. Be aware of the practical usefulness of repetition, which can indicate the purpose or function of a document in the life of ancient Israel or the early church.

THE CASEBOOK

1. Notice the repeated pattern in Jonah 1:1-2 and 3:1-2 and in Job 1:6-12 and 2:1-6. How does the repetition in each case add structure and balance to the text? Do you notice any other functions or benefits of the repetitions?
2. Note the repeated sentence in Jeremiah 7:4. Explain its function in the context.
3. Look at the repeated pattern in Leviticus 18:7-17. Separate out the components of the repeated sentence and explain what each means. What is the overall intent of this series of prohibitions? What relationship is missing? How do you account for its absence?
4. What repeated pattern do you find in Hebrews 11? Analyze the pattern and explain how its repetition contributes to the message and effect of the chapter?
5. What pattern is repeated in Revelation 2-3? How does the repeated pattern influence your understanding of the book and of the genre of apocalyptic literature? Locate the cities mentioned here on a map. What does this tell you about the audience of the book?

9

The Clue of the

BROKEN PATTERN

Last year there was a rash of burglaries in a posh neighborhood a couple of miles from the station. They all had the same m.o.—a house hit while the residents were away. Entry through a backyard window. Alarm disabled. Jewelry and cash missing.

Enter Dr. Marcus Meese, a psychiatrist who lived in the neighborhood. His was one of the first residences hit. He was president of the neighborhood association, so he gave us a hard time from the beginning. He was all up in our business wanting to know every detail about the investigation—what we had done and were going to do to catch the perp. He got his neighbors all riled up claiming we weren't doing enough (like this was the only case we were working), that it was our fault the crimes hadn't been solved. He rode us hard and really played the media against us.

Then, as we were going over the police reports for what seemed like the millionth time, we noticed something unusual in the report on Meese's house. In addition to a nice-sized haul of Mrs. Meese's jewelry and a few hundred bucks, there was also a laptop on the list. It was the only electronics item stolen from any of the houses. The thief had walked past a couple dozen laptops and tablets at the other places that had been hit, so it was very curious that Meese's was the only one taken. It was a distinct break in the pattern, and it cried out for an explanation. We put Meese under close surveillance at that point and pretty soon came up with the evidence to pin the whole string of break-ins on him.

Turned out he had set up the first couple of heists as an insurance scam by faking the one at his own house and the theft of his wife's jewelry. On impulse, he decided he wanted a new laptop and reported it stolen as well. In the meantime, he developed a taste for the capers. It wasn't that he needed the dough. He got off trying to prove he was smarter than the cops. His practice specialized in "stress relief," and with a little help from anti-anxiety meds, sometimes helped along with booze, he could coax out all kinds of details from his patients about their valuables without them remembering that they had told him. The case was the perfect example of the principle that the breaks in a pattern are sometimes more telling than the pattern itself.

In the Bible, the Clue of the Broken Pattern can be detected by the careful reader when there is a violation of the basic structure of a pattern in a text. This can take different forms. It may be that something is left out, something is added, an element is expanded, or the order of material has changed. To spot the Clue of the Broken Pattern, the pattern itself has to be recognized first, which requires close attention to the details. Once a pattern is detected, its various iterations must be studied. The break in the pattern may serve the ideological agenda of the text as a literary technique in the service of the writer's rhetorical purposes. It may also reflect editorial activity by a later writer who ignored or overlooked the underlying pattern.

Picking up where we left off

Since you have to find the pattern before you can see where it's broken and why, we thought we'd begin with a few cases from the Clue of the Repeated Pattern that come from a couple of big-time patterners, namely, Amos and Matthew.

Amos

We've already discussed Amos 1–2, which repeatedly use the sentence "Thus says the LORD, 'For three transgressions of X, and for four, I will not revoke the punishment'" to introduce oracles against different nations: Aram/Syria (1:3–5), Gaza/Philistia (1:6–8), Tyre/Phoenicia (1:9–10), Edom (1:11–12), Ammon (1:13–15), Moab (2:1–3), Judah (2:4–5), and

Israel (2:6-16). You can already tell just from this lineup of guilty parties where the big break in the pattern is. The one against Israel sticks out like a bloodhound at a poodle show. While all the others are handled in two or three verses, Amos throws the book at Israel by going on for a painful eleven verses about all it's done wrong.

This pattern makes it clear that the Israelites were the prophet's target all along. In fact, the whole passage is kind of like a target, naming off nations all around Israel while all the time zeroing in on it. If you imagine people in ancient Israel hearing these oracles spoken or read, you can picture them lulled into a false sense of security as all their neighbors are called out one by one until, suddenly, they feel the noose tightening around their own collective neck and realize they themselves are on the hot seat. Well played, Amos! It's a textbook example of how to ensnare a bad guy with a comfortable repeated pattern broken just at the right moment.

THE CLUE OF THE BROKEN PATTERN: a violation of the basic structure of a pattern in a text

A closer look, though, shows that the final oracle is not the only variation. There's no "says the LORD" at the end of the oracles against Phoenicia (1:9-10), Edom (1:11-12), and Judah (2:4-5), as there is after the other oracles. Some detectives think this is because the evidence has been tampered with by adding these oracles into the lineup. Maybe so. Or maybe the variation raises questions about whether "says the LORD" was part of the m.o. of the passage to begin with. A Bible detective has to consider every possible angle and can't be too quick to jump to conclusions. The defense attorney tried to have the case thrown out because of this ambiguity, but the conviction for a broken pattern with the oracle against Israel is solid.

Matthew

A couple of the repeated patterns that we witnessed in Matthew also turn out to be broken when examined carefully. The Beatitudes in Matthew 5:3-11 follow a pattern of sayings that begin with "Blessed are," as described in the Clue of the Repeated Pattern. But as with the oracle against Israel in Amos 2, when you line up all of Matthew's "Blesseds," the last one stands out and breaks the pattern in two ways. First, it changes from third to second person. Instead of "they," it reads, "Blessed are *you* when people revile *you* and persecute *you* and utter all kinds of evil against *you* falsely on my account." Second, it is much longer that the previous "Blesseds," because it continues, "Rejoice and be glad, for your reward is great in heaven, for in the same way they persecuted the prophets who were before you."

Why these differences? It's unclear, although a good guess is that this last beatitude is directed at the "Matthean community," the original intended audience of the book with whom the author was familiar and maybe a part of. These two verses and a few other passages in Matthew (10:18, 39; 16:25) suggest that this audience was experiencing some kind of social or political persecution. It's also interesting that the second-person form is more similar to Luke's version (Luke 6:22–23). So perhaps Matthew got the second-person address from Q (on this, see the Clue of the Doublet) and kept it because it spoke directly to his audience. Whatever the reason, the break in the pattern was definitely intentional. Matthew was too well organized for it to be an accident. Remember that this is the scribe who turned in a very neat report on Jesus's life with a beginning, ending, and five clearly delineated discourses between them. The discourses are all marked with "When Jesus had finished . . ." (Matt. 7:28; 11:1; 13:53; 19:1; 26:1). Here also there's a pattern break. It's a small but important one. The conclusion to the fifth discourse reads "When Jesus had finished saying *all* these things . . ." The word "all" is new and tells you that this is the last of the ending statements. It provides a conclusion not just to the fifth discourse but to all five of them. It's the Bible's way of saying, "Move along, folks, there's no more to see here."

Part of the plan

Are you starting to see how one or more broken patterns can be the key to cracking a case of biblical interpretation? To seal the deal, we're going to trot out another example of a case that's even more high profile than Matthew and Amos.

Back to the beginning

We're talking Genesis 1, where it all began. It doesn't get much more mainstream media than that. The problem is, the media always pick up on the wrong thing when they report on this case. They only talk about science or history, creation versus evolution. They don't examine the facts in the case from the standpoint of Bible detection and the evidence from broken patterns. But there are several big patterns in Genesis 1, and the whole case of what's going on here revolves around those patterns and the points where they're broken.

The patterns are pretty obvious because the document reads like a court reporter's log. The first thing you notice is that there's a pattern of days. Creation takes place over six days with God resting on the seventh, which is the Sabbath. This means that the account spills over into Genesis 2 and includes the first three verses of that chapter. Some rookie Bible cops who decided to add chapter and verse divisions in the Middle Ages failed to cordon off the right amount of real estate. There's a lesson here for Bible investigators: sometimes you have to ignore the numbers and go by the evidence in the text. So in this case, the full scene is Genesis 1:1-2:3. After that, you bump into another case involving Adam, Eve, and a talking snake, but cut off your investigation too soon and you miss crucial evidence.

The time frame for the case in Genesis 1 is a full week. Each day of the week is important, and each day is plainly marked in the text by another pattern—a couple of them actually. The days are counted off like morning roll call. The only thing is, the calendar being used was ancient Israel's where day began at sunset rather than at midnight, like ours does (except for the guys pulling night shift), so evening preceded morning for them. That's why the formula "There was evening and there was morning, day X" comes at the end of each day's account rather than at the beginning (vv. 5, 8, 13, 19, 23, 31). Each starts with God on the witness stand and the lead, "God said," which you get in verses 3, 6, 9, 11, 14, 20, 24, and 26. (This doesn't count the two occurrences of "God said" in verses 28-29, which are off the record because they're not followed by creative acts and so are not part of the creation formula.) There are two more "God saids" than "evening and mornings," that is, two more opening formulas than there are concluding formulas. There are six concluding formulas, one for each day, leading up to the Sabbath, when God rested. That makes sense; the numbers match. But there are eight opening formulas. Something doesn't add up. Literally. Let's look further into the patterns. In between the opening and the closing formulas are the accounts of each day's creation, and those accounts also follow a pattern. It's not as regular as the others. Creative activity can be a messy process, after all. But the pattern is still recognizable. Here's how it all lays out:

1—Let . . . and there was . . . God saw [it] was good . . . God separated . . . God called

2—Let . . . God made . . . and separated . . . it was so . . . God called

3—Let . . . it was so . . . God called . . . God saw it was good . . . Let . . . it was so . . . God saw it was good

4—Let . . . it was so . . . God made . . . God saw it was good

5—Let . . . God created . . . God saw it was good . . . God blessed

6—Let . . . it was so . . . God made . . . God saw it was good . . . Let . . . God created (3 x) . . . God blessed . . . God said (2 x) . . . it was so . . . God saw everything that he had made, and indeed, it was very good.

You don't have to be a Detective I to immediately notice some important breaks in the pattern. There's a big one on day 3 where the pattern is repeated on the same day, so that there are two creative acts for the day—gathering the waters on earth to form dry land and calling for vegetation. The same thing happens on day 6, where there are two instances of "Let," referring to the creation of land animals and the creation of human beings. There is also further pattern breakage on the sixth day. The verb "created" occurs not just once but three times; God speaks directly to the humans, which does not happen with any other part of creation; and there is the summative statement à la Matthew that God saw that *everything* in creation was *very* good. Recognizing that days 3 and 6 correspond to one another, if we outline Genesis 1:1–2:3 in another way, a separate pattern emerges:

Day 1:	light	Day 4:	sun, moon, stars
Day 2:	dome (sky)	Day 5:	birds, fish
Day 3:	seas and dry land	Day 6:	land animals
	vegetation		humans

Day 7: Sabbath

The first three days correspond to the last three: light on day 1 and the light-giving bodies on day 4; separating waters with the dome on day 2 and the animals that live in the sky and seas on day 5; dry land and the vegetation that grows on it on day 3 and animals and humans who live on the land and consume the vegetation on day 6. It's all very neatly wrapped up with patterns, which only serves to draw your attention even more closely to places where the patterns are broken. One set of breaks—the loading up of day 6 with extras in verse 31—obviously had to do with the creation of humans as the climax and high point of creation (deserved or not). But what about the pattern of days of creation? Let's review the facts and just the facts.

Fact #1: There are six days reserved for creation. This fact is established by the testimony of Genesis 2:1-3, which has God resting on the seventh day, the Sabbath, and by the count kept in the concluding formula of the pattern of narration for each day's creation—"there was evening and there was morning, day X."

Fact #2: According to the testimony of the opening formula ("God said") and of the rest of the daily narrative pattern, which repeats on days 3 and 6, creation took place in eight installments.

We're not mathematicians, but the way we learned it in our day, eight and six are not equal, and we're pretty sure that's still true. There's not a contradiction exactly between these two facts, but there is a definite tension, especially since the repeats of the narrative pattern on days 3 and 6 break with the pattern for the other four days. It is a peculiarity, and detectives don't like unexplained peculiarities. It boils down to a matter of motive. Why would the narrator of Genesis 1:1-2:3 choose to tell the story this way as opposed to having just six installments to match the six days or extending the time period to eight days to match the number of installments? This is where you have to use your investigative intuition. Here's our gut feeling; see if it matches yours: The writer knew of an account of creation in eight steps and wanted to accommodate it to six days in order to provide a rationale for the Sabbath. As explained in the chapter on the Clue of the Etiology, it was a powerful rationale to have the Sabbath woven into the fabric of the cosmos and for even God to observe the Sabbath. Rather than mess with the account that he knew, the writer just doubled up on two days to fit it into six. You can take that a step further to appreciate the different light it sheds on the Genesis creation story. It was never about history or science as we know it. It was about getting people to observe a religious holiday. There were obviously no eyewitnesses around to corroborate our hunch, but we're willing to bet dollars to donuts that we're on the right track.

Moody Paul

You've demonstrated an aptitude for noticing broken patterns and for applying your intuition to explain the reasons behind them. Let's get a little more exercise on both fronts by looking at a couple of New Testament cases, one that requires some broad familiarity with the literature to pick out the pattern that's broken, and the other where the evidence is so inconclusive that we're mostly dependent on our guts.

The first case is Galatians 1:1–6:

> Paul an apostle—sent neither by human commission nor from human authorities, but through Jesus Christ and God the Father, who raised him from the dead—and all the members of God's family who are with me, to the churches of Galatia: Grace to you and peace from God our Father and the Lord Jesus Christ, who gave himself for our sins to set us free from the present evil age, according to the will of our God and Father, to whom be the glory forever and ever. Amen. I am astonished that you are so quickly deserting the one who called you in the grace of Christ and are turning to a different gospel.

That opening represents a break in a pattern, a departure from Paul's usual way of beginning a letter. For comparison purposes, here are the openings of the other six letters considered genuine to Paul.

> Romans 1:1–10: Paul, a servant of Jesus Christ, called to be an apostle, set apart for the gospel of God, which he promised beforehand through his prophets in the holy scriptures, the gospel concerning his Son, who was descended from David according to the flesh and was declared to be Son of God with power according to the spirit of holiness by resurrection from the dead, Jesus Christ our Lord, through whom we have received grace and apostleship to bring about the obedience of faith among all the Gentiles for the sake of his name, including yourselves who are called to belong

to Jesus Christ, to all God's beloved in Rome, who are called to be saints: Grace to you and peace from God our Father and the Lord Jesus Christ. First, I thank my God through Jesus Christ for all of you, because your faith is proclaimed throughout the world. For God, whom I serve with my spirit by announcing the gospel of his Son, is my witness that without ceasing I remember you always in my prayers, asking that by God's will I may somehow at last succeed in coming to you.

1 Corinthians 1:1–7: Paul, called to be an apostle of Christ Jesus by the will of God, and our brother Sosthenes, to the church of God that is in Corinth, to those who are sanctified in Christ Jesus, called to be saints, together with all those who in every place call on the name of our Lord Jesus Christ, both their Lord and ours: Grace to you and peace from God our Father and the Lord Jesus Christ. I give thanks to my God always for you because of the grace of God that has been given you in Christ Jesus, for in every way you have been enriched in him, in speech and knowledge of every kind—just as the testimony of Christ has been strengthened among you—so that you are not lacking in any spiritual gift as you wait for the revealing of our Lord Jesus Christ.

2 Corinthians 1:1–4: Paul, an apostle of Christ Jesus by the will of God, and Timothy our brother, to the church of God that is in Corinth, including all the saints throughout Achaia: Grace to you and peace from God our Father and the Lord Jesus Christ. Blessed be the God and Father of our Lord Jesus Christ, the Father of mercies and the God of all consolation, who consoles us in all our affliction, so that we may be able to console those who are in any affliction with the consolation with which we ourselves are consoled by God.

Philippians 1:1–5: Paul and Timothy, servants of Christ Jesus, to all the saints in Christ Jesus who are in Philippi, with the bishops and deacons: Grace to you and peace from God our Father and the Lord Jesus Christ. I thank my God every time I remember you, constantly praying with joy in every one of my prayers for all of you, because of your sharing in the gospel from the first day until now.

1 Thessalonians 1:1-3: Paul, Silvanus, and Timothy, to the church of the Thessalonians in God the Father and the Lord Jesus Christ: Grace to you and peace. We always give thanks to God for all of you and mention you in our prayers, constantly remembering before our God and Father your work of faith and labor of love and steadfastness of hope in our Lord Jesus Christ.

Philemon 1-5: Paul, a prisoner of Christ Jesus, and Timothy our brother, to Philemon our dear friend and co-worker, to Apphia our sister, to Archippus our fellow soldier, and to the church in your house: Grace to you and peace from God our Father and the Lord Jesus Christ. When I remember you in my prayers, I always thank my God because I hear of your love for all the saints and your faith toward the Lord Jesus.

Did you spot the pattern that Galatians breaks? If you said that in Galatians *Paul doesn't thank God for them* as he does in most of his other letters, you deserve a commendation—especially since we didn't really play fair. Galatians doesn't express Paul's thanks, but neither does 2 Corinthians. They both break the pattern. In 2 Corinthians, Paul replaces his usual expression of thanks with a blessing. Part of the reason for this is that the relationship between Paul and the Corinthian church was strained because Paul thought they had paid attention to some visitors who attacked him.

Which takes us to Galatians, where Paul skips the thanksgiving altogether because he is seriously annoyed with them. This is clear from his language, which accuses them of turning to a different gospel (v. 6) and perverting the real gospel (v. 7), and then he twice curses those who would teach such a different gospel (vv. 8-9). By "curse" we mean that he damns them to eternal punishment in hell, and he's not kidding. What he's worked up about is the teaching that gentiles who converted to Christianity had to, in effect, convert to Judaism first and be circumcised before they could be Christians. That could deter more than a few guys from changing religions. There were also some challenges to Paul's authority, which is why he gets very defensive in Galatians, as explained in the Clue of the Doublet. If you notice the pattern break and Paul's bad mood, it helps you look for things in the letter that account for them. Like when you're summoned to the captain's office, it softens the blow a little to know what the reason is going in. What's distinct about this case is that the pattern occurs over multiple books and not just within the same writing. It's another reminder that picking up on a clue sometimes requires familiarity with what's going on in more than one neighborhood at the same time.

All you need is love

The other New Testament case we'll look at calls for intuition to interpret. It's in the Gospel of John, near the end. The setting is after Jesus's resurrection. Peter and some of the other disciples decide to go fishing. They're not having much luck until Jesus appears and tells them to throw the net on the other side of the boat, which leads to a huge haul. When they get back to shore, Jesus is there like the Chief at the annual Boys and Girls Club breakfast, getting ready to cook. After they've eaten (what else?) fish for the most important meal of the day, Jesus strikes up a conversation with Peter. Here's how it goes:

> "Simon son of John, do you love me more than these?" He said to him, "Yes, Lord; you know that I love you." Jesus said to him, "Feed my lambs." A second time he said to him, "Simon son of John, do you love me?" He said to him, "Yes, Lord; you know that I love you." Jesus said to him, "Tend my sheep." He said to him the third time, "Simon son of John, do you love me?" Peter felt hurt because he said to him the third time, "Do you love me?" And he said to him, "Lord, you know everything; you know that I love you." Jesus said to him, "Feed my sheep." (John 21:15–17)

Seems simple, but there's a complication when you look at the Greek. Two different verbs are involved. Jesus starts out using the verb *agapaō*, which is sometimes defined as "Christian" love, although it's certainly not limited to Christians. It means to have a deep, long-lasting, and unselfish concern about someone and his or her well-being. Peter replies using the verb *phileō*, which is brotherly affection or friendship, and is maybe not quite as strong as *agapaō*. The same thing happens the second time. But on the third time, *Jesus breaks the pattern by switching to Peter's verb*. Peter gets his feelings hurt. Is that because Jesus "reduced" verbs or because he asked the same question a third time? There's no right or wrong answer. At least, no one is sure what the right answer is. The change of verbs is obvious in Greek, and it's easy to impute meaning to it. On the other hand, a lot of New Testament sleuths think there was no real difference in the everyday use of the two verbs. It's hard to communicate the difference between the two verbs in English, which only has one verb for "love." You could substitute the verb "like" for *phileō*, but that probably makes for too strong a contrast. Peter's response might be better understood if we were to translate, "You know I love you, bro." Maybe that means the same thing as what Jesus was asking, but maybe it's a little more ambiguous. You're really on your own on this one, and your intuition is as good as ours. You'll just have to wait until you join the big precinct in the sky to find the author of the Gospel of John, if you can figure out who that was, and ask him. Or you can ask Peter, who's supposed to be minding the pearly gates to the place. Be sure to give him our love.

Plans change

Whatever the meaning of the exchange between Jesus and Peter in John 21, the passage is the work of a single author. That's not necessarily true of the passages we'll consider next. The patterns in these texts seem to reflect cases of breaking and entering by later revisers.

Hair for brains

You don't have to have a degree in Bible criminology to know that Samson is the strongest dude in the Good Book, though he may also be the dumbest. It's hard to imagine the Bible neighborhoods without his presence. But the tales about him in the book of Judges may not be original to the book. Why? You guessed it—he breaks the pattern of stories of the other judges. The book of Judges is nothing if not patterns. The main pattern is spelled out in Judges 2:18–19, which needs to come with a spoiler alert because it tips off biblical sleuths regarding the outcome of each of the stories they're about to read (see the Clue of the Telegraphed Information): "Whenever the LORD raised up judges for them, the LORD was with the judge, and he delivered them from the hand of their enemies all the days of the judge; for the LORD would be moved to pity by their groaning because of those who persecuted and oppressed them. But whenever the judge died, they would relapse and behave worse than their ancestors, following other gods, worshiping them and bowing down to them. They would not drop any of their practices or their stubborn ways."

The pattern is clearer than the assembly instructions for our new filing cabinets from Pier One (then again, what isn't?):

> The Israelites sin.
> The Lord is angry and turns them over to _____ (name of foreign oppressor).
> There is a period of oppression for _____ years.
> The Israelites cry out to the Lord for help.
> The Lord raises up _____ as a judge.
> The Lord's spirit comes on the judge.
> The judge defeats the oppressor.
> The land has rest for a period of _____ years.

Then it all starts over again, like the recycled plot of a bad TV cop show.

You can take this pattern and fill in the blanks for the judges that follow: Ehud (Judg. 3:12-30), Deborah (Judg. 4-5), Gideon (Judg. 6-8), and Jephthah (Judg. 10:6-12:7). Then you come to Samson. The Samson stories start out more or less according to the pattern with the first three elements wrapped up in one: "The Israelites again did what was evil in the sight of the LORD, and the LORD gave them into the hand of the Philistines forty years" (Judg. 13:1). But then there's no cry for help and no notice of the Lord raising up Samson as a judge. There are references to the Lord's spirit coming upon Samson (Judg. 13:25; 14:6, 19; 15:14) for individual feats of strength, but not for a single, decisive defeat of the oppressor. Besides, it's never entirely clear in the stories whether Samson's strength comes from his long hair or the Lord's spirit falling upon him. He kills a lot of Philistines in his final exit, but that's not the end of Philistine oppression, which continues in the book of 1 Samuel. And there's no mention that the land of Israel had rest, only that Samson had judged for twenty years (Judg. 16:31b), which is a doublet of 15:20 (see the chapter on the Clue of the Doublet).

So the Samson narratives break the pattern for judges in several respects. It could be that the creator of the book of Judges found the stories of Samson in a collection and adopted them wholesale. But you have to wonder why that editor/compiler didn't conform the stories more to the pattern established for the other judges. Whatever the reason, the stories of Samson the pattern breaker look to us like they're an add-on as a substantial supplement to the book of Judges.

Musical interlude

Let's lighten the mood by putting on Pharrell Williams's "Happy" and reading Paul's letter to the Philippians. Paul was in prison—he doesn't say where. The Philippians hear about his imprisonment and send one of their members, a man named Epaphroditus, to check on Paul and take gifts to him, showing their love and concern (Phil. 2:25; 4:18). After fulfilling his mission, Epaphroditus became seriously ill and almost died (2:26-27). Now that he has recovered, Paul is sending him back, along with the letter, to express his thanks for their interest in him. Paul deals with some other issues as well, but the letter is largely one of encouragement; joy is a major theme of the book, with words for "joy," "rejoice," and "be happy" occurring sixteen times. A good example is the beginning of chapter 2: "If then there is any encouragement in Christ, any consolation from love, any sharing in the Spirit, any compassion and sympathy, make my *joy* complete: be of the same mind, having the same love, being in full accord and of one mind. Do nothing from selfish ambition or conceit, but in humility regard others as better than yourselves. Let each of you look not to your own interests, but to the interests of others. Let the same mind be in you that was in Christ Jesus" (Phil. 2:1-5).

The positive energy continues in verses 12-18:

> Therefore, my beloved, just as you have always obeyed me, not only in my presence, but much more now in my absence, work out your own salvation with fear and trembling; for it is God who is at work in you, enabling you both to will and to work for his good pleasure. Do all things without murmuring and arguing, so that you may be blameless and innocent, children of God without blemish in the midst of a crooked and perverse generation, in which you shine like stars in the world. It is by your holding fast to the word of life that I can boast on the day of Christ that I did not run in vain or labor in vain. But even if I am being poured out as a libation over the sacrifice and the offering of your faith, I

am *glad* and *rejoice* with all of you—and in the same way you also must *be glad* and *rejoice* with me.

The repeated expressions of joy don't constitute as tight a pattern as we have seen in other Bible cases. But they still represent Paul's m.o. in Philippians. In fact, it's enough of a change from his usual tone in other letters to qualify as a pattern break in and of itself. In the midst of this joy-fest, verses 6-11 appear in the form of a poem in many English translations:

> who, though he was in the form of God,
>> did not regard equality with God
>> as something to be exploited,
> but emptied himself,
>> taking the form of a slave,
>> being born in human likeness.
> And being found in human form,
>> he humbled himself
>> and became obedient to the point of death—
>> even death on a cross.
> Therefore God also highly exalted him
>> and gave him the name
>> that is above every name,
> so that at the name of Jesus
>> every knee should bend,
>> in heaven and on earth and under the earth,
> and every tongue should confess
>> that Jesus Christ is Lord,
>> to the glory of God the Father.

These verses interrupt Paul's expressions of joy and his encouragement to the Philippians to share in that joy with an ode of praise to Christ that our New Testament colleagues agree was probably an early Christian hymn. Some of them, especially the veterans, think that the hymn was probably inserted by a later writer. They emphasize the contrast between the direct address of encouragement to the Philippians in the surrounding verses and the abstract praise of Jesus in the song. Others point out continuity between Paul's stress on humility and unselfishness in verses 3-4 and Christ's self-emptying to take on human form at the start of the hymn. They suggest that Paul himself included the hymn to continue this thought. We're out of our jurisdiction here and don't have a firm opinion either way. There is agreement that the poem breaks the pattern in verses 1-5 that continues in verses 12-18, and no one, at least in our Bible Division, thinks that Paul wrote the poem. So even if he included it, he interrupted himself by choosing to sample it at this point in his letter.

Neither of the suspects in these cases of broken patterns by later writers left their signatures. So we can't be sure beyond reasonable doubt that they were secondary. But we're dealing with a different standard of proof in Bible cases—preponderance of the evidence. That's what we shoot for as Bible detectives; it's the best we can hope for.

WHY THIS CLUE MATTERS

Broken patterns can give insights into both the rhetorical and ideological purpose of a biblical passage and its history of composition. In some cases, the break shows what the real objective of the text is, the real point that it is driving at. In other cases, it introduces information that is extraneous from and even at odds with the main force of the text and that therefore points to a secondary hand. In both instances, the broken pattern is a key piece of evidence for deducing the message in a passage and how that message may have changed or been interpreted over time.

THE CLUE OF THE BROKEN PATTERN CAN HELP US . . .

1. Be aware of both the macrostructure and content of a document and the microelements within a particular portion of the document.
2. Examine perceived patterns carefully for changes or inconsistencies.
3. Inquire into what the point of a given pattern is and how it fits with a larger piece of literature.
4. Consider how variations in a pattern may affect the overall point of a text.
5. Look into the reasons for variation and whether they further the larger agenda or differ from it.

THE CASEBOOK

1. Compare Joseph's interpretations of the dreams of the cupbearer and baker in Genesis 40:12–13, 18–19. Where do you see the repetition of a pattern? Where does the pattern break? What significance or artistry does this add to the story?
2. Matthew's genealogy for Jesus in Matthew 1:1–16 breaks a pattern found in other genealogies in the Bible by its mention of five women. Identify the five women and review their stories. What messages does this alteration of the usual pattern convey?
3. Beginning in Matthew 5:21 and running through the rest of the chapter, Jesus repeats a pattern in his teaching about the law. Pick out the elements of the pattern and any variations you notice. Is Matthew casting Jesus's teaching as a new and different law from that of the Hebrew Bible or as a renewal of the Hebrew Bible law that gets at its real significance? Explain how the repeated pattern and any breaks in it contribute to the message of the passage.
4. The book of Hebrews ends following the pattern of a letter, but it does not follow that pattern in its beginning. What other differences do you notice with New Testament letters? How would you classify the genre of this book? How does your understanding of the genre of Hebrews affect how you read it?
5. Take another look at the story of Jephthah in Judges 10:6–12:7. In what ways does it vary from the pattern of the preceding stories of the judges? Notice that the story of Jephthah interrupts the list of the so-called minor judges in Judges 10:1–5 + 12:8–15. Could this help to account for the variations?

PART TWO

DUSTING FOR PRINTS

... clues that require more specialized training in methods and tools from the detective's bag of tricks.

10

The Clue of the

TELEGRAPHED INFORMATION

The department recently posted this flier as part of a public awareness campaign:

> If you witness a crime, it is your responsibility to drop a dime. Just dial the precinct number and leave the 411 on the voice-mail tape. Then hang up the phone. It's as simple as that. On the flip side, if you prefer, you can do it online. There's a slide show with the instructions on the department web page: BibleDetectives.org. Be sure to use upper- and lowercase letters. You can address an email to one of us, then hit the return, and the cursor will move to the cc line. Type in another detective's name there, so that your letter will end up in both inboxes. We will create a new file and cut and paste your message to include in it. Your testimony may be crucial for solving a crime. So, at the risk of sounding like a broken record: If you witness a crime, drop a dime.

The department's goal was to make the message of the flier widely accessible, so you probably had no trouble understanding it. But a lot of the terms used in it are anachronistic and hark back to the days when our high-tech world was in its infancy, or still in the womb. How familiar these terms are depends on how old you are and where you come from. We're going to go through some of these, but we've left a few of them

("411," "flip side," "slide show," "inbox," "file") for you to investigate on your own.

Drop a dime—This comes from when there were pay phones on most street corners and other public places. It cost ten cents to make a local call. Now that everyone has cell phones, it's hard to track down a pay variety, and it costs at least a quarter if you do find one.

Tape—Watch a few episodes of Netflix's *Mindhunters* if you want the 411 on recording. Before digital there was reel-to-reel, and before CDs there were cassettes. (We're skipping eight-tracks, which made a brief appearance in the 1960s and '70s mostly to play music in cars driven by high school students and weren't used for general recording.) Mini-cassettes were used in telephone answering machines.

Hang up—This one's not completely gone yet, because there are still landlines. So you may very well have hung up a telephone handset back on its cradle. But when you "hang up" your cell, you're really just disconnecting a call. The device itself doesn't hang anywhere (unless you're one of those people who still has a flip phone with a holder on your belt).

Upper- and lowercase—Speaking of putting things in backward, this one comes from the specialized field of printing, so even though it's been around for a long time, it's not known to most people. Without photocopying and digitization, printing on paper required typesetting, which meant placing cast metal letters and symbols in reverse order on tracks so they could be inked and have their images imprinted on paper. The letters were kept in cases with the capitals in the upper compartment and the minuscules in the lower one.

Return—Ever wonder why the Enter button on your computer is also called Return? It's because computer keyboards were borrowed from typewriters, which had a movable carriage return that holds the paper between two rollers. The carriage moves from right to left with each keystroke. When you come to the end of a line, you reach up with your left hand and push a lever that *returns* the carriage all the way to the right. The technology changed by building on what was already in existence. You don't reinvent the wheel, you just improve it—and when you do you keep the name.

cc—If you wanted a backup copy of the document you were typing, you'd load two sheets of paper in the rollers with a piece of carbon paper between them. The acronym "cc" stands for "carbon copy" and was used on letters and memos to let the primary recipient know that a copy was being sent to another party. The format continued for emails, and it's easily adaptable. We can just say that "cc" now stands for carbonless copy.

Cut and paste—It's hard to believe, but cutting (with scissors) and pasting (with glue) are exactly what used to be involved if you wanted to move a section or photo from one document into another. It sure is a lot easier to press Control X, move the cursor, and press Control V, no?

Sound like a broken record—The only reason eight-tracks and cassettes replaced records was because record players were bulkier and harder to carry around. You couldn't have a record player in your car. It would be next to impossible to change a record while going down the freeway at 55 mph (the national speed limit from 1974 to 1987 as a gas-saving measure). With a cassette player you could eject the cassette, turn it over, and reinsert it all with one hand. But the sound was never as good. And if the tape broke, the only thing you could do was throw it away and buy another one. If your record got scratched, the needle might skip and play the same thing over and over again—78, 45, or 33⅓ times a minute. Irritating, yes. But once you moved the needle you could still listen to the rest of the record.

One of the main corporations we have to thank for the proliferation of technology is AT&T, which stands for American Telephone and Telegraph. The telegraph was the first modern telecommunications device. It was invented by Samuel Morse in the 1830s and '40s. It transmitted electronic signals that could be coded to send messages over wire stretched between stations. Morse also invented the code that was used to send messages. Morse sent the first message from Washington, DC, to Baltimore in 1844. It read, "What hath God wrought?" In the US Civil War of the 1860s, the telegraph proved invaluable, especially for the Union army, for planning, coordinating, and intelligence gathering. It was the fastest way to send information, such as that obtained by spies. That's how it took on the sense of divulging information unwittingly, as when a boxer telegraphs punches, allowing an opponent to block them, or a basketball player telegraphs passes, making them easy to intercept. Telegraphed information today would arrive much slower than an email, especially since Western Union, the main telegraph company, closed the telegraphy branch of its company in 2006. As with the previous examples, the expression "telegraphed information" has outlived the technology.

In the Bible, telegraphed information is present when the text anticipates something that will happen later on, often an event or aspect of the story itself. This clue can function in different ways. At times it indicates some sort of literary reworking. At other times, it simply reveals an author's technique or style, in which case it is part of the artistry of biblical storytelling. However, in some instances it is an attempt to clue in the audience reading the text at a later point in time in order to relate it to their concerns. If it is intended for a later audience, the telegraphed information stands out because it doesn't make sense in its literary context. If the telegraphed information anticipates something in the story, it can only be detected in retrospect, unless readers already know the larger narrative. The Clue of the Telegraphed Information can also provide hints about the audience and context for which a text was originally written.

The Clue of the Physical Description is often a kind of telegraphing because physical descriptions in biblical stories usually hint at the role or roles a character will play. In this chapter, though, we're going to look at some other instances of telegraphing that are unrelated to physical descriptions and are usually much harder clues to uncover.

Close-range telegrams

Since telegraphy isn't really used anymore, you might think that it's irrelevant for law enforcement. And you'd be right in terms of that specific technology. But the concept of instantaneous long-distance communication that telegraphy made real is an enormous asset to police work. It negated the correlation of distance with time and paved the way for further long-range telecommunication methods. It didn't matter if the perps were across town, across the state, or across the country, for the first time you could get ahead of them and have police waiting for them. Distance wasn't important.

The same is true in the Bible, which can telegraph info about events or texts later in a story, in a book, or in a whole division of the canon. Just to prove it, that's how we've organized the folders we pulled from the case files drawer for this clue. The folders are a little yellowed, because we went all in and searched for cases involving telegraphs. You can substitute newer technology like email or texting and come out with the same results.

A simple case of telegraphing is the sons of Eli—Hophni and Phinehas—in 1 Samuel 2:12–25. This story relates the sending of multiple telegrams about the same issue. Verse 12 tells you that the sons were scoundrels. Five verses later in verse 17 their sin is identified as very great because it treated God's offering (and hence God) with contempt. Next, in verses 22–25, Eli hears about his sons' wicked deeds and eschews the use of telegrams, deciding that a face-to-face is warranted. He cautions his sons that their sin is against God directly and could not be mitigated by a third party. According to verse 25, the sons ignore their dad's warning because it was God's will to kill them. Pretty easy to guess what's coming down the pike. Sure enough, a couple of chapters later in 1 Samuel 4:11, we learn that Hophni and Phinehas are killed in a battle with the Philistines in which the ark of the covenant is captured. The only reason the telegram doesn't cover a shorter distance is that the narrator uses the rest of chapter 2 after verse 25 and all of chapter 3 to build a contrast between Eli's sons and Samuel. The telegraphing in this case, therefore, has a purpose larger than just hinting at the death of Eli's sons; it alludes to Samuel's replacement of Eli and his house as Israel's leading priest. It also provides a theological reason: God had determined to kill Eli's sons in order to put Samuel in their place.

> THE CLUE OF THE TELEGRAPHED INFORMATION: an anticipation of something that will happen later on in the story

Another nice telegram occurs following David's sin with Bathsheba in 2 Samuel 11. At the very end of 2 Samuel 11 we find the statement that the Lord considered what David had done to be evil. The next thing you know, the prophet Nathan shows up, and like a sneaky ancient Lt. Columbo, he gets David to pronounce judgment on himself. Nathan takes charge of the punishment phase and tells David that the child he fathered with Bathsheba will die and that the Lord will raise up trouble from his own house, which is a telegram in its own right anticipating David's son Absalom's revolt. Because these two chapters are so negative toward David and the surrounding chapters can be read as very positive, and because chapter 12 alludes to Absalom's revolt but nothing in the revolt story refers back to Nathan's oracle, some Bible dicks think that the Bathsheba story (2 Sam. 11–12) was added later. It's a viable theory. The telegraphing alone isn't enough to win a conviction, but it's an important piece of evidence.

Telegraphing is also alive and well in the New Testament. Matthew and Mark both report that one of the accusations made against Jesus during his trial before the high priest and other Jewish authorities was that he had said he would destroy the temple and rebuild it in three days (Matt. 26:61; Mark 14:58) and that this was one of the things people ridiculed him for on the cross (Matt. 27:40; Mark 15:29). While neither of them reports Jesus actually saying such a thing, they don't deny it either. Neither of them interprets the saying, but it's an evident allusion to his death and resurrection after three days. By "allusion" we mean "telegram." Jesus or Matthew or Mark or all three sent the same one. We don't know when Jesus is supposed to have said these words, but it had to be within the last week of his life when he was in Jerusalem, according to Matthew and Mark. For both of them, Jesus was crucified a short time later, so we can add another close-range telegram to the collection.

Up-front summaries

When telegraphed information covers a whole book of the Bible, we like to call it "proleptic (or anticipatory) synthesis." That means it's an up-front summary of what the book is about—its main theme(s) or argument(s). Think of it as the nutshell technique—it sums up the main point of a book in a neat package at its beginning. All the examples in the previous section on short-range telegrams were about death, so we'll try to be more positive here.

Gospelgrams

The New Testament gospels, or at least those of Matthew, Mark, and John, are the best examples of this kind of messaging. Matthew 1:1 is a nice bridge between the short-range telegram and the longer proleptic synthesis. It reads, "An account of the genealogy of Jesus the Messiah, the son of David, the son of Abraham." And that's how Matthew divides the genealogy that follows, as he explains in verse 17: "So all the generations from Abraham to David are fourteen generations; and from David to the deportation to Babylon, fourteen generations; and from the deportation to Babylon to the Messiah, fourteen generations." If you count, you'll find that there's actually one more generation in the middle section than in the other two. So Matthew may not have been great at math, but he was terrific at telegraphing. Not only is the first verse a telegram of the genealogy, but it's also a good proleptic synthesis of the whole gospel. Matthew was writing for a Jewish or Jewish Christian audience and wanted to emphasize that Jesus was the descendant of Abraham, hence a solid Jew ethnically, and a descendant of David, hence qualified to be the Messiah or Christ (see the Clue of the Weird Social Custom on the meaning of these titles as "anointed").

Mark does pretty much the same thing, but he actually sends a double telegram just to be sure we get the message. The Gospel of Mark begins, "The beginning of the good news of Jesus Christ, the Son of God" (Mark 1:1). The identity of Jesus as God's Son is Mark's main theme, so this verse is a proleptic synthesis of that theme broadcast (by telegraph, of course) for the rest of the gospel. It is reinforced in the first story that Mark relates, which is about Jesus's baptism. When he comes up out of the water, a dove descends on him and a voice from heaven announces, "You are my Son, the Beloved; with you I am well pleased" (Mark 1:11). The telegram is then re-sent in the last story of the original gospel that reports Jesus's death. As he expires on the cross, a Roman centurion observes the scene and remarks, "Truly this man was God's Son" (Mark 15:39). Jesus's divinity is the essence of the "good news" that Mark recounts. The Greek term is *euanggelion*, from which we get "evangelism" and similar words. It is also translated "gospel." Mark may have invented the term at least as a genre designation for the story of Jesus's life. So in a sense he telegraphs not only the main theme of his book but also that of all Christianity. That's an even more significant telegram than Samuel Morse's "What hath God wrought?"

John spends the first eighteen verses, often called the "prologue," telegraphing key words and ideas from his gospel—*word, life, light* and *darkness, witness, the world, new birth, children of God, power, flesh, glory, grace,* and *truth.* It's a long telegram, but it can be boiled down to the first line: "In the beginning was the Word, and the Word was with God, and the Word was God" (John 1:1). Talk about a spoiler! It's a lot like Matthew and Mark in the sense that the first verse synthesizes the verses that follow—Jesus's genealogy in Matthew, Jesus's baptism and death in Mark—as well as the major theme of the whole gospel.

Luke is the odd man out of the gospels in this respect. He doesn't use a proleptic synthesis in his gospel. But he makes up for it in his volume 2—the book of Acts. The opening scene of the book relates Jesus's ascension. The last thing he says to his disciples as he goes up to heaven is, "You will receive power when the Holy Spirit has come upon you; and you will be my witnesses in Jerusalem, in all Judea and Samaria, and to the ends of the earth" (Acts 1:8). The verse is a kind of outline for the spread of early Christianity as Luke recounts it: the first fifteen chapters of the book deal with its growth in the Jewish region around Jerusalem, and the second half of the book focuses on Paul's work among the gentiles as he moves toward Rome, which was the gateway to the Roman Empire and the known world. The transition from the sphere of Judaism to the larger gentile world was pivotal in Luke's presentation. It was also more complicated than Acts suggests, to judge by Paul's preoccupation in his letters with questions about whether gentiles should have to keep the law and be circumcised. So the telegram in Acts 1:8 reflects the theology of the book, which tends to tamp down controversies and present the growth of early Christianity as a consolidated, harmonious process.

Old Testament nutshells

While the gospel writers may have perfected the technique of proleptic synthesis, they didn't invent it. We have some nice examples in the Hebrew Bible files. It's not a hard technique to master, but it does require some advance planning. You have to have a good idea of what you're going to say before you write it all down. The author of Qoheleth, or Ecclesiastes, knew what to say, and said it over and over and over again. Not that it was that difficult to remember. It was just one word—"vanity." Vanity, vanity, vanity. Actually, verse 2 uses the word five times:

> Vanity of vanities, says Qoheleth,
>   vanity of vanities! All is vanity.

The word really means "meaninglessness, worthlessness." So "vanity of vanities" means "absolutely devoid of meaning or value." That's how the author assesses the meaning, or lack thereof, of life. Qoheleth's view of life is the epitome of the expression "Same old, same old" (Eccles. 1:5-9). This single-word telegram is the essence of the book, and the writer sends it to you at the very start—in the second verse, right after the heading (v. 1). For the folks in Forensics, who prefer technical, scientific names, that's a monolexical proleptic synthesis.

The writer of the book of Judges also knew what to say and when to say it. The writer probably had a collection of stories about military heroes. We've already seen in the Clue of the Broken Pattern how Judges 2:18-19 articulates the circular pattern of sin, punishment, repentance, deliverance, and rest for the whole book. You'd miss the entertainment if you skipped the stories, but there's not a lot of forward progress theologically or even historically, since it's the same story over and over in a sense. At the end of the book, the writer telegraphs the way forward by repeatedly observing that there was no king in Israel in those days. A couple of times the writer adds that everyone did what was right in their own opinion. That's how the book ends (Judg. 21:25). These texts, especially the last one, are a series of telegraphed info about the beginning of the monarchy, which is the subject of the books of Samuel and Kings that follow. The isolation of the allusions to kingship in the last five chapters of Judges contrasts with the circular pattern represented by the stories of judges earlier in the book and suggests that the two parts may be from different writers. One of them sees hope in repentance, the other in the institution of kingship. Both use telegrams, but they send mixed signals.

More telegraphy

The use of the telegraph in one book (Judges) to send information about subsequent books (Samuel and Kings) hints at how far-reaching telegraphed information can be. And while Judges and Samuel are next-door neighbors in the Hebrew Bible (English Bibles typically follow the order of the Greek Septuagint and place Ruth between Judges and Samuel, but in the Hebrew Bible Ruth follows Proverbs in the section called Writings), there are examples of telegraphed material that transcends multiple books. Being aware of this can help with one of the items that should be on your bucket list—reading the entire Bible. When you hit a telegraphing text and figure out the extent of the story or information it's telegraphing, you can skip right over it. Okay, so technically, you're not reading the whole Bible, but it's a good workaround. One step at a time, right?

Fast-forwarding

A good example is the promise to Abraham in the book of Genesis. One version of that promise, Genesis 15:13-14, reads like this: "Then the LORD said to Abram, 'Know this for certain, that your offspring shall be aliens in a land that is not theirs, and shall be slaves there, and they shall be oppressed for four hundred years; but I will bring judgment on the nation that they serve, and afterward they shall come out with great possessions.'" It's not clear how the four hundred years were calculated, but they obviously cover the period from Abraham till the exodus from Egypt. That takes you through chapter 15 in the book of Exodus, which is almost halfway through the book. If you keep reading just a few more verses, you can jump a lot further: "'As for yourself, you shall go to your ancestors in peace; you shall be buried in a good old age. And they shall come back here in the fourth generation; for the iniquity of the Amorites is not yet complete.' When the sun had gone down and it was dark, a smoking fire pot and a flaming torch passed between these pieces. On that day the LORD made a covenant with Abram, saying, 'To your descendants I give this land'" (Gen. 15:15-18). Again, the time frame is a little odd—one hundred years is a long time for a generation, which is usually closer to twenty years. But our focus for this investigation is on the first part of that statement, which refers to the "return" of Israel to Canaan under Joshua. The last line of the quote contains a direct promise that the Lord will give Israel the land (of Canaan). Now you can skip a lot further in your Bible speed-reading project—all the way to the end of the book of Joshua, since that is where the Israelites take possession of the land of Canaan.

If you were reading carefully, you might have already taken a leap at the end of Genesis 12. That's where the first of three stories in Genesis about the "endangered ancestress" occurs (see the chapter on the Clue of the Doublet). In all three, the patriarch (Abraham in Genesis 12 and 20; Isaac in Genesis 26) claims that his wife is his sister while they are visiting a foreign country (Egypt in Genesis 12; Gerar in Genesis 20 and 26), because he is afraid that the people of that country will kill him in order to take his beautiful wife. His fear proves groundless, and the foreigners are quite principled and reasonable. In Genesis 12 Abraham (a.k.a. Abram) and Sarah (a.k.a. Sarai) go to Egypt to escape famine. After he hears how beautiful Abraham's "sister" is, the pharaoh brings Sarah into his house, which probably means he added her to his harem.

Pharaoh rewards Abraham with lots of livestock and other property, making him a wealthy man. But the Lord afflicts Pharaoh's house with plagues because of Sarah. Sum up the story in outline form, and here's what you get:

> Famine in Canaan
> Journey to Egypt to escape the famine
> Plagues on Egypt
> Abraham enriched
> Abraham and Sarah sent away with their wealth

The summary resembles the story of Israel in Genesis and Exodus. Abraham and Sarah in Genesis 12 are a living, breathing proleptic synthesis of what will happen to Israel. Their experiences in Egypt telegraph Israel's later history all the way through the exodus. The synthesis is more subtle than Genesis 15, so it's easy to miss. It also doesn't get you as far down the road of Bible reading as Genesis 15, so if you miss the summary in Genesis 12, you haven't really lost anything. But it's a good reminder to keep your eyes open for symbolism in the Bible, even in something as mundane as a telegram.

Telegraphy after the fact

The kingdoms of Israel and Judah came to their respective ends as the result of invasions by different Mesopotamian empires. Israel went first. Its capital, Samaria, was besieged and destroyed in 722/721 BCE by the Assyrians. Following typical Assyrian practice, the leaders of the revolt were executed and the remaining members of the upper classes were taken captive and resettled in other parts of the empire. People from elsewhere were brought in to take their place. The poorer people were probably mostly left where they were. There are indications that a portion of the population had got out of Dodge and fled to Judah before the Assyrians arrived. The story of Israel's end is told in 2 Kings 17.

Judah lasted another 135 years or so until 587/586 BCE, when Jerusalem was destroyed by the Babylonians, the southern cousins of the Assyrians. Babylonian policy regarding the treatment of conquered populations was different than that of the Assyrians. The Babylonians didn't swap populations, but they did take upper-class people captive to Babylon, and that's what they did with the citizens of Jerusalem. That marked the beginning of the period known as the Babylonian captivity or exile, which lasted until 538 when the Persians, who had conquered Babylon, followed their policy of allowing captive peoples to return to their homelands.

The story of Judah's fall is at the end of 2 Kings. But the experience of defeat and exile was a traumatic one and is reflected in different ways in a lot of other places in the Hebrew Bible. Some of them are telegraphic. One such passage is also one of the best-organized texts in the Bible— Deuteronomy 28. It's a very long chapter (sixty-eight verses) consisting of a few blessings followed by lots and lots of curses. Down around verse 49 the curses start to get very real as they talk about the Lord bringing the army of a nation from far away to devastate the land and besiege the cities. The description of the effects of siege, including starvation and cannibalism, becomes quite graphic. Look, we're cops. We've seen a lot of bloody, gory sights, but these verses get to us. We can't bring ourselves to quote them here. You'll have to check them out for yourself. The realism is so strong probably because they are describing actual experiences of siege warfare that took place in the context of the destruction of Jerusalem and the beginning of the Babylonian exile. In other words, the last segment of the curses in Deuteronomy 28 telegraphs information about the Babylonian exile because these verses were written after that event. It's a case of telegraphy after the fact by later addition.

The same kind of telegraphy occurs in 1 Kings 8. The context is the dedication of the temple under Solomon. In conjunction with the sacrifices of dedication, Solomon offers a lengthy prayer. It's one of those prayers that is addressed as much to the people who hear it as to God. Solomon posits a series of hypothetical situations with the basic request that the Lord hear the prayers that are directed to him from the temple or toward the temple. The situations include: when someone sins against a neighbor (vv. 31-32), defeat in war (vv. 33-34), drought (vv. 35-36), famine (vv. 37-40), when a foreigner is converted (vv. 41-43), defeat, again (vv. 44-45), and exile (vv. 46-51). The double mention of defeat and the extralong request for attentiveness during exile suggest that the prayer has been retouched (see the chapters on the Clues of the Doublet and the Broken Pattern). The real audience of verses 46-51 especially was probably the people in exile. The extension of the prayer in those verses was likely intended to encourage the readers to pray to the Lord toward the temple and to ask for forgiveness in the hope that this would be their ticket back home. That is, that the Lord would forgive them and grant them mercy before their captors so that they would be allowed to return home. It is a prayer by telegraphy by later addition that put words in Solomon's mouth he never would have said.

In John 21, after Jesus switched verbs in asking Peter for the third time if he loved him (see the Clue of the Broken Pattern), Jesus went on to add, "Very truly, I tell you, when you were younger, you used to fasten your own belt and to go wherever you wished. But when you grow old, you will stretch out your hands, and someone else will fasten a belt around you and take you where you do not wish to go" (John 21:18). Believe it or not, that's a telegram, but it's still in Morse code, so to speak, because the intrusive narrator of the gospel steps in with a parenthetical interpretation: "(He said this to indicate the kind of death by which he would glorify God)" (John 21:19). The amazing thing is that Peter seems to have understood what Jesus meant, because he asks, "What about him?" (John 21:21), referring to the "disciple whom Jesus loved," a title that the author of the book adopts (probably pseudepigraphically) for himself.

There is no further account in the Gospel of John or in the New Testament about Peter's death. According to the apocryphal book the Acts of Peter (chapter 37) and other early traditions, Peter was crucified upside down at his own request because he thought he was not worthy to die as Jesus had. This is supposed to have taken place under the emperor Nero in 64 CE. John 21:18 assumes Peter's martyrdom but says nothing about the way in which he died. Peter's death happened long after Jesus but also long before the Gospel of John was written. The allusion to Peter's death in John 21:18 is a telegram containing information that transcends the bounds of the New Testament but was evidently known to the original, intended audience of the Gospel of John.

WHY THIS CLUE MATTERS

Although the terminology—telegraphing—may be outmoded because the technology has developed, the idea of long-distance, virtually instantaneous communication is as important to the Bible as it is to law enforcement. Telegraphed information gives readers advance clues about an author's theology and major themes that are to be worked out in a piece of literature. It hints at an author's style and concern for aesthetics in his or her literary work. Telegraphing can also reveal who the intended audience for a piece of literature was or if a text was expanded by later addition with a particular audience in mind.

THE CLUE OF THE TELEGRAPHED INFORMATION CAN HELP US . . .

1. Recognize advance synthesizing in a piece of literature.
2. Be sensitive to anticipation in a text of later events or details.
3. Appreciate an author's skill at preparing readers for developments in a story or document.
4. Discern the historical or cultural situation that a text was composed to address.
5. Pick out later additions by the change in circumstances that they assume.

THE CASEBOOK

1. Explain how the condemnation of Jeroboam in 1 Kings 13:34 telegraphs what will happen to his royal house or dynasty (consult 1 Kings 15:25-30). What other information about the history of the kingdom of Israel might 1 Kings 13:34 telegraph?
2. Compare 2 Kings 8:12 with 2 Kings 10:32-33; 12:17-18; 13:3-5, 22-25. The terminology of 2 Kings 8:12 is different from that of the other passages. Is it still a case of telegraphing? Why or why not?
3. Read Samuel's warning about making a king in 1 Samuel 8:11-17. To what period in Israel's history does this passage seem to allude? What does that suggest about its date of writing?
4. Explain how Isaiah 6:9-13 might be understood as telegraphing for Isaiah's career as a prophet. Does the passage also telegraph information about the vocation of prophets in general as portrayed in the Bible?
5. Read Paul's letter to Philemon. What is Paul trying to get Philemon to do? Is there any place in the letter that telegraphs his intention?

11

The Clue of the

NAME

We hope the fact that we love our jobs has become abundantly clear as we've led you on this clue-by-clue tour of the inner workings of the Bible detective business. Being a biblical sleuth can be an immensely rewarding and fulfilling occupation, and we've been extremely fortunate to have experienced the richness it has to offer. A big perk is that even if it isn't the cushiest job in the world, there's usually not a great deal of pressure on those of us who work the Bible beat. In firefighter's terms, we spend a lot more time rescuing cats from trees than we do battling blazes. Maybe that's what led to the career crisis we went through a few years back.

The thrill was gone. Things were stale. The well had run dry. We had hit a wall. However you choose to describe it, one thing was obvious—stagnation had set in. We thought maybe we needed to clear our heads and take a vacation, but that didn't do the trick. A switch to the night shift for a while didn't help matters either. Our hand-wringing and existential angst continued for several months until one day out of the blue the mystery was solved by—what else?—a clue.

The Clue of the Name is present when the meaning of a person's name is connected, either explicitly or not, to the events of the story in which it is mentioned. Every person mentioned in the Bible doesn't have a name, but there are still just short of two thousand names in the text (many of them are shared by more than one person). The key words in the sentence above are "either explicitly or not." Sometimes this clue is easy to see because the person's name is clearly identified as having some connection with the events of the story. Elsewhere that link isn't explicitly made, although careful investigative work can uncover the connection. It was those latter cases that helped us turn the corner and snap out of our funk, and here's how it happened.

One day when we were moping around the office feeling sorry for ourselves, our boss came by looking for someone to inspect the files on the book of Ruth to see if they contained the Clue of the Name. Neither of us had ever spent time working on that particular clue, so we jumped at the chance. Besides, we figured the job would be a breeze. At four chapters long with eighty-four verses total, how hard could inspecting Ruth be? We thought we'd be in and out of there in no time, and be playing darts in our favorite watering hole just as happy hour was getting started. Boy, were we wrong. (Read Ruth 1-4, and pay attention to the names of the characters.)

Practically every person in Ruth is a walking, talking Clue of the Name, but almost none of them admit to it. The only one who does fess up is Ruth's mother-in-law, who actually has two names in the story that are both clues. When we first meet her she has lost her husband and her two sons, and when she and Ruth arrive back in her hometown of Bethlehem after being away for a while, her friends greet her the only way they know how—by calling her "Naomi," the name she had left with. She immediately sets them straight and tells them she is now living under an alias.

> "Call me no longer Naomi,
>> call me *Mara*,
>> for the Almighty has dealt *bitterly* with me.
> I went away full,
>> but the LORD has brought me back empty;
> why call me Naomi
>> when the LORD has dealt *harshly* with me,
>> and the Almighty has *brought calamity* upon me?" (Ruth 1:20–21)

This Clue of the Name, like many other examples we'll look at, is designed around wordplay. The Hebrew form of her original name means "pleasant," which she thinks doesn't fit anymore because of all the bad breaks she's had. She opts instead for "Mara," which translates as "bitter" and better reflects her current state of mind. This is an example of an explicit Clue of the Name because it has a clear connection with the story that Naomi/Mara herself points out, but it takes knowledge of Hebrew to catch the pun it contains.

The names of the deceased members of the family also contain clues, but they are harder to spot. "The name of the man was *Elimelech* and the name of his wife Naomi, and the names of his two sons were *Mahlon* and *Chilion*" (Ruth 1:2a). Elimelech's name means "my God is king," and since that doesn't have anything to do with the story, it's not an example of the Clue of the Name. But his sons' names are previews of what comes next in the story—they mean something like "weak" and "sickly." That those names are tip-offs of what's in store becomes apparent the only other time the brothers are mentioned a few verses later. "Both Mahlon and Chilion also died" (Ruth 1:5a). Is any biblical death notice less surprising than that one? If you know Hebrew, you can see it coming from a mile away. Despite the obvious connection their names have with their demise, Mahlon and Chilion are not explicit examples of the Clue of the Name because that link is not directly stated, as it is in the case of Naomi/Mara.

> THE CLUE OF THE NAME: the meaning of a person's name is connected to the events of the story in which it is mentioned

Ruth, the heroine of the story, has a name that vaguely resembles the Hebrew word for a female companion. This meaning aligns very nicely with her role in the book as the person who accompanies Naomi back to Bethlehem from Moab, but if it's an example of the Clue of the Name, it remains an implicit one because the meaning of her name is never mentioned. So too with Boaz, the man Ruth eventually marries and who saves the day by becoming the father of the child who will turn his grandmother Naomi from bitter to pleasant again. Boaz's name looks a lot like the Hebrew for "in him is strength," which sums up nicely his role in the story, but that connection isn't explicitly made. The only other named person in the story is Orpah, Naomi's other daughter-in-law, who chose not to accompany her to Bethlehem. (The baby is given the name Obed, but he isn't really a character in the narrative.) The meaning of Orpah's name is disputed, but many have argued that it is related to the Hebrew word for "neck." Because we're not sure what it means, we can't make the argument that Orpah's name has any association with what takes place in the story, so it's not an example of the Clue of the Name.

Nonetheless, five of the seven named characters in the book of Ruth can plausibly be associated with the clue. While that percentage is not maintained throughout the rest of the Bible, there are still a large number of individuals who are carriers of the clue, and so it clearly merits inclusion in this training manual.

A method to our madness

It isn't possible to wade through the nearly two thousand names in the Bible to determine which ones carry the clue and which do not. Plus, you would have to study every single occurrence of a name in the Bible, not just its first appearance, because the clue could be present in just one passage that mentions it. To simplify the task, we've come up with a taxonomy of the Clue of the Name to give some structure and order to that massive pile of data. Based on our Ruth investigation, it's clear there are two main forms of the clue—those that explicitly mention the connection between a name and what's going on in the story, and those that don't. After batting around different ideas, we decided to label those two classes of clues with a nod toward our love of horror movies. With those two categories in mind, we developed the following four simple guidelines to help a detective recognize and classify the Clue of the Name. You'll see how these rules work in action when we look at specific examples of the clue in the sections that follow, so for now we'll just briefly explain them.

1. *Be on the lookout for both zombies and vampires.* In some cases, characters are clearly identified as carriers of the Clue of the Name. When characters are marked in an explicit way, we're calling them zombies because their association with the clue is immediately recognizable. (You definitely know a zombie when you see one.) Then there are the characters who are carriers of the clue even though they're not explicitly marked as such. These we're calling vampires, because they can pass as normal and nothing calls attention to their special status as clue carriers. It goes without saying that vampires are much more difficult to detect, and that's why the Clue of the Name is treated in the second chapter of the "Dusting for Prints" section of this manual that deals with the more challenging clues.

2. *Be aware of your surroundings.* The Clue of the Name can pop up anywhere, but there is a clear pattern of behavior regarding where it's likely to be found. In particular, it's most at home in birth stories and descriptions of people being given a new name. In such passages the clue tends to take its zombie form, but it has been known to also appear as a vampire.

3. *Listen for zombies.* When it is found in its zombie mode, certain expressions and phrases often signal that the Clue of the Name is about to make an appearance. The detective familiar with these telltale signs can usually anticipate the arrival of a zombie with a high degree of confidence. No such early warning system exists for vampires, which normally show up without notice.

4. *If you suspect a zombie or vampire is nearby but you're not sure, seek help immediately.* Zombies can sometimes be hard to detect, but vampires are always elusive. Recognition of the clue is especially challenging for the detective who is unfamiliar with the original languages of the Bible. Aids and resources are available for those who need assistance, and you are strongly encouraged to take advantage of these opportunities.

Zombie birthdays and other special occasions

Hunting zombies is the shooting-fish-in-a-barrel part of a biblical detective's job. Once you know what to look for, you can't miss them. In its classic zombie form, the Clue of the Name is found in a birth story and it usually contains three elements: (1) the child's name; (2) a Hebrew or Greek word that is usually etymologically related to the name; and (3) a word or phrase that links the two and explains their causal relationship. The third element is not always present, but the other two must be there for it to be a zombie, although they can be in reverse order. Here's an example in which we've numbered all three parts. "And the angel of the LORD said to her, 'Now you have conceived and shall bear a son; you shall call him (1) Ishmael, (3) for the LORD has (2) given heed to your affliction'" (Gen. 16:11). Ishmael's name and the verb "given heed" come from the same Hebrew root, and the word "for" highlights the causal connection between the two. As in the case of Naomi/Mara, the name has been given because of something that has occurred in the story. (Sometimes the name refers to something that will occur later on in a story.) That's the way your typical zombie comes into existence, and you can see the same pattern (minus the numbers) in the following examples.

Zombie case #1—the sons of Jacob

The highest concentration of zombies is found in Genesis 29-31. In these chapters the first eleven of Jacob's twelve sons (and his non-zombie daughter—more on her later) are born to four different women, and in each case all three parts of the zombie formula are present. We'll list only a few of them here, and we'll include just the relevant sections so you can see how similar they are.

> And she named him *Reuben; for* she said, "Because the LORD has *looked on* my affliction; surely now my husband will love me." (Gen. 29:32)

> Again she conceived and bore a son, and said, "Now this time my husband will be *joined* to me, because I have borne him three sons"; *therefore* he was named *Levi*. (Gen. 29:34)

> Then Leah said, "God has endowed me with a good dowry; now my husband will *honor* me, because I have borne him six sons"; *so* she named him *Zebulun*. (Gen. 30:20)

Jacob's sons are the Bible's largest group of zombie siblings, but there's a question whether there are eleven or twelve of them. He definitely had a dozen sons, but is the last one a zombie? Here's the account of how his mother Rachel gave birth to son number twelve: "When she was in her *hard labor*, the midwife said to her, 'Do not be afraid; for now you will have another son.' As her soul was departing (for *she died*), she named him *Ben-oni; but his father called him Benjamin*" (Gen. 35:17-18). Whenever he's mentioned again in the Bible, Jacob's youngest son is always referred to as Benjamin, and never by the name Ben-oni that his mother gave him with her dying breath. Her name for him means "son of my sorrow," which has an obvious connection to her death during labor and so would make him a zombie. But elsewhere in the Bible he goes by another name. We're prepared to give him the benefit of the doubt and include him among his zombie brothers so Jacob can have his twelfth, but with an asterisk attached because he's the one who gave him the name that hides his son's true identity.

Keep in mind the fourth of the guidelines we gave you earlier: if you suspect a zombie or vampire is nearby but you're not sure, seek help immediately. That help sometimes comes in the form of a footnote that explains the wordplay to readers who don't know the original language. Some translations of the Bible frequently do this; for example, the NRSV provides notes with the English meanings of the names of all of Jacob's sons as well as most of the names of the zombies we discuss in this chapter.

Zombie case #2—Eve

Eve is the mother of all zombies. She has the distinction of being the very first zombie and one of only two female zombies in the Bible. (Naomi/ Mara is the other, and she's also the only self-made zombie because she renames herself.) Zombie status isn't bestowed on Eve at birth, but at a later point when Adam does the honors. Come to think of it, that's something else that sets Eve apart—she's the only person whose spouse makes him or her a zombie. Even though she's not a newborn, we can clearly discern the three elements of the Clue of the Name in the passage that describes her creation. "The man named his wife *Eve, because* she was the mother of all *living*" (Gen. 3:20). The wordplay in this verse is the close resemblance between the Hebrew words for "Eve" and "living." She immediately exercises her role as mother of all the living by giving birth to Cain, who is himself a zombie. "Now the man knew his wife Eve, and she conceived and bore *Cain*, saying, 'I have *produced* a man with the help of the LORD'" (Gen. 4:1). This also makes Eve the only zombie who gives birth to another zombie.

Zombie case #3—Isaac

The circumstances surrounding the birth of Isaac deserve a close investigation, because there's something odd about them. His name comes from a Hebrew root that means "to laugh," and the description of his birth makes that connection. "Abraham was a hundred years old when his son *Isaac* was born to him. Now Sarah said, 'God has brought *laugh-*

ter for me; everyone who hears will *laugh* with me'" (Gen. 21:5–6). The oddity is that additional clues have been strategically placed in the story prior to this point. Several times in the preceding chapters words from the same Hebrew root are used, and they are always found in contexts related to Isaac's birth. In one of them Abraham can hardly contain himself when he is informed that he and Sarah will become parents. "Then Abraham fell on his face and *laughed*, and said to himself, 'Can a child be born to a man who is a hundred years old? Can Sarah, who is ninety years old, bear a child?'" (Gen. 17:17). And then in the next chapter the same Hebrew root is used four different times when Sarah hears similar news. "So Sarah *laughed* to herself, saying, 'After I have grown old, and my husband is old, shall I have pleasure?' The LORD said to Abraham, 'Why did Sarah *laugh*, and say, "Shall I indeed bear a child, now that I am old?" Is anything too wonderful for the LORD? At the set time I will return to you, in due season, and Sarah shall have a son.' But Sarah denied, saying, 'I did not *laugh*'; for she was afraid. He said, 'Oh yes, you did *laugh*'" (Gen. 18:12–15).

Zombie case #4 — Samuel

The final birth story we'll examine is Samuel's, and once again all three parts of the Clue of the Name are present. "Hannah conceived and bore a son. She named him *Samuel, for* she said, 'I have *asked* him of the LORD'" (1 Sam. 1:20). To the untrained eye, this looks like every other example we've considered, but it's not. This verse should be marked off with police tape and given a wide berth because it's definitely a crime scene. What we have here is a blatant case of identity theft that escapes the notice of most readers. The Hebrew form of Samuel's name has nothing to do with asking, so the connection that his mother Hannah attempts to make simply doesn't work. But it does fit perfectly for another character who will make his first appearance (without a birth narrative, and now we know why) eight chapters from now — Saul. The Hebrew root Saul's name comes from means "to ask," and so it's quite likely that his birth story has been appropriated and recycled to serve as Samuel's. Whoever did it probably wanted to get caught because additional clues are strewn around that call attention to the Saul connection. Before and after the naming verse, there are echoes of Saul's name through the use of words that come from the same root. One occurs prior to Hannah's pregnancy when the priest Eli tells her, "Go in peace; the God of Israel grant the *petition you have made* to him" (1 Sam. 1:17). The other comes after the child's birth, when Hannah says, "For this child I prayed; and the LORD has granted me the *petition that I made* to him" (1 Sam. 1:27).

Zombie case #5—Jacob

To fill out the picture, we should mention a couple of other prominent biblical characters who became zombies, but they didn't attain that status until after they were well along in years. These occur in the context of name changes. Jacob is a very interesting case of the Clue of the Name. He becomes one at birth when he is given the name Jacob (Gen. 25:26), but then he is renamed later in life after an all-night wrestling match with a mysterious opponent. "Then the man said, 'You shall no longer be called Jacob, but *Israel, for* you have *striven* with God and with humans, and have prevailed'" (Gen. 32:28). This makes Jacob/Israel a double zombie, and you'll find another example of one in the Casebook assignment at the end of this chapter.

Zombie case #6—Peter

We're really conflicted about what to do with Peter. In a passage only in Matthew's Gospel that has the feel of a zombie-making moment, Jesus says something to him that sure looks like the Clue of the Name. "And I tell you, you are *Peter*, and on this *rock* I will build my church, and the gates of Hades will not prevail against it" (Matt. 16:18). The Greek words for "Peter" and "rock" are almost identical, so there's a nice wordplay present, and a connection is made to the events of the story, which checks that box as well. But here's the problem—what's happening here isn't the same as what takes place in the story of Jacob mentioned above. Jacob is given a brand-new name, but we can't say the same thing about the Peter episode because just two verses earlier he's referred to as "Simon Peter" (Matt. 16:16). In fact, the first time we meet him, when he's called to be a follower of Jesus back in the fourth chapter of the gospel, he's called "Peter" (Matt. 4:18). As far as we can tell, he was always known as Peter. Jesus is not renaming him but merely giving new significance to a name he's always had. So what does that make him?

A vampire stakeout

Other carriers of the Clue of the Name haunt the pages of the Bible in relative anonymity—the vampires. They look, talk, and act like the characters they rub shoulders with, but they are creatures set apart. The meanings of their names also have some association with the texts they inhabit, but unlike with zombies, those connections remain largely hidden. They roam their stories undetected by many readers, recognized only by those with the ability to spot them. We've already met two vampires in Mahlon and Chilion, the sons of Naomi/Mara. Their names point to their early deaths, although nothing in the story calls attention to that fact. On rare occasions footnotes in the text expose the presence of vampires, but in most cases knowledge of biblical languages is required to identify them.

Vampire case #1—Adam

The Bible's first vampire is the Bible's first person. The complicating issue is that sometimes the Hebrew word *adam* is used in the generic sense of a person, and in other places it appears to function as a personal name. Most of the time he's mentioned in Genesis 2–3 it's with the definite article "the" (*ha-adam*), and in those verses he is usually referred to as "the man" in translation. But in a few places the definite article isn't there, like in Genesis 2:20b, and then the word can be rendered as a name. "But for Adam there was not found a helper as his partner" (cf. Gen. 3:17, 21). After he and Eve are expelled from the garden of Eden, the switching continues—when their son Cain is born he is "the man" (Gen. 4:1), but when their third child, Seth, comes along, he's identified as "Adam" (Gen. 4:25). In the final references to him before he dies, he's consistently "Adam" (Gen. 5:1–5). The evidence from the first creation story in Genesis 1 complicates things further because the word *adam* is found twice there, once with the definite article and once without, and both times it's a collective term to refer to humanity at large (Gen. 1:27–28). Because his name is also generic and can refer to all of humanity, Adam's role as the first human being who personifies the rest of us is subtly being highlighted. That idea is never explicitly stated in the story, as he gradually becomes just "Adam," and that's what makes him a vampire.

Vampire case #2—Benjamin

Let's briefly return to Benjamin, to whom we gave honorary member-ship in the zombie club in the last section, even though his father, Jacob, changed his name at birth (Gen. 35:17-18). Perhaps he deserves that aster-isk after all, because without it Ben-oni/Benjamin would not have pulled off the rarest of double plays that makes him the only biblical character who is both a zombie and a vampire. The name Benjamin actually has two possible meanings because it can be translated as either "son of the right hand" or "son of the south." (This is a rare case in which footnotes can help identify a vampire, because the NRSV lists both meanings.) If we opt for the latter alternative, it can be interpreted as a way of distinguishing him from the rest of his brothers, who were all born outside the land in Aram (to the north) whereas he was born in Canaan.

Vampire case #3—Eglon

Eglon is the victim in what is sometimes called "the world's oldest locked-door murder mystery," which also features a judge named Ehud. Here are the facts as we have them:

> Then he presented the tribute to King Eglon of Moab. Now *Eglon was a very fat man.* When Ehud had finished presenting the trib-ute, he sent the people who carried the tribute on their way. But he himself turned back at the sculptured stones near Gilgal, and said, "I have a secret message for you, O king." So the king said, "Silence!" and all his attendants went out from his pres-ence. Ehud came to him, while he was sitting alone in his cool roof chamber, and said, "I have a message from God for you." So he rose from his seat. Then Ehud reached with his left hand, took the sword from his right thigh, and thrust it into Eglon's belly; the hilt also went in after the blade, and *the fat closed over the blade,* for he did not draw the sword out of his belly; and the dirt came out. Then Ehud went out into the vestibule, and closed the doors of the roof chamber on him, and locked them. (Judg. 3:17-23)

It's one of the most vivid killings described in the Bible, and the account is also notable for the level of detail it contains. Among those details are two references to Eglon being overweight. The first reference is particularly suspicious because its phrasing sounds like it could be wordplay. A pun could be hiding behind "Eglon was a fat man," and even if you're not reading the text in Hebrew, you might be able to sniff it out by paying a visit to a dictionary or similar resource to see what his name means. Eglon means "young calf," and it comes from a Hebrew root that is associated with being round.

Vampire case #4—Dinah

Dinah is born after Jacob has had a string of ten consecutive sons (Benjamin, the combo zombie-vampire, comes along a little later), and the report of her birth is brief and to the point compared to those of her siblings. "Afterwards [Leah] bore a daughter, and named her Dinah" (Gen. 30:21). The contrast with the earlier birth announcements is quite stark—there's no mention of what her name means or how it might be related to the story. That kind of abrupt shift is the sort of thing biblical detectives file away in the backs of their minds, figuring it might come in handy one day. That day arrives the next time we see Dinah, four chapters later, and she is all grown up. Genesis 34 relates an unusual story that some believe might be an example of an ancient practice called "marriage by abduction." It explains how a man named Shechem forced Dinah to have sex with him and then decided he wanted to marry her. When her brothers found out about what Shechem had done, they were outraged that their sister and their family had been dishonored. They allowed the marriage to proceed with the condition that Shechem and the rest of the men among his people be circumcised. All this was a setup, and while the men were recovering from their circumcisions, the sons of Jacob killed them and plundered their city.

Since her birth and this story are the only two times Dinah is mentioned in the Bible (except for her appearance in a list of family members in Genesis 46), it's reasonable to wonder if there might be some connection between the two passages. A Bible dictionary or similar tool will tell you that Dinah's name comes from a Hebrew root that conveys meanings associated with justice and punishment, which are the central themes of the episode involving Shechem and his people.

Vampire case #5—Jezebel

She might be the most despised woman in the entire Bible, and she has the name to prove it. "Jezebel" literally, if somewhat coarsely, means "Where is shit?" It goes without saying that this was not her real name, but a distortion of it that was meant to be an insult. With minor changes to two vowels, it's a variation of a name meaning "Where is Prince?" that laments the death of a god of her native land. So it simultaneously maligns Jezebel and the god Baal for whom she was originally named. She's a reviled figure in the Bible because she was an opponent of the worship of Yahweh and she convinced her husband, King Ahab of Israel, to reject Yahweh and follow Baal (1 Kings 16:31–34; 18:18; 19:1–3). The description of her death exceeds even Eglon's in terms of its gruesomeness.

> When Jehu came to Jezreel, Jezebel heard of it; she painted her eyes, and adorned her head, and looked out of the window. As Jehu entered the gate, she said, "Is it peace, Zimri, murderer of your master?" He looked up to the window and said, "Who is on my side? Who?" Two or three eunuchs looked out at him. He said, "Throw her down." So they threw her down; some of her blood spattered on the wall and on the horses, which trampled on her. Then he went in and ate and drank; he said, "See to that cursed woman and bury her; for she is a king's daughter." But when they went to bury her, they found no more of her than the skull and the feet and the palms of her hands. When they came back and told him, he said, "This is the word of the LORD, which he spoke by his servant Elijah the Tishbite, 'In the territory of Jezreel the dogs shall eat the flesh of Jezebel; the corpse of Jezebel shall be like *dung* on the field in the territory of Jezreel, so that no one can say, This is Jezebel.'" (2 Kings 9:30–37)

In a mocking response to the question posed by her name ("Where is shit?"), Jezebel bites the dust, and all that remains of her has been defecated on to the ground after passing through canine digestive tracts. This Clue of the Name can easily escape detection by those who don't possess the necessary language skills, but here too the character's true nature might still be uncovered by the clever detective who notes that she is detested and scorned in such strong terms that Jezebel is the very sort of character whose name is ripe for ridicule.

Vampire case #6—Barabbas

The last biblical vampire we'll consider was a prisoner who had the good fortune to be doing time in the same facility where Jesus was being held as he awaited execution.

> Now at the festival he [Pontius Pilate] used to release a prisoner for them, anyone for whom they asked. Now a man called Barabbas was in prison with the rebels who had committed murder during the insurrection. So the crowd came and began to ask Pilate to do for them according to his custom. Then he answered them, "Do you want me to release for you the King of the Jews?" For he realized that it was out of jealousy that the chief priests had handed him over. But the chief priests stirred up the crowd to have him release Barabbas for them instead. Pilate spoke to them again, "Then what do you wish me to do with the man you call the King of the Jews?" They shouted back, "Crucify him!" Pilate asked them, "Why, what evil has he done?" But they shouted all the more, "Crucify him!" So Pilate, wishing to satisfy the crowd, released Barabbas for them; and after flogging Jesus, he handed him over to be crucified. (Mark 15:6–15; cf. Matt. 27:15–26; Luke 23:18–25; John 18:39–40)

The name Barabbas means "son of the father" in Aramaic, a language related to Hebrew that was spoken during the time of Jesus. Since by definition every son has a father, the name doesn't really set Barabbas apart from other men, but within the Gospels it does link him in a special way to Jesus. He often refers to God as his Father, and he does so in Mark's Gospel just prior to the passage quoted above when he is arrested in the garden of Gethsemane (Mark 14:36). Consequently, there is an ironic dimension to the release from prison of a man named "son of the father" rather than Jesus, who is also "son of the Father." This irony is dramatically heightened in Matthew, the Synoptic Gospel in which Jesus calls God his Father the most, when Barabbas's full name is given. "At that time they had a notorious prisoner, called *Jesus Barabbas*. So after they had gathered, Pilate said to them, 'Whom do you want me to release for you, *Jesus Barabbas* or *Jesus who is called the Messiah*?'" (Matt. 27:16–17). Now the choice is between two prisoners who are both named Jesus, and the addition of that name to the account in Matthew should cause the perceptive detective to start snooping around. The Jesus also known as the Messiah refers to God as his Father nearly twenty times in Matthew's Gospel, including three times in the chapter just before this one (Matt. 26:29, 42, 53), and that underscores the point Matthew is trying to make in this scene —they put to death the wrong "Jesus son of the father" and let the vampire walk.

WHY THIS CLUE MATTERS

The Clue of the Name is important because it functions as a reminder. It reminds us that something as commonplace and mundane as a name isn't always so ordinary after all, and there could be more going on in a story than meets the eye. Biblical names can be laden with meaning, but we often miss that fact. The zombie form of the clue reminds us that at times we miss it because it's so obvious we skip right over it, while the vampire form reminds us that at other times it's so hidden we have to work hard or we won't discover it. Both forms remind us that when we read the Bible in translation, there's a divide between its original readers and ourselves. What would have been immediately apparent to them sometimes eludes our notice, but every time the Clue of the Name helps us solve another mystery of the text, the distance between us narrows.

THE CLUE OF THE NAME CAN HELP US . . .

1. Appreciate the presence of wordplay and patterns in the Bible.
2. Become more aware that we are reading in translation.
3. Make use of dictionaries and other resources.
4. Develop critical reading skills.
5. Ask questions that lead to alternative ways of interpreting a passage.

THE CASEBOOK

Find the Clue of the Name in the following chapters and explain why each is a zombie or a vampire. (Keep in mind that you may have to consult a Bible dictionary or other resources to identify vampires.)

Genesis 4
Genesis 17
Genesis 25
Exodus 2
1 Samuel 4
2 Samuel 4
Esther 1
Job 1
Qoheleth (Ecclesiastes) 1
Isaiah 7–8
Matthew 1
Mark 5
Acts 23
Revelation 9

12

The Clue of the

ANACHRONISM

Every PD unit has its ongoing games, pools, and contests to try to keep morale up. We have the anachronism list. Next to the wanted posters on the bulletin board in the break room, we keep a running list of items relating to law enforcement that are out of proper time sequence in movies. If you find one that makes the list, we buy you lunch. Here is the list so far. The entries aren't in any particular order because . . . well . . . they're anachronisms. See what you think:

> Francis Ford Coppola is still miffed about a shot that includes some long-haired hippie types in the background of *The Godfather*. They were perfectly at home in 1972 when the film was made but too far in the future for its setting in the 1940s and 1950s.
> Keeping with the gangster theme, *Goodfellas* (1990) has a scene showing a Boeing 747 taking off right after telling you that the year is 1963. Problem is, the 747 didn't make its first flight until 1969 and wasn't used commercially until the year after that. The movie also features a 1965 Chevy Impala. So it was ahead of its time on land and in the air.
> We can forgive Clint Eastwood for showing men wearing pants with belt loops in his 1992 *Unforgiven*. This particular accent on clothing didn't come along until the twentieth century, and the movie takes place in 1881. But it's easy to miss a belt loop, and they would come in handy for holding your gun belt in place.

A little sloppier is the voice of someone screaming to call 911 when Malcolm X's house is firebombed in the movie that bears his name (1992) when 911 service didn't exist until 1968, three years after Malcolm was assassinated.

Also in the category of telephones in movies named after their main characters, *Bernie* could not have used an iPhone in 1996 when he was intercepting calls to the woman he had murdered no matter how much of a true story the movie was based on, since iPhones were introduced in 2007.

There's an even bigger logo before its time in *The Untouchables* (1987), which features the Canadian maple leaf painted on a bunch of boxes in the 1930s. That particular design of the maple leaf was only adopted for the Canadian flag in 1965.

In *The Shawshank Redemption* (1994) Andy Dufresne (played by Tim Robbins) covers the hole he uses to escape his prison cell with a poster of Raquel Welch from her movie *One Million Years BC*, which was released in the United States in February 1967, the year after Andy escaped in the story. This one has taken on a life of its own on the bulletin board, with people scribbling in other anachronisms they've found in the film, from twist tops on beer bottles in 1949, to later model cars in the prison parking lot, to comic books and music that are too early, to the existence of the Internal Revenue Service under that name, to the April 15 due date for filing income taxes.

Top (or bottom) of the list is *The Green Mile* (1999), set in Louisiana in 1935. One of its main characters is the electric chair used to execute convicts on death row known by the film's title. The chair didn't replace gallows as the method of execution in Louisiana until the 1940s, which throws the whole plot of the movie out of whack. In the book on which the movie was based, the setting was three years earlier—1932. The date was moved in the film to include the scene of Fred Astaire dancing in *Top Hat*, which came out in 1935. So getting it right is important for filmmakers when it comes to their industry, but not to anyone else's.

The Shawshank Redemption and *The Green Mile* were both based on books by Stephen King. We haven't checked whether any other anachronisms in the movies are holdovers from the novels. And we're not out to disparage Mr. King, whose imagination and writing schedule are far more productive than ours will ever be. Our hats are off to him. It just shows nobody's perfect. And if it makes him feel a little better, there are anachronisms in the Bible, that is, things that are "out of time" in some way and don't fit the chronology or period of the story. Such an item could be a person or group, a place, a practice, or an object. It might also be an idea or concept that is "at home" at a later (or sometimes an earlier) time. Because you need to be aware of historical events both within and outside the Bible to spot an anachronism, they can be hard to detect, but they provide useful information about the composition of the text. They can also raise issues regarding historicity, and they can sometimes indicate the ideological agenda or bias of the writer or editor of a biblical passage.

Dig it

The ghouls down in Forensics are all a little bent, but they're basically good people. They've helped us out on a lot of cases, establishing time of death, trajectory of entry and exit wounds, identification of victims, and so on. They're also a great resource for throwing a killer Halloween party. In the Bible Division we have our own forensic team—archaeologists. They're a pretty misunderstood lot too. Many people think of them as treasure hunters, and that was true a few generations back. But the field has gotten a lot more sophisticated in the last seventy-five years. They've pointed us to some case files that have received the anachronism stamp based on the evidence they've dug up.

Misplaced camels

There's a herd of mentions of camels in the book of Genesis. Most of them are in the story in Genesis 24. Abraham's servant took ten of his master's camels (Gen. 24:10) loaded with all kinds of riches and gifts and went to the home of Abraham's brother Nahor in upper Mesopotamia (Aram Naharaim) looking for a wife for Isaac. There he found Rebekah. Camels are mentioned as a measure of wealth for Abraham (Gen. 12:16) and Jacob (Gen. 30:43) and as Jacob's means of travel back to Canaan from Aram Naharaim (Gen. 31:17; 32:7, 15). But these mentions are as suspicious historically as a three-humped dromedary. It's not that camels weren't around, but they weren't domesticated until much later. To crunch the numbers, the stories of Abraham, Isaac, and Jacob would fall somewhere in the range from 2000 to 1500 BCE. Camels started being used in human commerce and as part of the economy around 1000 BCE. The difference is more than twice the age of the United States, and it tells us that whoever is responsible for these stories was living in a much later time period than the one they're set in.

In-Philtrators

Move the date of appearance back a couple hundred years, and you have almost the exact same scenario for Philistines. The Philistines are mentioned in Genesis 21 and 26 where Abraham and Isaac are living among them and making deals with them. Again, the problem is, archaeology—including Egyptian reliefs—indicates that the Philistines entered Canaan in the thirteenth century as one group of sea peoples from the western Mediterranean. That's not quite as wide a gap as for the domestication of camels, but it's still about equal to the age of the United States. When they finally arrived, the Philistines left an indelible impression, lending their name to the land—Palestine, which comes from "Philistine." But to make them Abraham's contemporaries is like saying the Beatles were once the opening act at a Beethoven concert.

It's about time

This next anachronism is literally *the* chronological problem of all time because it concerns the BC/AD axis. Hang on to your caps. This one has more moving parts than Marty McFly's DeLorean DMC-12 in *Back to the Future*. So when was Jesus born? Easy, right? Zero BC/AD. Unfortunately, it's a bit more complicated. Let's do a little time travel. Head back to AD 525. That's the year the BC-AD axis was invented by a short monk named Dionysius Exiguus or "Dennis the Little," who wanted to change the pagan calendar that was in use at the time to one based on Jesus's birth. He calculated 753 years from the founding of Rome to Jesus's birth, and that's where he nailed the hinge.

Now, set the chronometer back to around AD 75, when the Jewish historian Flavius Josephus dated the death of Herod the Great shortly after a lunar eclipse. There were several lunar eclipses in Herod's time, but the one in 4 BC is most likely the one Josephus is referring to. Why is Herod important? In AD 75 or 80, when the gospels were written, Matthew and Luke both place the birth of Jesus during the reign of Herod. According to Matthew 2:16, Herod killed all the baby boys in Bethlehem who were two years old and younger. Putting all this together, it looks like Jesus was born sometime between 7 BC and 4 BC (or BH for Before Himself).

THE CLUE OF THE ANACHRONISM: elements that are 'out of time' in some way and don't fit the chronology or period of the story

Bu-u-u-ut . . . now look in on Luke (Luke 2:1–2). He dates Jesus's birth during a census taken while Publius Sulpicius Quirinius was military governor or legate of Syria. We talked about him a little in the chapter on the Clue of the Inconsistency. To refresh your memory, Quirinius was appointed legate in AD 6. During the same year, Herod Archelaus, son of Herod the Great, was removed as ethnarch of Judea, and Judea and Samaria were placed under direct Roman rule as provinces. One of Quirinius's first duties was to carry out the census in Judea, which made him very unpopular because the purpose of the census was to acquire a base list for taxation. Luke's dating of Jesus's birth to the governorship of Quirinius is a long-standing chronological issue. A lot of sleuths think that Luke just got it wrong, because he was trying to make the connection with the census in order to explain why Joseph went from Nazareth where he lived back to his family home in Bethlehem where Jesus was born. Whatever the reason, something is out of whack about the dates here. Jesus couldn't have been born before 4 BC, at zero BC/AD, and after AD 6. In other words, it's a big, old anachronism.

We would be in the dark about matters such as these without archaeologists and others who work in the trenches of the forensic unit. So let's pause here for a moment to doff our caps to them before we move on.

Internal affairs

Forensic evidence from archaeology or ancient records isn't always available, and that's okay because it isn't always necessary. Sometimes the IA folks can dig up enough to prove that something is amiss time-wise. The evidence comes from close reading and comparison of biblical texts. If you are good at weaseling out the anachronisms in the following cases, you might think about checking out a career in IA investigation.

There oughta be a law

You know those weird laws that are on the books in every state—the ones that are so out of date that nobody knows they exist, much less enforces them? Like cows have the same rights as motorists in Farmington, Connecticut. Or restaurants in Kansas aren't supposed to serve pie à la mode on Sundays. And it's illegal for women to adjust their stockings in public in Bristol, Tennessee, and Denison, Texas. That's the way laws work. They're drafted to address particular situations, and situations always change. You don't pass laws to prevent "what ifs"; you pass them to prevent things that have happened from happening again.

That's the basic reason why the law of Moses in the Bible is an anachronism. Take a glance at the laws in Exodus, Leviticus, and Deuteronomy. They're all about things like what to do when an ox gores someone or a donkey falls into a pit, and what sacrifices from your livestock and harvest you're expected to make and how to treat slaves and how to handle real estate transactions. In other words, the law presupposes a settled, agricultural society, not a bunch of nomads wandering in the wilderness, as we pointed out in our treatment of the Clue of the Inconsistency. An anachronism is a temporal inconsistency. Sure, there are laws that apply in both settings, like "Thou shalt not kill," "Thou shalt not steal," "Thou shalt not commit adultery." But even in the Ten Commandments, the law about keeping the Sabbath is applied to household, slaves, livestock, and resident aliens living in towns, and the law against coveting names household, animals, and fields (see the Clue of the Doublet on the differences between the Exodus and Deuteronomy versions). Remember that the initial setting of the law is Moses on Mount Sinai before the wilderness wandering even begins.

What we're saying is that the laws in the Torah or Pentateuch don't come from Moses but from a much later time. The collection of laws that we have in the Torah is Priestly and comes from the exile (586-539 BCE) or later. That doesn't mean that all the laws in it are that late; only that their compilation into a collection dates from that time. The person who gets credit for this in Jewish tradition is Ezra the priest, who read the law for the people (Neh. 8). Ascribing the law to Moses is a very clever anachronism because it turns the law into a kind of constitution for Israel established at its beginning as a people and handed down by God to one of Israel's greatest heroes. There is also internal confirmation of the anachronism within the Torah itself. Exodus (34:28) and Deuteronomy (4:13; 10:4) both make it clear that what Moses brought down from Sinai (called Horeb in Deuteronomy) was the Ten Commandments and only the Ten Commandments. It would have taken two very large and heavy tablets of stone with a lot of small writing to contain all the laws in the Torah. So even taking the Bible's account at face value, all the laws outside of the ten are a later aggregation, in other words—all together now—an anachronism.

Law and order

Once you wrap your mind around the anachronism of the Mosaic law, it's a lot easier to see other anachronisms in the Hebrew Bible. It's not that they stem from the law exactly, but they're related to the phenomenon of wanting to locate later social structures and developments at the beginning of Israel's history to give them more legitimacy and clout. The prominence of the law of Moses and the influence of the priestly class in the formation of the Bible are reflected in the books of 1 and 2 Chronicles. Here it's David who is used in a deft anachronistic move. In 1 Chronicles 23-26 he organizes the priests and Levites by families right down to the gatekeepers and musicians and specifies their roles in the service of the temple. Yet, this is a temple that isn't built yet and that David will never see. His son Solomon builds it after David is dead. The divisions mentioned in Chronicles are those of the Second Temple period, after its rebuilding in 520-515 BCE. Many of the names are also known from this period, including that of Jehezkel = Ezekiel (1 Chron. 24:16), which may be the prophet who has a book in the Bible named after him. One hint that the lists are an anachronism is that there is nothing at all about David doing anything like this in the books of Samuel and Kings, which were the Chronicler's main source.

That's not to say that the author of Samuel and Kings didn't use anachronism. It was a time-honored tradition among Bible writers, if not exactly time honoring. In the book of Kings, the author used a major anachronism to explain why God rejected Israel and favored Judah. The author evaluated every king of Israel and Judah as either righteous or evil depending on how faithful the king was to the law in Deuteronomy. For kings of Judah it was about fifty-fifty, with a few more on the evil side. But the kings of Israel were all bad. Every last one of them. And all for the same reason: they all participated in the "sin of Jeroboam."

First Kings 12:26-33 tells how Jeroboam, the first king of the divided kingdom of Israel, got scared that all his subjects would go to the temple in Jerusalem to worship and eventually defect as a result. So he built a couple of replacements for the temple in the towns of Dan and Bethel and encouraged his people to worship there. These became the national shrines of Israel, so all the kings of the country supported them and worshiped in them. Bad mistake, according to the author of Kings, because this violated the principle of centralization in Deuteronomy 12, which specified that proper worship could be conducted only at "the place" that the Lord chose. That place turned out to be Jerusalem, where Solomon built the temple. That meant that all the kings of Israel were guilty of improper worship.

In reality, though, Jeroboam couldn't have violated the law of centralization because it wasn't in existence when he was alive. It was instituted by a king of Judah named Josiah (2 Kings 23), who ruled 640-609 BCE. The story says that he acted on the basis of a copy of the law that he found in the temple, but this is a literary device for introducing the anachronism. The measures Josiah took to impose centralization were all brand-new and were probably part of his political program to consolidate authority in Jerusalem in preparation for a revolt against Assyria. The law book that was "found" under Josiah was a version of the book of Deuteronomy that was probably written at Josiah's direction. Deuteronomy 12 changed the way sacrifices were carried out. Before, it was fine to offer sacrifices to the Lord anywhere. There are passages, like 1 Kings 18:30, that assume the presence of altars to the Lord outside of Jerusalem and are okay with them. Exodus 20:24 even gives instructions for building such an altar. Sacrifice was previously connected with eating meat. You would burn parts of the animal—the fat and entrails—as an offering to the deity and eat the rest. Deuteronomy 12 made a distinction between secular slaughter and religious slaughter. That way, you could eat meat at home without having to go to Jerusalem, which was the only place you could sacrifice. Why does Deuteronomy 12 lay all this out in such detail? Because it was changing the typical practice to accommodate the law of centralization. The book of Kings drags poor old Jeroboam through the mud for a crime he couldn't have committed because the law against what he did wasn't on the books yet.

PEA

The Forensics staff are always saying things in briefings like "deoxyribonucleic acid—that's DNA to you nonscientists." So we've come up with some snooty slang of our own, one example of which is "pseudepigraphic anachronism" (PEA). That's the term we're using for when an author writes under the guise of another person, usually a famous person from the past. A variation of PEA is when an editor inserts something in a previously written piece of literature so that it passes as the work of the original author. This sort of thing happens quite often in the Bible. The law of Moses is an example. Moses didn't write the various laws and collections in the Torah; they were ascribed to him later through the process called *midrash*—interpretation. Laws were interpreted for new situations and explained by adding new laws and provisions.

The book that gets the prize for the most anachronisms is . . . drum roll, please . . . Psalms. The book of Psalms is a collection of musical poetry from throughout Israel's history. It's a collection of collections really, since it is composed of five sections or "books" (Pss. 1-41; 42-72; 73-89; 90-106; 107-150). The separate books show both the sense that the larger book of Psalms is a compilation and that someone has gone through and tried to organize the different psalms into some kind of cohesive unit. One of the main ways the editor or editors did this was by connecting the psalms with stories in David's life through the use of headings or superscriptions to the individual psalms. This is where the PEAs come in. They aren't the doing of the authors of the psalms. If you read the psalms, it becomes clear that their contents often don't match the headings. The headings are anachronistic in that they try to match events in David's life with psalms that were written hundreds of years later. It's like when Lt. La Rosa opens an old case file and then puts a new label on it with his name and the date and time he opened it. His label tells us nothing about the contents of the file. Drives us nuts.

Seventy-three of the 150 psalms have headings that mention David. That's too many to look at them all, so we'll just pull out a couple of the most famous, assuming La Rosa hasn't gotten hold of them in the last couple of months. The opening line of Psalm 23 ("The Lord is my shepherd, I shall not want") is right up there with the Lord's Prayer as one of the best-known passages in the Bible. Its heading reads simply, "A psalm of David," not connecting with any one episode but with David's life as a whole, especially his youthful beginnings as a shepherd, but also with his reputation as a musician. Its last line goes (see if you can quote it), "I will dwell in the house of the LORD forever." Don't get hung up on the "forever." It doesn't mean eternity in the Hebrew Bible, just a very long time. The NRSV translation, "my whole life long," works well. In the ancient Near East, a god's house was his or her temple. The psalmist envisions a life praising the Lord in his temple in Jerusalem. But that temple wasn't built when David was alive, so the attribution of the psalm to David in the heading is anachronistic.

An even better example is Psalm 51. It's a psalm of repentance and forgiveness. The heading assigns it to David after his sin of adultery with Bathsheba had been discovered. Notice verse 18:

Do good to Zion in your good pleasure;
    rebuild the walls of Jerusalem.

The request to rebuild Jerusalem's walls assumes that they were torn down. When was Jerusalem in need of rebuilding? The answer is, after its destruction at the hands of the Babylonians in 586 BCE, more than four hundred years after David lived. In fact, it was Nehemiah in 444 BCE who led the rebuilding effort, and that seems a likely date for this psalm. The heading places it hundreds of years ahead of its time.

Like father, like son. As with David and Psalms, there are some books pseudepigraphically associated with Solomon because of his reputation for great wisdom and his many wives. You might call all these cases implied PEAs. Implied because in the Psalms the phrase "of David" is ambiguous. It probably means "by David," but it might also mean "for David" or "to David," as in a dedication. In the same way, the book of Proverbs begins with "the proverbs of Solomon." Even so, there are different sections to the book: There's another "proverbs of Solomon" at 10:1 and a third one at 25:1. Then, chapter 30 is attributed to someone named Agur, and chapter 31 to a king named Lemuel. All this means that the book is a collection of collections, like Psalms, and we would not be surprised to find anachronisms.

They are certainly present in the other two books implied to be by Solomon—Ecclesiastes and Song of Songs, or Song of Solomon. The book of Ecclesiastes (also known by its Hebrew title, Qoheleth) doesn't actually name Solomon, but the opening line, "the words of the Teacher (*qoheleth*), the son of David, king in Jerusalem," and the setup in the first two chapters, where a rich king with plenty of time on his hands decides to do experiments to find the meaning of life, point to Solomon as the implied author. Solomon is mentioned in the Song that bears his name, which is a collection of erotic literature. Here's the thing: both books contain Persian words—*pardes* (park, orchard) in Song 4:13 and Ecclesiastes 2:5 and *pitgam* (sentence) in Ecclesiastes 8:11—as well as a lot of late Hebrew terms and expressions. Since Judah only came into contact with Persia beginning in the sixth century BCE and Solomon lived in the tenth century, this linguistic evidence suggests that both Ecclesiastes and Song of Songs were written substantially later than Solomon.

Another kind of PEA is the piggyback variety. This kind is especially common in the prophetic books. Maybe that's because they get past, present, and future mixed up, because they're . . . well . . . prophets. The best known example is the book of Isaiah, which many Bible detectives think is three books in one: chapters 1–39*, 40–55, and 56–66. The first thirty-nine chapters contain material that goes back to the eighth-century prophet Isaiah, although they may also have passages that were added later. (That's what the asterisk means.) Chapters 40–55 were appended by a later writer in the sixth century. Then chapters 56–66 were piled on even later. For lack of better names, these sections are referred to as First, Second, and Third Isaiah.

See how they sort of pretend to be from the original Isaiah just by adding on to his work? The transition from First to Second Isaiah is pretty dramatic, partly because chapters 36–39 were borrowed from the book of 2 Kings (see the Clue of the Doublet). Second Isaiah begins this way:

> Comfort, O comfort my people,
>   says your God.

Speak tenderly to Jerusalem,
    and cry to her
that she has served her term,
    that her penalty is paid,
that she has received from the LORD's hand
    double for all her sins.
A voice cries out:
"In the wilderness prepare the way of the LORD,
    make straight in the desert a highway for our God.
Every valley shall be lifted up,
    and every mountain and hill be made low;
the uneven ground shall become level,
    and the rough places a plain." (Isa. 40:1-4)

The penalty paid by Jerusalem was the captivity of its people in Babylon. That captivity is over, and the return journey to Jerusalem from Babylon is envisioned as a joyful procession on the highway built by the Lord through the desert. If you keep reading in Second Isaiah, you come across even more concrete signs of its date. At the end of chapter 44, God says this of Cyrus:

"He is my shepherd,
    and he shall carry out all my purpose";

and this of Jerusalem, "It shall be rebuilt"; and this of the temple, "Your foundation shall be laid" (Isa. 44:28). Cyrus was the first king of the Persian Empire. He conquered Babylon and instituted a policy of allowing captives to return to their homelands. This happened in 539-538 BCE, two hundred years after the time of the original Isaiah.

The NT presents its own set of challenging PEAs, mostly related to Paul. We don't know who wrote most of the books of the New Testament. Take the Gospels, for instance. We know them as Matthew, Mark, Luke, and John, after the traditions that developed in early Christianity. But the books themselves never name their authors, so those are just aliases. They are anonymous, not pseudepigraphic. The letters of Paul are a different story. There are thirteen books in the NT that bear his name as author, although the books themselves are titled according to their audiences—Romans, 1 Corinthians, 2 Corinthians, Galatians, Ephesians, Philippians, Colossians, 1 Thessalonians, 2 Thessalonians, 1 Timothy,

2 Timothy, Titus, and Philemon. The first nine are places; the last four are people. The book of Hebrews isn't listed because it doesn't purport to be by Paul. It's like the Gospels—anonymous but not pseudepigraphic. Just to show that the question of pseudonymous authorship is a thing, there are two books that aren't in the NT—the letter to the Laodiceans and 3 Corinthians—that claim to be by Paul. None of our NT colleagues think these two books are genuine, and some of them have doubts about nearly half of the NT books attributed to the apostle. They're not unanimous (Bible detectives rarely agree completely about anything, including where to go for lunch), but a lot of them don't think Paul wrote all thirteen. In fact, they agree on only seven. They all think Paul wrote Romans, 1 and 2 Corinthians, Galatians, Philippians, 1 Thessalonians, and Philemon, but they disagree on the rest. When you get them debating the topic, things can get pretty heated. The arguments are mostly about differences in vocabulary and writing style, and they get pretty technical. We won't bore you with the details, but . . .

A more relevant issue involving Paul and anachronism concerns his view of women. A couple of NT passages attributed to Paul give the order for women to be quiet in church. One of them is in 1 Timothy 2:8–15, which first says that men should pray and then tells women how to dress (vv. 8–9). As if that didn't strike close enough to home, the next four verses give these instructions: "Let a woman learn in silence with full submission. I permit no woman to teach or to have authority over a man; she is to keep silent. For Adam was formed first, then Eve; and Adam was not deceived, but the woman was deceived and became a transgressor." Whoever penned these words obviously never worked for a lady captain. The thing is, it probably wasn't Paul. First Timothy, along with 2 Timothy and Titus, form a subcategory of Paul's letters called the "Pastorals," and they're among the books that NT sleuths think are pseudepigraphic, that is, not written by Paul. One of the reasons for that judgment is that these letters deal with issues that Paul's other letters, at least the "Big Seven," don't touch—like the hierarchical differentiation of genders.

As it happens, there is one passage in 1 Corinthians 14:33b–36 that sounds a lot like the one in 1 Timothy. Here's part of it: "As in all the churches of the saints, women should be silent in the churches. For they are not permitted to speak, but should be subordinate, as the law also says. If there is anything they desire to know, let them ask their husbands at home. For it is shameful for a woman to speak in church." If you look at the context, it's clear that these verses are an intrusion.

The NRSV puts them in parentheses as a way of calling attention to their being out of place. First Corinthians 14 is talking about spiritual gifts, especially speaking in tongues up through verse 33a, and this topic picks up again in verse 37. The passage about women looks like a later insertion.

The same thing happened in 1 Corinthians 11:3–16. This passage doesn't say anything about women keeping silent. It makes a strange argument against men praying with their heads covered and for women covering theirs. It builds the same hierarchy of men over women based on the creation story in Genesis 2 as you find in 1 Timothy 2. But it also seems to be a later addition. In verse 2, Paul says, "I commend you because you remember me in everything and maintain the traditions just as I handed them on to you." Then in verse 17, he picks up on that thought and writes, "Now in the following instructions I do not commend you, because when you come together it is not for the better but for the worse." The intervening verses interrupt the continuity and change what Paul meant by "the traditions" from his teachings about Jesus and the unity of the church to ritual distinctions between women and men. Because of these passages, Paul has been branded a sexist pig and woman hater. We're not card-carrying members of the Paul fan club or anything like that, but we think he may have gotten a bum rap on this one, all because of a couple of anachronisms.

Before we wrap up this chapter, we want to express our sincere hope that Stephen King feels better about his anachronisms. It's got to be tough to write a thousand-page novel about the past and not have a few anachronisms creep in. As we've seen in this chapter, the Bible has more anachronisms in it than any Stephen King novel, and it's still the best seller of all time.

WHY THIS CLUE MATTERS

The Clue of the Anachronism is important because it shows that the Bible is a complicated collection of literature that developed over a long period of time. As readers, we need to keep two sets of dates in mind while reading the Bible—the time when a story or document is set, and the time when it was written. Anachronisms help us to identify those two sets and not confuse them. An anachronism often signals the date of writing of a biblical work and thus its intended audience and purpose. It can also sometimes signal a later addition or insertion into an earlier work. Anachronisms show not only how the Bible grew over time but also how it was interpreted and applied to different situations.

THE CLUE OF THE ANACHRONISM CAN HELP US . . .

1. Separate the setting of a story from its time of writing.
2. Locate the approximate time when a biblical text was written.
3. Identify the concerns that the text was intended to address.
4. Pick out later additions and supplements to a book or passage.
5. Understand that the Bible, for all of its timeless teachings, is very much the product of specific times and places.

THE CASEBOOK

1. The description of Goliath's armor and weapons in 1 Samuel 17:5-7 has been seen as reflecting items from different time periods and cultures. Do some online investigating to see if you can identify similar artifacts. Sketch a drawing of what Goliath would have looked like.
2. Amos 9:11 reads:

On that day I will raise up
   the booth of David that is fallen,
and repair its breaches,
   and raise up its ruins,
   and rebuild it as in the days of old.

This is an addition to Amos that does not fit with the time, place, or tone of the previous material in the book. Try to explain why. Hint: Focus on what is meant by the expression "booth of David" and on the verbs "repair," "raise up," and "rebuild."
3. The book of Jonah is generally viewed as a kind of anachronism, one that used the brief mention of the prophet Jonah in 2 Kings 14:25-26 as the springboard for a story directed at a much later time. What evidence can you find to support this understanding?

4. Acts 11:26 states that followers of Jesus were first called "Christians" in Antioch. This has been considered an anachronism by some scholars. Others have not questioned the date of the term but have suggested that it may have originally been a derisive way of referring to the followers of Jesus. What arguments can you find to support these different interpretations?

13

The Clue of the

HIDDEN MEANING

Back in the late 1990s a book came out that had a lot of people convinced it was going to revolutionize the Bible detective profession. Quite a few of our colleagues who got swept up in the wave of enthusiasm it created thought we were about to enter a new age of biblical sleuthing and all our job descriptions would have to be rewritten. We never drank the Kool-Aid, but it made for some interesting times.

The author's name was Michael Drosnin, an American journalist, and the title of his book was *The Bible Code*. Drosnin claimed that with a computer's help he had discovered within the Hebrew Bible a previously unknown secret code that mentions many significant events that have occurred throughout history. According to Drosnin, the assassinations of prominent people, World War II, the Holocaust, the dropping of the atomic bombs, Watergate, the first moon landing, the Gulf War, the Oklahoma City terrorist attack, and many other events are all referred to in the Bible if you know where to look. Drosnin said his research showed him that it's possible to find any day's main story referred to in the Bible if that story is big enough, and he stated boldly that anything that can possibly happen is encoded in the biblical text.

The book was a huge success, as it quickly climbed to the tops of the best-seller lists and undoubtedly made Drosnin a lot of dough. He followed it up a few years later with *The Bible Code II*, in which he said the Bible also predicts the 9/11 attacks. In that book he additionally proposed a theory for the origin of the Bible code itself—it was written by an extraterrestrial life-form that also brought the human DNA genetic code to Earth. Drosnin claimed an alien left the key to the code in a metallic obelisk that remains hidden near the Dead Sea to this day. Perhaps it was the alien, or the over-the-top doomsday message of the books, but the Bible Code eventually became its day's Segway—something that intrigued people and showed a lot of promise but never quite lived up to its initial hype after you took it out for a spin.

Drosnin's premise and approach have been debunked by mathematicians, computer scientists, and other experts who have pointed out serious flaws in them. Despite those critiques, Drosnin continued to pursue his goal of becoming the world's foremost Bible decoder and published a third book—*The Bible Code III*—in which he warns of a Bible-predicted imminent nuclear terror attack.

The Bible Code's millions of copies sold and its translation into multiple languages demonstrate the fascination people have with the text of the Bible, particularly the concealed mysteries and dark secrets they believe (hope?) it might contain. Curiosity about this dimension of the Bible goes back to its earliest days, and Drosnin is just one of the latest (and most successful) people to tap into it and personally profit from it. A Google search for the phrase "codes in the Bible" results in a whopping sixteen million hits. Compare that to the approximately six million hits for "Morse code," a code we know actually *does* exist, and you can see what we mean. It's likely that many of those sixteen million sites are skeptical about or dismissive of the existence of a Bible code, but that number still points to the high level of interest in the topic.

Despite Michael Drosnin's best efforts to convince us otherwise, we have no idea if there are secret codes like his in the Bible (although we seriously doubt it). But something we do know with certainty is that many of the folks engaged in the quixotic quest to discover a code that probably doesn't exist are missing out on something that's staring them right in the face from many pages of the Bible—the Clue of the Hidden Meaning. If they were to turn their attention to it instead of the code, they would be well rewarded.

The Clue of the Hidden Meaning is found in biblical passages that convey significance beyond what is stated on their surface level. On occasion the Bible explicitly acknowledges that sort of double significance. This example from John's Gospel relates part of a conversation Jesus has with some people about the temple in Jerusalem. "Jesus answered them,

'Destroy this *temple*, and in three days I will raise it up.' The Jews then said, 'This temple has been under construction for forty-six years, and will you raise it up in three days?' *But he was speaking of the temple of his body.* After he was raised from the dead, his disciples remembered that he had said this; and they believed the scripture and the word that Jesus had spoken" (John 2:19-22). Here Jesus uses the term "temple" in a symbolic or metaphorical sense, but his listeners understand it literally, so the exchange takes place on two levels with different meanings. In this case the author informs the reader that this is going on, but that's not typically done in the Bible, and so the reader usually has to figure out two things: (1) that there are multiple levels of meaning in a passage, and (2) what the meaning on each level is.

The Clue of the Hidden Meaning is planted throughout the Bible, which also makes it difficult to spot. If you limit your search to just one style of writing or a certain part of the text, you're liable to miss out on evidence of it elsewhere. Most of this chapter is devoted to a particular manifestation of the clue that can be particularly hard to pin down—euphemisms that fill in for other words and phrases an author deems inappropriate or prefers not to use for some reason. These can be especially difficult to identify, particularly when a text is being read in translation.

THE CLUE OF THE HIDDEN MEANING: biblical passages that convey significance beyond what is stated on the surface level

There's also a certain genre of writing used a couple of times in the Bible that is full of the Clue of the Hidden Meaning because it uses a lot of symbolic and veiled language to communicate its message. An additional way this clue makes itself known is in certain linguistic or numerical patterns imposed on a text that convey a meaning different from what the words themselves are communicating, and we'll consider a couple of examples of those.

This clue reminds us that we shouldn't take everything at face value when we read the Bible because sometimes the meaning of a passage resides on a level different than its surface one. Reading any text, not just the Bible, entails shifting between different levels since the meaning isn't always located where we expect to find it. With that in mind, a good guideline for this clue is the following: If something you are reading can

have more than one sense, you have come across the Clue of the Hidden
Meaning.

Blowing their cover

One place you'll always find the Clue of the Hidden Meaning is in a euphemism, a word or a phrase used in place of another that is deemed
inappropriate because it's too risqué, rude, or unpleasant. The biblical
authors can be incredibly blunt at times, but they occasionally resort
to euphemisms when they discuss certain topics. This allows them to
address these topics, but in a way that is indirect and roundabout. The
technical term for this type of communication is "circumlocution" (literally, "talking around" something), but being detectives, we prefer to
stick to jargon we're familiar with and call it like we see it—these authors are engaging in cover-ups.

There are certain aspects of life many people prefer not to discuss
publicly (even though they think about them all the time), and among
them the Big Three reign supreme: (1) death, (2) certain bodily functions, and (3) sex. Let's peek under the covers and see how the biblical
writers sometimes tiptoe around these areas.

The big sleep

The number of alternative ways people have come up with to talk about
the end of life is impressive and undoubtedly reflects the deep-seated
fears we have about it. A list we've consulted of euphemisms in English
for death tallies up to well over one hundred expressions, and some
of them point to the amazingly creative capacity of the human mind.
(Surprisingly, the one that's the title of this subsection isn't on that list.)
The expressions the Bible uses for death can be equally colorful, and
they show that its authors drew from an extensive menu of options
when they broached the subject of human mortality. Those euphemisms
include the following:

> When David's time to die drew near, he charged his son Solomon,
> saying: "I am about *to go the way of all the earth.* Be strong, be
> courageous." (1 Kings 2:1–2)

"Therefore, I will *gather you* to your ancestors, and you shall *be gathered* to your grave in peace; your eyes shall not see all the disaster that I will bring on this place." (2 Kings 22:20)

They were *snatched away* before their time;
    their foundation was washed away by a flood. (Job 22:16)

They are exalted a little while, and then *are gone*;
    they *wither and fade* like the mallow;
    they are *cut off* like the heads of grain. (Job 24:24)

Then Jesus gave a loud cry and *breathed his last*. (Mark 15:37)

After saying this, he [Jesus] told them, "Our friend Lazarus has *fallen asleep*, but I am going there to awaken him." (John 11:11)

I think it right, as long as I am in this body [literally, "in this tent"], to refresh your memory, since I know that my death [literally, *"the putting off of my tent"*] will come soon, as indeed our Lord Jesus Christ has made clear to me. (2 Pet. 1:13-14)

The verb "to die" is an extremely common one in the Bible, but on occasion authors prefer to use less direct ways of referring to the end of a person's life. When they do so, the rest of the passage can usually help the reader determine the meaning of the euphemism, but a certain ambiguity remains nonetheless. With the exception of a couple of them, like "breathed his last," if the italicized words were simply listed on a page, you wouldn't automatically assume that they were references to death. At the same time, when you read them in the context of the passages in which they're embedded, it becomes apparent that they are all in fact ways of speaking about life's final frontier. Their capacity to mean more than one thing is what makes these expressions examples of the Clue of the Hidden Meaning.

Rest stops and periods

Bodily excretions are another taboo topic for many, and in a few places the Bible gingerly sidesteps it by talking around it. The text's most graphic discussion of defecation is in a passage that talks about latrines and the proper etiquette one should follow when making use of those facilities. It contains a couple of euphemisms that are lost in translation in the NRSV, and it ends with a description of a literal cover-up. "You shall have a designated area outside the camp to which you shall go. With your utensils you shall have a trowel; *when you relieve yourself outside,* you shall dig a hole with it and then cover up your *excrement*" (Deut. 23:12–13). The Hebrew of the italicized phrase translates literally as "in your sitting outside," and so it does not contain an explicit reference to relieving oneself. In the same way, the term "excrement" is a less-than-literal rendering of the Hebrew "that which has gone out of you." There are several different words for feces in biblical Hebrew, but the author preferred to use this euphemism, perhaps because it stresses the need for one to take personal responsibility in matters of hygiene—if it has come out of you, it's yours to deal with.

Speaking of literal cover-ups, two other passages use that language in connection with biblical figures answering nature's call. One describes the aftermath of King Eglon's death at the hands of the judge Ehud, as the former's attendants wait outside the room where he has been killed. "After he [Ehud] had gone, the servants came. When they saw that the doors of the roof chamber were locked, they thought, 'He must be *relieving himself* in the cool chamber'" (Judg. 3:24). The other is part of a scene in which David has the opportunity to kill Saul but chooses not to do so. "He came to the sheepfolds beside the road, where there was a cave; and Saul went in to *relieve himself.* Now David and his men were sitting in the innermost parts of the cave" (1 Sam. 24:3). As in the previous example, the NRSV's translation of the italicized phrase isn't exact because the Hebrew does not literally say that Eglon and Saul were relieving themselves. It rather makes use of an expression that calls to mind the position one sometimes assumes when engaged in that act—the passages say that each man "was covering his feet." The Hebrew euphemisms in all these cases involving bodily excretions have more than one meaning, and so the passages contain further examples of the Clue of the Hidden Meaning.

We'd like to pause for a moment to call your attention to a Bible perp who busily works behind the scenes and is sometimes guilty of serious infractions that can easily escape detection. The Italian words

traddutore traditore literally mean "translator, traitor," and they highlight the fact that whenever a text is translated, a type of injustice is
done to it. It's impossible to fully convey all the meaning and nuance
of something expressed in one language in another. Things will always
be left out or distorted along the way. A word that has been translated
never has the exact same meaning in both languages, and so translators
are always traitors because of the built-in limitations of their craft.
But translators can also intentionally act as traitors, and we often see
evidence of this in the way they deal with euphemisms. In the cases we
just looked at, the decision was made to translate the Hebrew phrases
"to sit outside" and "to cover one's feet" as "to relieve oneself" rather
than to render them literally. But such a decision has ramifications.
On the positive side, the sense of the expression is made clear and the
reader knows exactly what it means. But the trade-off is that the euphemism completely disappears and is replaced with something that
expresses its meaning but lacks its distinctiveness. In the interest of
clarity, the euphemism is euphemized.

Biblical detectives need to keep an eye out for the traitorous translator because he can make our job harder. Such vigilance is necessary
at all times, but especially when the Clue of the Hidden Meaning takes
the form of a euphemism. When we read the Bible in translation, there
are always at least two sets of fingerprints on the scene—those of the
author and those of the translator. While the translator might appear
to be the author's accomplice, sometimes it seems they're working at
cross-purposes. The translator shows up after the author has left the
scene and sometimes does his work so diligently that he wipes away
every trace of the author's prints and only his own remain. That's what
happened when Eglon and Saul relieved themselves instead of covering their feet. Some translations (like the NRSV) render the Hebrew
expressions literally in a footnote, but not all do. If you can't read the
text in its original language and it's not mentioned in a footnote (or
you don't read the footnote), you'll never know you're in the presence
of a euphemism.

When menstruation is mentioned in the Bible, it is usually described
as a flow of blood, but euphemisms have been used in a few places. In
one story Rachel steals her father Laban's household gods before she and
Jacob embark on a trip to Canaan, but Laban pursues the couple in an
effort to recover his property. Rachel manages to avoid being caught by
pretending she is having her monthly period, but she does not employ

the terminology commonly used in the Bible for that condition when she speaks to her father. "Now Rachel had taken the household gods and put them in the camel's saddle, and sat on them. Laban felt all about in the tent, but did not find them. And she said to her father, 'Let not my lord be angry that I cannot rise before you, for *the way of women* is upon me.' So he searched, but did not find the household gods" (Gen. 31:34-35). A legal passage in Leviticus has a different way of referring to a woman's period, but it also includes the more usual way of describing it. "If a man lies with a woman *having her sickness* and uncovers her nakedness, he has laid bare her flow and she has laid bare *her flow of blood*; both of them shall be cut off from their people" (Lev. 20:18).

Even without the explicit reference to a flow of blood, the contexts of both these passages strongly suggest that "the way of women" and "her sickness" are references to menstruation, but since other senses are possible for these expressions, they should be considered examples of the Clue of the Hidden Meaning.

Biblical know-how

The sex-related euphemisms in the Bible can be grouped in two main categories: (1) the things people do, and (2) the body parts they do them with.

The things we do for love

Perhaps the most widely known of all biblical euphemisms is one that describes sexual intercourse, and it is "to know," as in "Now the man *knew* his wife Eve, and she conceived and bore Cain" (Gen. 4:1a). This is a delicate way of referring to something that one might be hesitant to bring up in polite company, but some of the other verbs in the Bible commonly used for sexual relations leave little to the imagination even if they're technically euphemisms. "To go into," "to come into," and "to enter into" come to mind. Beyond that, other talk-arounds run the gamut between those two extremes and demonstrate that covering up what goes on under the covers has a long and venerable history that can be traced back at least as far as the Bible.

When Isaac had been there a long time, King Abimelech of the Philistines looked out of a window and saw him fondling [literally, *playing with*] his wife Rebekah. (Gen. 26:8)

You shall not *uncover the nakedness* of your father's brother, that is, you shall not *approach* his wife; she is your aunt. (Lev. 18:14)

If a woman approaches any animal and has sexual relations [literally, *stretches out*] with it, you shall kill the woman and the animal; they shall be put to death, their blood is upon them. (Lev. 20:16)

Then let my wife *grind* for another,
      and let other men *kneel over* her. (Job 31:10)

It is actually reported that there is sexual immorality among you, and of a kind that is not found even among pagans; for a man is living with [literally, *has*] his father's wife. (1 Cor. 5:1)

Now concerning the matters about which you wrote: "It is well for a man not to *touch* a woman." (1 Cor. 7:1)

Male-related terminology

Here's a tip to keep in mind—the traitorous translator can sometimes help you establish a profile for a euphemism that then enables you to identify others of the same type. In a passage that criticizes the Israelites for following other gods, Isaiah employs sexual imagery to describe the nature of their offense.

Behind the door and the doorpost
      you have set up your symbol;
for, in deserting me, you have uncovered your bed,
      you have gone up to it,
      you have made it wide
and you have made a bargain for yourself with them,
      you have loved their bed,
      you have gazed on their *nakedness*. (Isa. 57:8)

The Hebrew term for the word in italics means "hand," which of course makes little sense in this context. But if we bring in evidence from Israel's neighboring cultures, where the word "hand" was sometimes used as a metaphor for the penis, things fall into place. Once again, the euphemism has been euphemized, as the translator opts for "nakedness" rather than "hand" for "penis," but the jump from "hand" to "nakedness" is still a red flag that lets us know we've hit on the Clue of the Hidden Meaning.

This is when a biblical detective should see if some dot connecting is in order. Once the linkage of the two words has been established, other occurrences of the term "hand" can be investigated to see if they might be euphemisms for "penis." Our review of the files has identified a likely suspect in a passage from the book of Ezekiel that describes how the people will react in terror to the punishment God is sending their way.

All *hands* shall grow feeble,
   all knees turn to water. (Ezek. 7:17)

The reference to knees turning to water is odd, and some translations understand this to be an allusion to involuntary urination out of fear. It's not inconceivable that the word "knee" could itself be a euphemism for "penis" in this verse. If it is, that increases the likelihood that "hand" means the same thing. The verb translated here as "feeble" supports the meaning of "penis" for "hand" because it can carry the meanings "to slacken, sink, drop." The verse is therefore likely describing a fear that is so paralyzing that it results in impotence and incontinence.

A passage in Isaiah contains an image so unusual that an experienced detective will immediately cordon it off and start working through the euphemism protocol. "On that day the Lord will shave with a razor hired beyond the River—with the king of Assyria—the head and *the hair of the feet*, and it will take off the beard as well" (Isa. 7:20). What exactly is "the hair of the feet"? A literal interpretation of the phrase gets us nowhere fast, so we can tentatively ID it as a euphemism. It was common in antiquity to remove all the body hair of prisoners of war as a way of shaming them, and this verse describes that practice. The same investigative technique employed above can be used here. Israel's neighbors often referred to the foot as a euphemism for the penis, and that appears to be its meaning in this verse where "the hair of the feet" is a euphemism for pubic hair, so other biblical uses of the word can be interrogated as other possible examples of it. Here are three additional passages that contain this form of the Clue of the Hidden Meaning:

> But Zipporah took a flint and cut off her son's foreskin, and touched Moses' *feet* with it, and said, "Truly you are a bridegroom of blood to me!" (Exod. 4:25)

> When Boaz had eaten and drunk, and he was in a contented mood, he went to lie down at the end of the heap of grain. Then she [Ruth] came stealthily and uncovered his *feet*, and lay down. At midnight the man was startled, and turned over, and there, lying at his *feet*, was a woman! (Ruth 3:7-8)

> When Uriah came to him, David asked how Joab and the people fared, and how the war was going. Then David said to Uriah, "Go down to your house, and wash your *feet*." (2 Sam. 11:7-8)

Even though the word is translated literally by the NRSV in these three passages, the larger contexts of the stories indicate that the men's genitals are being referred to rather than their actual feet.

A third part of the body that sometimes does double duty and refers to the penis is the thigh. You really have to be on your toes for this one, because the translator sometimes completely does away with the euphemism. In some cases, unless you're reading the passage in its original language, you wouldn't even know it makes mention of a body part, let alone the thigh. In both of the following examples, the Hebrew original of the italicized words is "coming out of the thigh of X."

> The total number of people *born to Jacob* was seventy. Joseph was already in Egypt. (Exod. 1:5)

> Now Gideon had seventy sons, *his own offspring*, for he had many wives. (Judg. 8:30)

Things are clearer in a couple of other cases that refer to the thigh and are always translated that way. Twice in the book of Genesis someone is asked to take an oath by placing his hand under someone else's thigh. The first involves Abraham and his servant. "Abraham said to his servant, the oldest of his house, who had charge of all that he had, '*Put your hand under my thigh* and I will make you swear by the LORD, the God of heaven and earth, that you will not get a wife for my son from the daughters of the Canaanites, among whom I live'" (Gen. 24:2–3). Later in the book Joseph engages in a similar ritual with his father, Jacob, here identified as Israel (Gen. 47:29). These passages reflect the practice common in the ancient world of swearing on the genitals that may also be the basis of the English verb "to testify," which is related to the word for testicles.

On rare occasions the translator is traitorous in the opposite direction by opting for a word or phrase that is more graphic than the original. Such a translation might be so suggestive that it signals it could be standing in for a milder euphemism. One might have that reaction after reading this passage from Leviticus: "When any man has a discharge from his *member*, his discharge makes him ceremonially unclean. The uncleanness of his discharge is this: whether his *member* flows with his discharge, or his *member* is stopped from discharging, it is uncleanness for him" (Lev. 15:2–3). While hardly offensive, the word "member" is not something many readers expect to find in the Bible. And they'd be correct, because it isn't actually in the text but is a racier translation of the Hebrew's rather pedestrian "flesh." The translator probably made this decision in order to specify which part of the man's body is experiencing the discharge, and in the process hinted at a possible euphemism. The same translation of Hebrew "flesh" as "member" is offered in Ezekiel 23:19–20, a passage that's likely to make biblical detectives think they've been transferred to the vice squad.

We conclude this examination of the male anatomy with two other verses that have euphemisms for the penis, but this time we'll leave out the italics so you can demonstrate your analytical prowess by picking them out on your own. We'll even make it more challenging by rendering the Hebrew literally and not give you the NRSV translation.

> No one whose testicles are crushed or whose pourer is cut off shall be admitted to the assembly of the LORD. (Deut. 23:1)

> The young men who had grown up with him said to him, "Thus you should say to this people who spoke to you, 'Your father made our yoke heavy, but you must lighten it for us'; thus you should say to them, 'My little thing is thicker than my father's loins.'" (1 Kings 12:10)

How did you do?

Female-related terminology

The Bible refers to female genitalia using some of the same euphemisms it does for the male, but it also introduces some new ones. This can escape the notice of even the most attentive readers, because here too the traitorous translator sometimes doesn't provide a literal rendering of the original Hebrew. "You built yourself a platform and made yourself a lofty place in every square; at the head of every street you built your lofty place and prostituted your beauty, *offering yourself* to every passer-by, and multiplying your whoring" (Ezek. 16:24–25). All the Hebrew grammatical forms in these verses are feminine singular, so there is no doubt that the addressee is female. Once again, the translator has substituted one euphemism for another because the Hebrew of the italicized words means "you have opened wide your feet." It could be argued that the word "feet" should be taken literally, as in the phrase "to spread one's legs," and in that case it's not a euphemism. But the only other verse in the Bible that uses this Hebrew verb suggests it is in fact a euphemism.

> Those who guard their mouths preserve their lives;
>   those who *open wide their lips* come to ruin. (Prov. 13:3)

That match strongly suggests that the Ezekiel passage contains a euphemism that refers to the parting of the lips of the female genitalia.

The same use of a term for both genders can be seen in a verse that discusses a woman's monthly period. "When a woman has a discharge of blood that is her regular discharge *from her body*, she shall be in her impurity for seven days, and whoever touches her shall be unclean until the evening" (Lev. 15:19). The italicized phrase is literally "in her flesh" in Hebrew, and so this is another word that can describe both male and female genitalia.

An additional body part that is sometimes identified with one's genitals might seem like an odd choice, but there is enough solid evidence to warrant including it in the Bible detective's manual. It is used in reference to females in a passage in Jeremiah.

> And if you say in your heart,
>   "Why have these things come upon me?"
> it is for the greatness of your iniquity
>   that your skirts are lifted up,
>   and *you* are violated. (Jer. 13:22)

This is one of a number of disturbing biblical passages that describe a woman being raped, and in this case it serves as an image for the punishment the Israelites will receive for their lack of faith. The translator uses the word "you" to leave no doubt as to what is being portrayed, because a literal translation of the Hebrew word "your heels" could lead to confusion. The association between the heel and the genitals is also found for males in the story of the birth of Jacob, which describes him holding that part of his twin brother's body when he and Esau are born. "Afterward his brother came out, with his hand gripping Esau's heel; so he was named Jacob" (Gen. 25:26a). The narrative that follows centers on which son's descendants will pass on the covenant, so the birth scene anticipates that theme by depicting Jacob grabbing the body part of his brother most closely associated with future lineage.

Finally, in a couple of places the mouth is cited euphemistically to refer to a woman's genitals; in the following verse from Proverbs it has a derogatory sense:

> This is the way of an adulteress:
>   she *eats*, and wipes her *mouth*,
>   and says, "I have done no wrong." (Prov. 30:20)

Note also the euphemistic use of the verb "to eat" to describe sexual intercourse.

We've devoted much attention to euphemisms because they're used often in the biblical literature and they present special challenges for biblical detectives, especially those reading the text in translation. In some of its other guises, the Clue of the Hidden Meaning is easier to spot because it's out in plain view. For instance, the many parables of Jesus in the New Testament are examples of the clue because their true meanings are not found on the surface but can only be discovered through careful reflection. To fill out the picture a bit more, we now consider a couple of other ways the Clue of the Hidden Meaning makes itself known.

Apocalypse then, not now

The New Testament book of Revelation, also known as the book of the Apocalypse, is full of examples of the Clue of the Hidden Meaning. But we warn you—the place is also a minefield. Many Bible detectives agree that Revelation is one of the worst crime scenes they've come across. Not because of what it contains (although there is quite a bit of violence in it), but because of what its readers have sometimes done to it. Too many of them—mostly Christians—have traipsed through the book and totally trashed it with complete disregard for the amount of carnage they've left behind.

Revelation and the book of Daniel are the Bible's two examples of apocalyptic literature, a style of writing rich in symbolism and coded language. Apocalyptic works are full of hidden meaning because they're written to give hope to an audience that's experiencing persecution. The authors attempt to encourage those who are suffering by letting them know that their oppressors' days are numbered, but they can't come right out and say that because it would just lead to more oppression. So they write in highly symbolic language that only their readers will understand.

The problem is that some folks believe the books were written for our times and symbolically describe things that are happening today. They're forgetting a basic principle taught in Bible Detecting 101—when you read the Bible, you're reading other people's mail. That is literally the case with Revelation, because its first three chapters relate the contents of letters addressed to seven churches in Asia Minor.

But that hasn't stopped some folks from believing that the author of the book, a man named John, has personally dropped a handwritten note in their mailboxes. This completely ignores the fact that Revelation was written for people who were experiencing persecution at the hands of the Roman Empire in the first two centuries of the common era. When the book is read with that context in mind, the meanings of the symbols become apparent and all the confusing imagery begins to make sense. We're not able to illustrate this at length here, so let's look at one passage in the hope that it will motivate you to delve deeper and study other parts of the book.

Read Revelation 17:1-6. This brief section describes a woman who symbolizes the Roman Empire. The reference to her seated on many waters indicates the vast geographic extent of the empire, and identifying her as a whore is a way of calling attention to the empire's immoral character (v. 1). In the next verse, the drunkenness and fornication of the people on earth express how all have come under the influence of the Roman Empire. The scarlet beast has the color of royalty and is therefore an allusion to the office of the emperor, whose "blasphemous names" are the titles that claim he is divine (v. 3). Later on in the chapter it is explained that the seven mountains the beast sits on are the famous seven hills of Rome, and the ten horns represent individual emperors (v. 9). The woman's opulent lifestyle depicted in the fourth verse is meant to suggest the wealth of the empire, and the reference to her "abominations" and "impurities" identifies the corrupt ways its wealth was acquired. The woman is identified as Babylon rather than Rome (v. 5) because the author wants to avoid directly naming the enemy out of fear that doing so would lead to more oppression. Finally, the description of the woman being drunk from the blood of saints and followers of Jesus is a not-so-subtle reference to the persecution Christians were forced to endure at the hands of the Roman authorities (v. 6).

Real Bible codes

Michael Drosnin was right about there being codes in the Bible; they just don't look anything like the one he claims to have found. One of them is in Revelation, and it might be the most well-known number in the entire Bible—666, "the mark, name, or number of the beast" (read Rev. 13:16–18). All sorts of candidates have been put forward as the person or organization the number represents. The prophet Muhammad, various popes, quite a few US presidents, a number of other world leaders, the United Nations, and the European Union have all been nominated for the dubious distinction, but those are all based on the Drosnin method of interpretation that relies on the premise that the Bible predicts future events.

Since we don't buy that approach, we think the designation 666 is pointing to someone in the author's own backyard who would have been known to the book's oppressed audience. The likeliest contender for the honor is the Roman emperor Nero, mainly because he did in fact persecute Christians and he's validated by the ancient practice of gematria whereby the letters of an alphabet are converted to numbers. When the letters in Nero's name and title are added up, they total 666. This passage is treated in more detail in the chapter on the Clue of the Messy Manuscript.

Gematria explains the use of another puzzling number in the New Testament that's related to Jesus's family tree. Read Matthew 1:1–17 and identify the code it contains. Matthew claims to organize Jesus's genealogical record in three time periods of fourteen generations each (Matt. 1:17). But the middle set has an extra generation, so Matthew slipped up. The number fourteen is important for Matthew because it's the numerical total of the letters in David's name, and he wants to connect Jesus to David because he's the one from whose line the Jewish Messiah will come. In fact, Matthew tips us off about what he's up to in the very first verse of his gospel. "An account of the genealogy of Jesus the Messiah, the son of David, the son of Abraham" (Matt. 1:1). Here again we have a biblical code, but it's not of the Drosnin type because it looks to the past rather than the future.

A final non-Drosnin code can be seen in the handful of biblical texts that are written in an acrostic format, as explained in the chapter on the Clue of the Repeated Pattern. An acrostic format puts the initial letter of each line in alphabetical order. This is done to allow for easier memorization of a passage because you know what letter begins each line, and to give a sense of wholeness or completion to the topic being addressed. Read Proverbs 31:10–31 and look for the acrostic it contains. That wasn't as easy as the previous example from Matthew, was it? Unless you're reading the text in Hebrew, you'll never find this pattern because it's virtually impossible to reproduce in translation. The passage identifies the qualities of a perfect woman, and perhaps it's presented in an acrostic arrangement to underscore that sense of perfection.

These three texts are examples of the Clue of the Hidden Meaning because each in its own way adds an additional layer of meaning to the surface one—the number of the beast provides information about its identity; Matthew's genealogy weaves Jesus's link with David throughout his entire family tree; and the acrostic in Proverbs helps to reinforce the ideal quality of the woman it is describing. And not a single one of them mentions Drosnin's alien.

WHY THIS CLUE MATTERS

Why does anything that is hidden matter? Because it holds the potential for us to learn about something we didn't even know existed. That means this clue matters only if it's discovered. If it remains hidden and unknown to us, we've learned nothing. But when we do uncover it, the Clue of the Hidden Meaning reveals important and interesting information we previously knew nothing about. Among the things we can learn are the following: (1) ancient people were sometimes reluctant to speak directly about some of the same topics that make us uncomfortable, and they too came up with creative ways to talk around them; (2) symbolic language played an important role in the biblical world by allowing people to communicate when it wasn't otherwise possible; and (3) there is evidence of coded language in the Bible, but it is always intended for its original audience and is not directed at people who will live in later times.

THE CLUE OF THE HIDDEN MEANING CAN HELP US . . .

1. Gain insight into the ways people long ago thought and communicated with one another.
2. Recognize that the meanings of texts often reside on more than one level.
3. Realize that the biblical literature was not originally written for us.
4. Appreciate the importance of reading the Bible in its original languages.
5. Make use of footnotes in Bibles and consult other tools that allow us to better understand the text.

THE CASEBOOK

Find the Clue of the Hidden Meaning in the following chapters. (Some of them require that you read footnotes in the text or consult other resources.)

Death
Job 17
Jeremiah 51
Acts 13
Ephesians 5

Sexuality
Genesis 18
Song of Songs 7

Isaiah 6
Isaiah 57
Jeremiah 13

Symbolism and Patterns
Psalm 119
Daniel 7
Matthew 13
Revelation 12

14

The Clue of the

MESSY MANUSCRIPT

A dozen years ago we got involved with the search for a shadowy international criminal known only as "Ryan." Dealing with Interpol was tricky at that time because of the fax machines—both ours and theirs—that printed out lousy photos and barely readable text. Long story short, we got the goods on Ryan, which no other law enforcement agency had been able to do. We were ready to make the arrest, but he skipped town before we could get a usable warrant. He didn't get far. The CIA took him down on the strength of our evidence. We did all the work, and they grabbed the glory.

The department called in the Bible Division to consult on the case, because we deal with problems of textual transmission all the time. One of the first things we learn in training is how many originals of biblical books are in existence today. We're talking manuscripts that bear the handwriting of the author—Moses, Samuel, Paul, or what have you. The official term for such a manuscript is "autograph." So, how many "autographs" of biblical books do we have? The answer comes as a surprise to most people. So take a guess. How many autographs of Bible books are socked away in the Vatican library or someplace where scholars can study them? The answer is none. Zero. Zip. Bupkus. We do not have an autograph of any biblical book. It would be an extraordinary find if one ever turned up, on par with discovering that Amelia Earhart has been working at a casino in Atlantic City all these years. What we have is copies, in reality copies of copies of copies of copies. The history of the

Bible from its writing to the print and electronic versions on the market today is a long, multistaged one that involves transmission through handmade copies of manuscripts in original languages as well as translations. Xerox machines didn't exist, so there was plenty of room for errors to creep in along the way.

The Clue of the Messy Manuscript refers to places in the Bible where there is a problem with the text of the passage. It can take different forms: something missing; a false ending or broken flow within a story; repetition or backtracking; something illogical in a story; a problem with versification or a chapter break. Many English translations resolve these problems, so the clue can be easily missed. Because of this, it is often hard to tell there is a problem unless something is mentioned in the footnotes of a study Bible.

THE CLUE OF THE MESSY MANUSCRIPT: places in the Bible where there is a problem with the text of the passage

It's a lucky break for Bible criminologists that ancient translations and copies of biblical writings are called witnesses. They aren't witnesses to the events that the writings describe but witnesses to the text of those writings. And like many witnesses, they sometimes sing like canaries and contradict each other. We have stacks and stacks of case files where the witnesses disagree. In order to interrogate those conflicting witnesses more easily, we've organized them in three piles. One pile contains cases where the disagreements, also called variants, are helpful for giving us a sense of what has gone on in the transmission of the text by copyists and even in the meaning of the story or text itself. The second pile consists of cases where the variants are kind of boring and don't tell us much. We're pretty sure which witness has the best rendition of the text, and the others don't make any real difference in the meaning of the passage, at least in our opinion. There are some famous passages in this pile, though, that might occasion a surprise or two. The third pile is composed of cases where the variants are substantial. Some of these are real challenges for figuring out what the best reading should be and how the variants came about. Without further ado, let's dive into the messier side of Bible detecting and call our first witnesses.

Pile #1: Variants that help put a puzzle together

Some witnesses can't wait to spill the beans, and they start singing before you can even ask a question. The manuscript differences in these
cases furnish insights into how they came about and also yield some
hints about the development and meaning of their contents.

A case of double murder

On the top of the heap is the case of David and Goliath in 1 Samuel 17,
which has been mentioned in connection with some other clues. It's
such a famous case that it's hard to avoid. Although it reads like a run-
of-the-mill street brawl, it also turns out to be a very complicated file
in some respects. One problem is the condition of its text and the witnesses to it. If you study the case, you begin to notice a few peculiarities, especially if the version of the Bible you're using has footnotes on
the text. For example, verse 4 gives Goliath's height as "six cubits and
a span," but there's a note in the NRSV that looks like alphabet soup:
"MT: Q Ms Gk *four*." This isn't secret code; it's just abbreviations. "MT"
is Masoretic Text, the standard version of the Hebrew Bible. "Q" stands
for Qumran, where the Dead Sea Scrolls were found, and "Ms" means
one of the manuscripts found there. "Gk" means Greek and refers to
the Septuagint, or Greek translation of the Hebrew Bible, abbreviated
LXX. What the note is saying is that a Dead Sea Scrolls fragment of this
verse and the Greek translation of it list Goliath as four cubits and a span
tall—6 feet 6 inches instead of 9 feet 6 inches! Keep reading. Verse 12 is
odd because it seems to be introducing David for the first time, yet we've
been reading about him since the start of chapter 16. Then in verse 23
Goliath is introduced again.

The strangest feature of the story, though, is in verses 50–51 where
David kills Goliath twice! The first time it is with his famous sling: "So
David prevailed over the Philistine with a sling and a stone, *striking down
the Philistine and killing him; there was no sword in David's hand.*" The second time is with Goliath's own sword: "Then David ran and stood over
the Philistine; *he grasped his sword, drew it out of its sheath, and killed him*;
then he cut off his head with it."

What the NRSV notes don't tell you is that the Hebrew (MT) version
of this story is about twice as long as the Greek (LXX) version, which

begins with the introduction of David in verse 12. This is because the Hebrew combines two (or more?) versions of the story. That's why there is a second introduction of David, two introductions of Goliath, and two versions of his death. It is a Clue of the Doublet that is corroborated by the textual witnesses. The version preserved in the Greek translation is older. You can see some development in the versions. The more the story was told and retold, the more popular it became and the more fantastic David's victory was. An example was Goliath's height, which shot up three feet in the course of transmission. This difference may have begun accidentally. The number "six" occurs in verse 7 and may have been accidentally written by anticipation in place of "four" in verse 4. But the larger number stuck because it made Goliath more formidable. The manuscript history of this story is a mess, but not as messy as the scene it describes.

The Case of the Malicious Monarch

This chapter on messy manuscripts is in the "Dusting for Prints" section of our manual rather than the "Smoking Guns" section because there are so many variants that have no trace in the NRSV or any other English version of the Bible. That means some of these cases are hard nuts to crack, and you're going to have to put in some overtime if you want to solve them.

In the Case of the Malicious Monarch, all the evidence is in the footnotes. If you read the story in 1 Samuel 11, King Nahash comes across as a really nasty character, and there doesn't seem to be any reason for his nastiness, other than the fact that his name means "snake," which might darken anyone's mood. Nahash was king of the Ammonites, the city-state of present-day Amman, Jordan. He attacked the Israelite city of Jabesh in Gilead, east of the Jordan. When the residents of the city offered to surrender and serve him, he agreed, on one condition—that he be allowed to gouge out everyone's right eye. Like we said, this guy was no choirboy. Given that the sudden loss of everyone's depth perception would have played havoc with traffic patterns citywide, the residents were reluctant to accept this condition. They sent for help to their kinsmen on the west side of the river, and Saul came to their rescue.

The NRSV has more information and a somewhat different slant on Nahash. If you compare its translation with other English versions, you will find an entire additional paragraph at the end of 1 Samuel 10, which makes for a very long verse 27 to conclude the chapter. Again, there's alphabet soup in the textual footnote in the NRSV, which lists Q Ms, and Josephus (an early Jewish historian whose writings include retellings of biblical texts) as supporters of the longer reading, while the MT lacks it. The missing paragraph has been restored based mainly on a Dead Sea Scrolls fragment. It was lost in the first place probably because of the repetition of the name and title "Nahash (king of) the Ammonite(s)," which is found both at the beginning of the added paragraph and at the start of the next chapter. A scribe's eye skipped from one of these to the next one and left out everything in between. The technical term for this mistake that we learned in the academy is "haplography." The reason for accepting the longer text as genuine is because the background it offers helps to make Nahash's behavior against the city of Jabesh more understandable, if not less nasty. He wasn't picking on Jabesh. He had been gouging out the right eyes of all the Israelites in the tribes east of the Jordan. The text doesn't explain his reason for this, but it is pretty easy to figure out. This was disputed land. Nahash viewed it as his and Ammon's, and he was marking Israelites as encroachers. How do you like that for irony? The explanation for why Nahash was plucking out people's eyes was lost in some manuscripts due to the wandering eye of a scribe.

The Case of the Stampeding Swine

The nature of the witnesses in New Testament cases is different. They developed over a shorter period of time, and we have a clearer idea of their relationship to each other and their individual characteristics and tendencies, so it is easier to assess their value as witnesses. At least that's what our colleagues on the NT side of the hall tell us. They've supplied us with a couple of files about valuable variants in celebrated cases. One, which we also discuss in the chapter on the Clue of the Inconsistency, is in Mark 5:1–13. Jesus had crossed the Sea of Galilee and was in the "country of the Gerasenes" (5:1), where he encountered a man who was possessed by demons and had broken the chains and restraints that had been used to try to control him. Jesus asked the man's name and was told, "My name is Legion; for we are many" (5:9). Jesus cast the demons out of the man and into a "great herd of swine" (5:11) "numbering about two thousand" (5:13) that was feeding nearby. The possessed pigs rushed down the bank and into the sea, where they drowned (5:13).

The expression "country of the Gerasenes" is curious. It is not clear how large this region is understood to be. Gerasa (known today as Jerash) was some thirty-five miles away from the Sea of Galilee. The thought of a couple thousand pigs stampeding that far to plunge to their deaths is pretty ridiculous, which is why other manuscripts of Mark have a different location—Gadara, which is still about ten miles from the sea, or Gergesa, which has not been identified for certain but is probably Kursi, on the shore of the sea. But Kursi was likely built as a pilgrimage site centuries later just because of this story. Matthew's version of the story locates this story at Gadara (Matt. 8:28), probably for the same reason.

Gerasa is most likely the original reading, because it is the most difficult one: you can see why someone might move the pigs' point of origin closer to the sea, but it is unlikely that a closer location would be changed to Gerasa, which is so far away. Then the question becomes, What gives with Gerasa? Why was it the location of the story to begin with? The answer may have to do with the name of the possessed man, or more accurately, the demons—Legion. This name immediately invokes images of the Roman army, which was composed of large divisions (six thousand men at full capacity) called "legions." Gerasa was a main city of the Decapolis, the region mostly east of the Jordan River that was culturally Greco-Roman. The Roman Tenth Legion was stationed near Gerasa shortly after 70 CE when Mark may have been written. The Tenth Legion's mascot was a wild boar. So-o-o-o, linking Legion with Gerasa may have been Mark's way of taking a shot at the Roman army, calling them a bunch of demon-filled pigs who subjugated the Jews and played a part in the destruction of Jerusalem in 70 CE. There is a legion of maybes in this theory, but it connects a lot of the dots.

The Case of the Numbered Name

The favorite horror film in the Bible Division is the 1976 version of *The Omen* starring Gregory Peck. His character is a diplomat named Robert Thorn, who secretly adopts a baby boy when his infant son dies moments after being born. He and his wife, who is unaware of the swap, name the kid Damien (what else?). All kinds of foreboding events and unnatural deaths take place around Damien as he grows up that lead the family priest, before he is impaled (of course), to suspect that Damien is the antichrist. When his (adopted) mom is murdered by the new nanny (the one she replaced inexplicably committed suicide), Pop seeks proof of Damien's real identity, and on advice from an archaeologist/antichrist expert, finds it in the number 666 that appears as a birthmark on his scalp. The discovery finally convinces Ambassador Thorn that he must kill Damien, and he hauls the boy, kicking and screaming, into a church for a ceremonial slaying by special dagger at the altar. The cops shoot him just before he plunges the dagger into the kid's heart, and the next thing you know the lad is at the joint funeral of mom and dad with the president of the United States, who has adopted him. The movie ends with a quote from Revelation 13:18, in doctored King James English: "Here is wisdom, let him that hath understanding, count the number of the beast, for it is the number of a man, and *his number is 666.*"

Being identified as the antichrist is kind of a mark of distinction. Everyone who's anyone has been called the antichrist by someone at some time. The club includes popes and presidents, prime ministers, and business magnates. Hitler is a popular candidate, as is Napoleon. Our three favorites for the title, chosen from a top-ten list on the Web (https://listverse.com/2016/01/06/10-individuals-surprisingly-identified-as-the-antichrist/), are: Bill Gates, King Juan Carlos I of Spain, and Danny DeVito. (We want to open an investigation into how Jesus claims the top spot on that list.) If your criterion is just people who are evil or hated, it's really hard to narrow it down to one person. You've got thousands upon thousands—maybe millions upon millions—of possibilities.

That's where the Clue of the Messy Manuscript helps, and it's part of the reason that Bible cops have a consensus nominee—Nero, or more precisely, Caesar Nero, which would be written in Hebrew as (ן)קסר נרו = QSR NRW(N) (the W is a vowel letter; the other vowels aren't written in Hebrew; "Nero" could be written with or without a final N). If you assign numbers to the letters such that the first nine letters of the alphabet are 1–9, the next nine are 10–90 by tens, and the remaining ones go up by hundreds, you get the following values according to the order of the Hebrew alphabet: ו/W = 6, נ/ן/N = 50, ס/S = 60, ק/Q = 100, ר/R = 200. Add those up and you get 666 with the final N, 616 without it. If you check out the textual footnote in the NRSV (and some other versions) for Revelation 13:18, you find: "Other ancient authorities read *six hundred sixteen.*" The reason for the variant is the two possible spellings of Nero's name.

Nero was long dead when Revelation was written (hence his "mortal wound" in 13:12). But he had been such an unpopular emperor that an urban legend was floating around that he would come back like an undead Elvis. Revelation borrowed that legend and cast Nero as the quintessential representative of the evil Roman Empire (à la Darth Vader without the light saber). John, the author of Revelation, was down on Rome because of the images of Roman gods and emperors that were everywhere and because of occasional persecution by Roman authorities in the region of Asia Minor (western Turkey) where the seven churches John was writing to were located (Rev. 1–2). So Nero, who had actively persecuted Christians, went from a terrible, but dead, emperor to an agent of the devil—in popular imagination and media, the antichrist, although that term is never actually used in Revelation. This interpretation shows that Revelation was written to address problems and issues in the first century during the rise of Christianity in the Roman Empire. That eliminates most of the proposals for antichrist that have been put forward in the two thousand years since. This file is a good reminder that the same biblical passage can contain multiple clues, because we also discuss Beast 666 in the chapter on the Clue of the Hidden Meaning.

Pile #2: Ho-hum—minor variants

Witnesses rarely agree completely. Was the subject's jacket navy or black? Did he come in closer to 4:00 or to 5:00? Did he have a cell phone or a portable calculator in his pocket? Did he say, "I'll see you there at 9:00" or "I'm going to hit the back nine"? While scum-sucking lawyers like to play them up at trial to get their dirtbag clients off, most of the time these minor differences don't have much impact on the investigator's job of identifying a suspect and making an arrest. Besides, it's usually easy to tell which witness is more reliable. The lady who works at the fabric store is a better judge of colors than the dude whose socks don't match. The banker with the Rolex beats the ditz whose deposit slip has the wrong date on it. We'll take the word of the kid who was texting while he spoke to us over that of the schoolteacher who doesn't own a cell phone on matters about electronics. And we'll take the nurse's word about what he said over that of the security guard with the hearing aid. We run into these kinds of differences all the time in the Bible Division. That's why this file pile is by far the biggest.

We have three criteria for putting files in this pile. First, the differences have to be minor in size, involving no more than a verse or two. Second, the differences must also be minor in significance; they don't appreciably change the meaning of the text or story. Third, we are pretty sure in every case which reading is the best one and which is the guilty party. Sometimes that's because of the date or quality of the manuscripts, but often it's because of logical reasons behind the changes. The cases we've chosen furnish good examples of these reasons. We've also selected these cases because they relate to well-known passages and stories from the life of Jesus.

Hail, Mary

Let's start with one that will make us unpopular right off the bat. Just remember, we aren't the bad guys here. We're just giving you the results from the annals of Bible investigation. Luke 1:28 reports the greetings of the angel Gabriel to Mary. The wording of the Douay-Rheims version of 1582 is widely known from Christian catechisms. All together now: "Hail [Mary] full of grace, the Lord is with thee: *blessed art thou among women.*" Most English translations done in, say, the last one hundred years—including the New American Bible, which was produced by Roman Catholics—don't contain that last clause, "Blessed are you among women." That's because Douay-Rheims was a translation of the Latin Bible (called the Vulgate), which was itself a translation done in the fourth century by Jerome. The King James Version, which worked from the Greek, also has the clause, but that's because its translators didn't have access to the best manuscripts. The clause is beautiful language, but it merely states the obvious. Mary was chosen as the mother of Jesus; clearly she was blessed among women (and among men).

A Christmas carol

Here's another oldie but goodie from Luke via the King James Version. "Glory to God in the highest, *and on earth peace, good will toward men*" (Luke 2:14). This time Jerome followed a better Greek manuscript, meaning that Douay-Rheims had a better reading as well. The difference is in the last phrase. Is it "peace, good will toward men" or "peace toward men

of good will"? It's a difference of one letter in Greek, and the best manuscripts have "men of good will." You might take issue with us about
whether this changes the meaning. We think the change is negligible
once you recognize that "peace" in the sense used here is a greeting more
than a wish. We also think there are bigger issues at stake—like why
only men are the recipients of the greeting, and if that's not the case,
why it keeps getting translated that way. Also, does "men of good will"
mean people who are innately good willed or people to whom God is
kindly disposed? These are big questions, but they transcend the minor
differences in manuscripts or translation in this verse.

Our Father

Switching to Matthew, the Lord's Prayer has this ending in the KJV: "For
thine is the kingdom, and the power, and the glory, for ever. Amen" (Matt.
6:13). You can tell it's the end of the prayer by the "Amen." The Lord's
Prayer is a very popular passage for recitation and song. (Thank you, Jim
Nabors, a.k.a. Gomer Pyle.) Those renditions always have the long ending.
Bu-u-ut, as you have no doubt already guessed, it's not in the best textual
witnesses. It also exhibits two tendencies of poorer witnesses and readings: (1) they are usually longer or "expansionistic," and (2) they often add
benedictions or doxologies praising God. You might want to keep these
tendencies in mind as we look at the next group of cases.

Missing verses

We each did a training rotation in the missing persons bureau. One of
the things we learned is that a lot of people who go missing don't want
to be found. There are a number of verses in the Bible that are missing if you go by the numbers. But there's another way of looking at it.
They're not missing but add-ons. It only looks like they're missing because the verse numbers are based on inferior manuscripts. The best
witnesses didn't include the "missing" verses in the first place. As Yogi
Berra would've opined: "It's missing 'cause it wasn't there." Here are a
few straightforward cases to give you a taste.

Matthew 17:21: "But this kind does not come out except by prayer
and fasting." You won't find this verse in many English versions. It's

not in the best manuscripts. The main reason for its addition is that essentially the same verse occurs in the parallel story in Mark 9:29. A scribe familiar with that version of the story either intentionally or accidentally added it to Matthew's version.

Matthew 18:11: "For the Son of Man came to save the lost." This verse is also missing in most English versions because, again, it was not in the best manuscripts. It's basically the same as Luke 19:10, although their respective contexts are different. Since it's found elsewhere in the Gospels, nothing is lost by its omission from Matthew.

Matthew 23:14: "Woe to you, scribes and Pharisees, hypocrites! For you devour widows' houses and for the sake of appearance you make long prayers; therefore you will receive the greater condemnation." This additional woe on the scribes and Pharisees is not in the best witnesses to Matthew, but it does appear in Mark 12:40 and Luke 20:47, so it's not lost from the New Testament.

Mark 7:16: "Let anyone with ears to hear listen." Once more, this verse is absent from the best manuscripts. It's another "listen up," in addition to the one Jesus says in verse 14. It's also paralleled by the end of Luke 8:8. So if ever there was an unnecessary verse, it's this one.

Mark 15:28: "And the scripture was fulfilled that says, 'And he was counted among the lawless.'" The verse is a quote from Isaiah 53:12, which early Christians thought referred to Jesus. The quote and reference to its fulfillment occur in Luke 22:37. But according to the best witnesses, it wasn't in Mark 15.

As far as we're concerned, these verses are like those folks who don't want to be found. We're not going to put out an APB on them.

Size doesn't always matter

The shortest reading may not always be the best one. There are some cases where it's really hard to decide.

Take Luke 23:34, for instance: "Then Jesus said, 'Father, forgive them; for they do not know what they are doing.'" This is one of the most famous of Jesus's final sayings. (As we discussed in the Clue of the Inconsistency, Jesus has several sets of last words.) In this location in Luke it appears to be intrusive because it interrupts the statements about what the soldiers did to Jesus—crucifying him (v. 33) and dividing his clothing in the rest of verse 34. Maybe that's why it's not in some ancient manuscripts. Still, the best witnesses do have it here. It might be an addition, but if so, it's probably a very early one.

John 4:9: the second half of this verse in the story of the woman at the well includes the statement "Jews do not share things in common with Samaritans." This explains what lies behind the woman's reaction of surprise that Jesus would speak to her to ask her for a drink of water. Jews and Samaritans did not get along. Not all manuscripts include the explanation, although the best ones do. It is another instance of an interruption of the story. Some English versions put it in parentheses. But again, it's likely a quite early insertion—maybe by the author of the Gospel of John.

Matthew 27:9: this one's not about added or missing text at all. The verse explains the priests' purchase of the Field of Blood with the thirty pieces of silver that Judas had returned to them as the fulfillment of an Old Testament prophecy by Jeremiah. Not all witnesses attribute the prophecy to Jeremiah, though. Quite a few of them have Zechariah's name instead. That's because there's nothing in the book of Jeremiah that sounds remotely close, but it does resemble Zechariah 11:12-13. That means the better reading has to be "Jeremiah," because it's inaccurate. "Zechariah" is a correction. The variant doesn't make sense otherwise, since no one would change the correct reference to an incorrect one.

Maybe it's not quite right to call these three variants insignificant, because they raise questions about authors' (and editors') shaping of the text. The last one even broaches the issue of an author's accuracy. But we think Matthew deserves a skate, especially since he was going by memory and didn't have a copy of the Bible sitting on his coffee table.

Pile #3: Biggies

Some manuscript differences get really messy. We're talking variations in the inclusion or location of entire stories or sections or genres of material. Plus, in some of these cases we're not sure which is the best reading. Around the precinct we call these unsolved mysteries "Jimmy Hoffas." Here are a couple of the most notorious examples.

The ending of Mark

No one is sure how the Gospel of Mark ends. That's because the witnesses attest three different endings to Mark—a surprise ending, a shorter ending, and a longer ending. They're like different directors' cuts of the same movie. The surprise ending is a surprise because it is abrupt. The book just stops in some manuscripts at Mark 16:8, as though the interview tape ran out in the recorder and the detective forgot to flip it over. It looks like a couple of later witnesses noticed the shortfall and tried to make up for it. So there's a shorter ending, which amounts to a single verse, and a longer ending, which runs for a dozen verses. The thing is, the best manuscripts have the surprise ending, so we have to go with it as the best one we have. But you have to admit that it's pretty unlikely the book ended this way originally. Looks like somebody dropped the ball, and the original ending was just lost. Bottom line: this one is going to be in the Unsolved drawer a long time.

The woman caught in adultery

We end on an up note, at least as far as solving cases is concerned. One of the most famous stories in the New Testament is about the woman who was caught red-handed committing adultery and was brought to Jesus for judgment. As has often been observed, it is more than a little curious that she was brought alone, since it takes two to do the adultery tango. Maybe that's part of the reason why Jesus started doodling on the ground and didn't respond right away. The men who brought her pointed out that the law of Moses commanded stoning to death in such a case. When they kept pressing Jesus, he said that the one without fault among them should throw the first stone. They gradually skulked away, leaving the woman alone with Jesus. When he noticed her still standing there, he said, "Has no one condemned you? . . . Neither do I condemn you. Go your way, and from now on do not sin again" (John 8:10-11).

It's a great story with a powerful message: nobody's perfect, so don't judge. You might have guessed from our inclusion of the story in this chapter that it isn't in the best witnesses for John. The best manuscripts don't have the story at all. Many of those that do have it mark it with signs like asterisks to show that it was included secondarily, or they have it in a different location—after John 7:36 or after Luke 21:38 or at the very end of Luke. There's not much doubt that this story was not original to John or the New Testament. It must have been a very popular story among early Christians, and some copyists couldn't resist including it. There are still plenty of open questions about where the story came from, whether it really happened, and how it became attached to John. But questions like those exist for every text in the New Testament. That's why the file on the woman caught in adultery is still active, even if it's not in the Unsolved drawer.

WHY THIS CLUE MATTERS

The Clue of the Messy Manuscript matters because there are no originals ("autographs") of any of the books of the Bible but only generations of handmade copies. Accidental errors and occasional deliberate changes by scribes crept in with every copy, and copies made from copies only compounded the problem. Not all manuscripts are of equal value. Biblical scholars use techniques of textual analysis and comparison to try to reconstruct the original text or at least get as close to it as possible. While many textual variants are minor and insignificant, some are quite important and involve large portions of a book or even a whole book. Such variants can alter a book's content and message. Even small variants can sometimes change the meaning of a passage. This clue reminds us that the composition and transmission of the Bible were a lengthy process that took place long before computers, photocopy machines, and printing presses. It raises issues about the different stages of this process and about the extent to which English translations can and should (or should not) obscure such difficulties.

THE CLUE OF THE MESSY MANUSCRIPT CAN HELP US . . .

1. Be aware of the textual footnotes in English Bibles.
2. Look for variant readings that are listed in the textual footnotes.
3. Understand the abbreviations used in the textual notes and the major witnesses to the text.
4. Recognize the kinds of textual variants that developed in the process of copying and transmission.

5. Carefully consider the differences in meaning that a textual variant may have in a passage.
6. Learn to appreciate the qualitative difference between minor, insignificant variants and variants that appreciably change the significance of a text.

THE CASEBOOK

1. Each of the following verses is absent in the best manuscripts. Examine them and the textual footnotes in your Bible. Try to come up with explanations for why the verse is "missing" from the original and why it was added later. What does the verse add to the passage? How does its absence detract from the passage's meaning, if at all?

> Luke 23:17
> Luke 23:34
> Acts 8:37
> Acts 28:29
> Romans 16:24

2. English Bibles represent the textual problem of the story of the woman caught in adultery in John 7:53–8:11 in different ways. A common way is to place the story in brackets. Some years ago, one prominent version put the story in a footnote but then, because of negative public response, moved it back into the text, in brackets, in later printings. What difference does it make, in your opinion, whether the story is in the footnotes or bracketed in the text? Should it be left out altogether? What would you recommend as the best way to communicate the textual variant regarding this story to Bible readers?

15

The Clue of the

PERSPECTIVAL BIAS

If we've learned anything from our years of sleuthing, it's that everyone has an axe to grind, even the Bible's authors. Make that, *especially* the Bible's authors. If you know what to look for and where to find it, you soon come to realize that there's definitely a lot of agenda pushing going on between the covers of the Good Book. If we're really blunt about it, our time in the trenches has taught us one thing above all else—much of the Bible is propaganda literature. Acknowledging that fact is a *sine qua non* for all serious biblical detective work, and much of our time is spent calling attention to it. Propaganda isn't necessarily misinformation or disinformation (it can take those forms), but it's always information—specifically, information intended to advance a cause or promote a perspective.

The Clue of the Perspectival Bias is found in passages that demonstrate how the Bible functions as propaganda. Of all the clues we've been discussing, this may be the most prevalent one, because the primary aim of virtually every book in the Bible is to convince and persuade its readers about something. At the same time, it's a tricky clue to detect because a particular type of investigation is needed to spot it. This one requires sophisticated interrogation techniques that put the text and its author on the hot seat until they give you the information you're looking for. The purpose of all that grilling is to get at two things—motivation and intent. Why was the text written? What impact is it supposed to have on its readers? In short, what's the author's endgame?

Here's a list of some of the many m.o.'s the Clue of the Perspectival Bias has been known to exhibit: (1) to justify positions; (2) to refute positions; (3) to legitimate practices; (4) to discredit practices; (5) to express theological points; (6) to challenge theological points; (7) to show sympathy or support for an individual or a group; (8) to criticize or condemn an individual or a group; (9) to reflect societal attitudes or norms; and (10) to reject societal attitudes or norms. This is the clue of a thousand faces, so let's say hello to one of them and conduct a quick workshop on how to interrogate.

> Thus both the daughters of Lot *became pregnant by their father*. The firstborn bore a son, and named him Moab; *he is the ancestor of the Moabites* to this day. The younger also bore a son and named him Ben-ammi; *he is the ancestor of the Ammonites* to this day. (Gen. 19:36–38)

> *No Ammonite or Moabite* shall be admitted to the assembly of the LORD. Even to the tenth generation, *none of their descendants shall be admitted to the assembly of the LORD*. (Deut. 23:3)

If you suspect a passage might contain the Clue of the Perspectival Bias, you should always begin with the same question: Is this text meant to have an effect on the beliefs or behavior of the reader? If you answer yes, in all likelihood you've hit upon an instance of the clue. When the question is asked of the two passages above, the answer is a definite yes.

Once you've established that perspectival bias is present, the next step is to determine its nature. Because the clue can take so many different forms, a follow-up question is necessary: What is the text's intended effect on the reader's beliefs or behavior? In the present case, the answer is clear. These passages are meant to cause readers to have a negative view of Moabites and Ammonites. That answer allows us to specify that these examples of the clue are representative of the eighth type listed above, because they criticize and condemn two groups of people. This last step is important because it goes beyond merely identifying the presence of the clue by placing it in a category as a particular type. That allows us to do two things that further the cause of biblical detecting—compare different forms of the clue to one another, and study various examples of the same form. If a text is intended to have an effect on the reader's beliefs or behavior, it is an example of the Clue of the Perspectival Bias.

This clue is quite complex. In the first place, note the origins and genres of the two passages we just looked at. One is part of a narrative about Lot in the book of Genesis that is itself embedded in a larger narrative that relates the events of Abraham's life. The other is a legal text from the book of Deuteronomy that is one of hundreds of laws in the Bible that cover many different areas of human life. The passages are separated by three other biblical books and are found in two completely different styles of writing, and yet they both share a perspectival bias against Ammonites and Moabites. As is the case with other clues, identifying this one demands broad familiarity with all the biblical literature and the ability to make connections between parts of it that otherwise might not appear to have much in common.

> THE CLUE OF THE PERSPECTIVAL BIAS: a text intended to have an effect on the beliefs or behavior of the reader

Also note that the perspective the Clue of the Perspectival Bias espouses is usually not the Bible's only position on the matter in question. It's a clue that always contradicts itself. We can see this regarding the present case in a verse from the end of the book of Ruth: "The women of the neighborhood gave him a name, saying, 'A son has been born to Naomi.' They named him Obed; he became the father of Jesse, the father of David" (Ruth 4:17). The child mentioned here is actually the son of Ruth, not Naomi, her mother-in-law, and throughout the book Ruth is regularly referred to as a Moabite. In other words, the great-grandmother of King David was a Moabite, which puts him well within the ten-generation range that excludes one from membership in the assembly of the Lord according to the book of Deuteronomy. What this example shows is that the Bible often contains multiple perspectives on the same issue that compete with one another but rarely negate each other. So, for the author of Ruth it's no big deal that David has Moabite blood coursing through his veins, while for the writer of Deuteronomy that's cause for him to step down from the throne, turn in his crown, and go back to his own people.

There's something else that makes this clue different from the others we've been tracking, and it has to do with authorship. The author personifies or represents a position that was likely shared by a group or circle of people. The writer or writers of the two above passages, from Genesis and Deuteronomy, were undoubtedly among those who had very little use for Ammonites and Moabites. In that sense, the Clue of the Perspectival Bias often reflects the thinking of a group of like-minded individuals. Their precise identities remain unknown, but the evidence from the clues they've left behind allows us to piece together some details about what membership in the group would have entailed. In this chapter we will study the mind-sets and tendencies of some of the Bible's most prominent and well-documented groups.

The priestly perspective

For a long time biblical detectives have been aware of the existence of a perspective in the Hebrew Bible that strongly pushes a priestly agenda. This perspective shows a keen interest in the nuts and bolts of organized religion but also exhibits a number of other quirks that set it apart from other biblical perspectives. It's likely that most of its members were priests themselves, but we should assume that the group included non-priest sympathizers who supported the views and propaganda the priestly class espoused. Here are some of the characteristics of this perspective you should keep in mind when you look for evidence of it.

Hangouts

The majority of the Pentateuch has come under the influence of the priestly perspective. Its impact on Deuteronomy, the last work in the Pentateuch, has not been as significant because that book has its own perspective that will be discussed in detail below. Other parts of the Bible that show evidence of priestly leanings include Chronicles and a few of the books of the prophets, some of whom acknowledge their own connections to the priesthood: "The words of Jeremiah son of Hilkiah, of the priests who were in Anathoth in the land of Benjamin, to whom the word of the LORD came in the days of King Josiah son of Amon of Judah, in the thirteenth year of his reign" (Jer. 1:1–2; see also Ezek. 1:2–3).

Aaron

The most prominent figure of the priestly perspective is Aaron, the brother of Moses. His leadership in it is unquestioned, and whenever Aaron is mentioned by name in the Bible, you can be sure the passage has a pro-priestly agenda. (A rare exception is in the golden calf story of Exodus 32, where he acts in an unpriestly way.) Aaron is such a central figure because the Bible presents him as the first priest of the Israelites, and you can read the description of his ordination ceremony in Leviticus 8 (cf. Exod. 29). His sons are also ordained with him in that chapter, and so all Aaron's offspring are likewise closely tied to this perspective (Exod. 28:1).

Interests and tendencies

This group is big into ceremonies and pageantry. As might be expected, the priestly perspective promotes all things related to institutionalized religion, especially if they somehow involve priests and religious leaders. So whenever you come across references to rituals, feasts, practices, and concepts associated with the Israelite religious practice, it's a safe bet you've found the Clue of the Perspectival Bias. This means that significant portions of the books of Genesis, Exodus, Leviticus, and Numbers express priestly propaganda because they all discuss these matters in some detail. This bias makes its presence known early because the first creation story in the Bible is priestly in nature due to its explanation of the origin of the Sabbath rest.

> And on the seventh day God finished the work that he had done, and he rested on the seventh day from all the work that he had done. So *God blessed the seventh day and hallowed it*, because on it God rested from all the work that he had done in creation. (Gen. 2:2-3)

> This is my *covenant*, which you shall keep, between me and you and your offspring after you: Every male among you shall be *circumcised*. (Gen. 17:10)

> This day shall be a day of remembrance for you. You shall celebrate it as a *festival* to the LORD; throughout your generations *you shall observe it as a perpetual ordinance*. (Exod. 12:14)

You shall observe *the festival of weeks*, the first fruits of wheat harvest, and *the festival of ingathering* at the turn of the year. (Exod. 34:22)

At the beginnings of your months you shall *offer a burnt offering* to the LORD: two young bulls, one ram, seven male lambs a year old without blemish. (Num. 28:11)

The temple has pride of place in the priestly perspective, and every nook and cranny of the building is measured and described in painstaking detail. A set of precise blueprints can be seen in a lengthy section at the end of the book of Ezekiel the priest, when he has a vision of the postexilic rebuilt temple (Ezek. 40-47). The same can be said of the tabernacle, a temporary structure that was the meeting place for God and the people while they wandered through the wilderness for forty years. Lengthy sections of the book of Exodus lay out all the specifics regarding its construction and furnishings, and these all come from priestly writers (Exod. 25-31).

Another special preoccupation of this group is record keeping. If something is listed, itemized, or otherwise catalogued for posterity in the Bible, there's a good chance the priests had a hand in it. *"These are the descendants* of Noah's sons, Shem, Ham, and Japheth; children were born to them after the flood" (Gen. 10:1). Passages that start this way, followed by a list of names, exemplify the priestly interest in genealogies. That's also the case with settlement records, references to censuses, and real estate transactions, like the one that describes Abraham's purchase of the plot of land on which he buried his wife Sarah (Gen. 23:16). Leviticus 6 is a listing of various types of sacrifices, a topic that would have been near and dear to the priests' hearts—the guilt offering (vv. 1-7), the burnt offering (vv. 8-13), the grain offering (vv. 14-18), the anointing offering (vv. 19-23), and the sin offering (vv. 24-30). The priests made sure all this information entered the public record so there would be no confusion for future generations.

Another trait of the priestly perspective is a preoccupation with matters of purity and cleanliness. These authors warn of the dangers of contact with blood, unclean foods, impure skin diseases, bodily emissions, and other things that can lead to contamination, so they maintain a strict separation between what is clean and what is unclean. "If a man has an emission of semen, he shall *bathe* his whole body in water, and be *unclean* until the evening. Everything made of cloth or of skin on which the semen falls shall be *washed with water*, and be *unclean* until the evening" (Lev. 15:16–17).

Favorite words/expressions

Most perspectives have their own distinct vocabulary that can help identify them more easily, and here are some of the most common words and phrases used by members of the priestly group. The presence of one of these in a passage does not guarantee that it is expressing the priestly perspective, but if other indications in the text point in that direction, the use of this terminology supports that identification.

be fruitful and multiply
bless
chieftain
circumcision
clean/unclean
congregation
covenant
descendants/generations
El-Shaddai as a name for God (often translated "God Almighty")
festival/feast
glory of God
holy
priest
Sabbath
sacrifice
separate
tabernacle
temple

Agenda

The priestly perspective's entire *raison d'être* is to affirm and validate any and all aspects of the institutionalized religion of the Israelites organized around worship of Yahweh. If your answer to the question

"What is the text's intended effect on the reader's beliefs or behavior?" includes such affirmation or validation, then you have uncovered the Clue of the Perspectival Bias in its priestly form. Knowing how this agenda is articulated is important because it reveals something about the authors' rhetorical strategy. According to the Bible, many of Israel's religious beliefs and practices began as instructions or laws that came directly from God during the formative years of the community. Careful investigative work by many generations of biblical detectives has demonstrated that in fact that religious system comes from much later time periods, but its origin has been relocated to the distant past by the biblical authors in order to give it more legitimacy through the divine stamp of approval.

The Deuteronomistic perspective

Deuteronomy is the fifth book of the Bible and one that most people are not very familiar with. This is understandable, because Deuteronomy is not very interesting or exciting to read, but it is an extremely influential book that gave birth to what is arguably the most dominant perspective in the Bible.

Hangouts

The Deuteronomistic group has left its mark on pretty much every corner of the Bible, with most books either endorsing the group's views or calling them into question, but the perspective is more obvious in some places than in others. Deuteronomy is its fountainhead, and it has been particularly influential on the six books that follow it (Joshua through 2 Kings), which have been so profoundly shaped by its message that they're collectively called the "Deuteronomistic History." Jeremiah is another biblical work associated with this perspective, with some claiming that Deuteronomy had a significant influence on the message and shape of the prophet's book.

Moses, Josiah, and Jesus

The book of Deuteronomy comprises a set of farewell speeches that Moses gives to the Israelite people prior to their entry into the promised land. For reasons that aren't completely clear (it's a famous unsolved mystery of the Bible), God denied Moses himself entry into the land, and the book closes with an account of his death on Mount Nebo as he scans the expanse of the land God has given the people (Deut. 34:1-8). Because the book's contents are ostensibly a record of his words, Moses is the person most closely connected to the Deuteronomistic perspective.

Another person biblical detectives commonly associate with this perspective, but who is relatively unknown to many readers, is Josiah, the king of Judah in the period 640-609 BCE. An account of his reign in 2 Kings 22-23 refers to a discovery during his time that had a tremendous impact on Israelite religion. While the temple in Jerusalem was being renovated, a book was discovered and brought to the king. The text refers to it as "the book of the law," and upon reading it Josiah realized that for a long time the people had been disobeying God because they were not worshiping in conformance with the divine will as outlined in the book. This caused Josiah to initiate a reform that introduced new religious practices that were in line with what was stated in the book of the law. The book is not identified in the story, but because the changes Josiah introduced and the theology he promoted adhere so closely to the message of Deuteronomy, it was probably somehow related to it. It makes a great story, but that's probably all it is, because it follows the outline of similar traditions from the ancient world in which the discovery of a previously unknown text causes a ruler to take things in a new direction. Even if it didn't happen exactly as 2 Kings 22 reports, the "discovery" of the book during his time establishes a strong link between Josiah and Deuteronomy.

Many other biblical characters are indirectly connected to the Deuteronomistic perspective because they buy into it even if they don't say so specifically. One who directly acknowledges this connection is Jesus, who quotes from or alludes to Deuteronomy on a number of occasions. In Mark, when he's asked what the greatest commandment is, Jesus recites two verses from Deuteronomy (6:4-5), and then adds another one from Leviticus for good measure (19:18). "Jesus answered, 'The first is, *"Hear, O Israel: the Lord our God, the Lord is one; you shall love the Lord your*

God with all your heart, and with all your soul, and with all your mind, and with all your strength." The second is this, *"'You shall love your neighbor as yourself.'* There is no other commandment greater than these" (Mark 12:29–31).

Interests and tendencies

Just as the priestly perspective is concerned with aspects of institution-alized religion, the Deuteronomistic perspective expresses interest in legal matters. Its focus on the law is the primary reason why the Deu-teronomistic perspective plays such a prominent role within the biblical canon. This is so because observance of the law came to be viewed as the primary way fidelity to the covenantal relationship between God and the people was expressed. *"If you heed these ordinances,* by diligently observing them, *the* LORD *your God will maintain with you the covenant* loyalty that he swore to your ancestors" (Deut. 7:12). This led to a *quid pro quo* theology in which those who follow the law are rewarded and those who choose not to follow it are punished. This reward-and-punishment understanding of the law and covenant is a defining trait of the Deuter-onomistic perspective. It's also the theological underpinning of virtually all the books of the prophets, which shows how widespread affiliation with this group is among the Bible's authors.

If a text exhibits this reward/punishment understanding of the way things work, it has been influenced by the Deuteronomistic perspective. It turns up often in the biblical literature, and it's the dominant way covenant is understood. You can see it in Job, who can't understand why he's suffering because he didn't do anything to deserve it. You can see it in Jonah, who struggles to accept that foreigners like the Ninevites can be accepted by God even though they're not part of the covenant community. You can find the perspective in the book of Proverbs, with its cause-and-effect view of life that says good people are rewarded and bad ones are punished. Some books challenge the Deuteronomistic per-spective and argue that it doesn't reflect the way the world works—like Qoheleth: "Again I saw that under the sun the race is not to the swift, nor the battle to the strong, nor bread to the wise, nor riches to the intelligent, nor favor to the skillful; but *time and chance happen to them all"* (Eccles. 9:11). While many might agree with that sentiment, it still remains a minority viewpoint within the Bible.

Other distinctive traits signal the presence of this perspective. The concept of covenant is internalized because it's no longer something that is primarily thought of in external terms. "Moreover, the LORD your God will *circumcise your heart* and the heart of your descendants, so that you will love the LORD your God with all your heart and with all your soul, in order that you may live" (Deut. 30:6). This had an influence on how Jeremiah reimagined the idea of covenant as an internal law (Jer. 31:33; cf. Ezek. 11:19). Another characteristic of the Deuteronomistic perspective is centralization, the idea that the temple in Jerusalem is the only proper place to bring sacrificial offerings to God. "But only at *the place that the LORD will choose* in one of your tribes—there you shall offer your burnt offerings and there you shall do everything I command you" (Deut. 12:14; cf. vv. 5, 11, 18, 21, 26). References to "this place" and "the place that God will choose" in contexts related to worship are clear indications of this form of the Clue of the Perspectival Bias. On the flip side of these passages are those that condemn shrines other than the Jerusalem temple and those that prohibit the worship of other gods.

The thematic concerns of the Deuteronomistic perspective just mentioned—the law, the system of reward and punishment, centralization of the cult in Jerusalem, the prohibition against worshiping other gods, as well as others—were used as the lens through which a large portion of the history of Israel was recounted. The resulting body of literature, known as the Deuteronomistic History, provides an overview of the approximately five-hundred-year period between the entry into the land and the exile that is presented in the books of Joshua, Judges, 1 and 2 Samuel, and 1 and 2 Kings.

We refer to it as a history, but it would be more accurate to call it propaganda because it is an exercise in theological interpretation rather than objective reporting. It's possible that some of the events recounted in the Deuteronomistic History are based on actual occurrences, but the presentation has been so heavily theologized that their historical significance is minimal. It doesn't take a great deal of detective work to discern the pattern used to shape how the story is told, because it's a decidedly Deuteronomistic one—prosperity and success are the result of remaining faithful to God, while failure and hard times stem from the refusal to obey the divine will. It's a refrain that's repeated over and over again, and every king's time on the throne is evaluated on the basis of his adherence to the law. The two options can be seen in the assessments of the reigns of Nadab and Amaziah, where the phrases in italics are the formulas commonly used to give a thumbs-up or thumbs-down to each ruler.

> Nadab son of Jeroboam began to reign over Israel in the second year of King Asa of Judah; he reigned over Israel two years. *He did what was evil in the sight of the Lord*, walking in the way of his ancestor and in the sin that he caused Israel to commit. (1 Kings 15:25–26)

> In the second year of King Joash son of Joahaz of Israel, King Amaziah son of Joash of Judah, began to reign. He was twenty-five years old when he began to reign, and he reigned twenty-nine years in Jerusalem. His mother's name was Jehoaddin of Jerusalem. *He did what was right in the sight of the Lord*, yet not like his ancestor David; in all things he did as his father Joash had done. (2 Kings 14:1–3)

Favorite words/expressions

commandments
covenant
decrees
did what was evil in the sight of the Lord
did what was right in the sight of the Lord
laws
Listen, O Israel
so that you may live
statutes
stipulations
that you may fare well upon the land
the place God will choose
this place
to go after/turn to/worship other gods
Yahweh your God

Agenda

The main aim of the Deuteronomistic perspective is to put forward an understanding of the covenant with Yahweh that centers on observance of the law. According to this perspective, the outcome of one's adherence or lack of adherence to the law is predictable and invariable—those who follow it will be rewarded, and those who do not will be punished. If during an interrogation your answer to the question "What is the text's intended effect on the reader's beliefs or behavior?" supports this understanding of the covenant and the purpose of the law, then you have uncovered an example of the Clue of the Perspectival Bias that has been left behind by the Deuteronomistic group.

The Davidic perspective

This perspective is different from the previous two in that its interest is in a single individual who is one of the Bible's central figures—King David. He was the founder of a political dynasty that lasted for more than four centuries, and the story of how it got started could have been ripped from today's headlines. It has something for everyone—political intrigue, psychological drama, sexual escapades, dysfunctional families, and more. This perspective explains and justifies the arc of David's career, and it can best be seen by reading against the grain and between the lines.

Hangouts

The Davidic perspective is most clearly seen in the latter part of the Deuteronomistic History. To be precise, David arrives on the scene in 1 Samuel 16 and continues as the main character until the report of his death in 1 Kings 2. That's a string of forty-two chapters in which he carries the story, but the biblical detective's work isn't limited to just the account of David's life. His specter casts a long shadow over the rest of the Deuteronomistic History thanks to the editorial efforts of those who wished to burnish his legacy. During the remaining forty-five chapters that recount the history of the monarchy, David's name is frequently mentioned, and it usually serves the agenda of the perspective by presenting him as the gold standard for kingship against which all subsequent rulers are measured.

David's life is also the subject of 1 Chronicles 11–29, part of a book that comes from a later time and presents a more streamlined version of the events. Chronicles has its own Davidic perspective, but because it's different from that of the Deuteronomistic History, we won't discuss it in detail here. It's not getting a free pass, though, because you'll have the opportunity to interrogate it on your own in the Casebook section at the end of the chapter. Those responsible for his story in Samuel present David as their leader and hero, but the David 2.0 of Chronicles who is the creation of later authors is a more idealized version of his former self because all the rough spots have been smoothed out and the negative elements removed.

Psalms also has a connection to David. Seventy-three (nearly one-half) of the psalms in the collection mention him by name in their superscriptions, and thirteen of those refer to events in his life (Pss. 3; 7; 18; 34; 51; 52; 54; 56; 57; 59; 60; 63; 142). But these titles are late additions to the text and really don't have anything to contribute to an investigation of the Davidic perspective. In addition, David is mentioned a number of times in the New Testament. The Gospel of Matthew gives Jesus the messianic title "Son of David" on several occasions (Matt. 9:27; 12:22–23; 15:22; 20:30–31; 21:9, 15), and in the book of Revelation Jesus refers to himself as the "descendant of David" (Rev. 22:16).

Known acquaintances of David

Besides his nemesis Goliath (1 Sam. 17), several other characters interact with David frequently throughout the story. His predecessor as king was Saul, who is presented as a paranoid and insecure leader, and he and David had a love-hate relationship that was dominated more by the latter, as Saul tried to take David's life on more than one occasion (1 Sam. 18–19). Two of Saul's children were especially close to David. He married Saul's daughter Michal, but their union was not a particularly happy one and did not produce any children (2 Sam. 6). In contrast, David's relationship with Saul's son Jonathan was marked by deep affection. At Jonathan's death David referred to him as his beloved and said that their love for one another exceeded that between a man and a woman (2 Sam. 1). Another of David's wives was Bathsheba, and the story of how they got together is one full of adultery, deception, and murder that puts the king in a most unflattering light (2 Sam. 11). Finally, the prophet Nathan makes two important appearances in the story as an intermediary who delivers messages to David from God (2 Sam. 7; 12).

Interests and tendencies

The David story in Samuel and Kings goes to great lengths to present its main character as a man above reproach who assumed the office of king in an honest and legitimate way. Two themes are revisited throughout the narrative to establish David's innocence: (1) God is in David's corner, and (2) David is in Saul's corner. Soon after meeting him for the first time, the reader is reminded several times that David has the divine stamp of approval. "David had success in all his undertakings; *for the* LORD *was with him*" (1 Sam. 18:14; cf. 18:12, 28). At key points in the story David consults God about military strategy or what his next move should be, and each time the deity gives him advice that leads to further success. "David inquired of the LORD, '*Shall I go up against the Philistines? Will you give them into my hand?*' The LORD said to David, '*Go up; for I will certainly give the Philistines into your hand*'" (2 Sam. 5:19; cf. 1 Sam. 23:2–4; 30:8; 2 Sam. 2:1; 5:23–24; 21:1). God is behind David's military victories and does not allow him to be captured by Saul. "David remained in the strongholds in the wilderness, in the hill country of the Wilderness of Ziph. *Saul sought him every day, but the* LORD *did not give him into his hand*" (1 Sam. 23:14; cf. 2 Sam. 8:6, 14).

One episode in his story above all others demonstrates the divine favoritism that David enjoyed. Read 2 Samuel 7. This chapter is sometimes referred to as "the Davidic Covenant" because in it God establishes a special relationship with David and his offspring, who are guaranteed permanent protection and support. "Your house and *your kingdom shall be made sure forever before me; your throne shall be established forever*" (2 Sam. 7:16). The passage offers a theological explanation for why the dynasty that began with David lasted so long—God's promise to him was fulfilled. As with other cases we've investigated, we shouldn't read this as history. This chapter was written long after the time of the purported events it is describing, and its main purpose is theological rather than historical.

In addition to God's support of David, we have David's support of Saul. The story goes to great lengths to show that David was devoid of any political ambition and that he played absolutely no role in his own ascent to power. On two occasions David has the opportunity to kill Saul, but he chooses not to, once when Saul enters a cave where David is hiding (1 Sam. 24:1-22) and another time when David goes into Saul's camp while he and his men are sleeping (1 Sam. 26:1-25). If he truly did want to be king, those were golden opportunities to seize the brass ring, but he declined, and each time he called attention to Saul's status by referring to him as "the Lord's anointed." When Saul loses his life in battle, David is overcome with grief and utters a long poem of lament to express his anguish (2 Sam. 1:1-27). He engages in all the typical rituals of mourning by weeping, tearing his garment, and fasting, and two more times in this episode he describes Saul as "the Lord's anointed."

David behaves in a similar way regarding Saul's offspring and does not treat them as potential political rivals. When two men assassinate Saul's son and bring his severed head to David, he has the men killed and doesn't rejoice over the death of the man who could challenge him for the throne (2 Sam. 4:1-12). David is equally respectful to the members of the next generation of Saul's line when he restores the family property to Saul's grandson and assures him that he will always have a place at the king's table (2 Sam. 9:1-13). All these parts of the story that demonstrate David's innocence and lack of political ambition are very lengthy and detailed, with each one taking up an entire chapter.

Favorite words/expressions

The Davidic group is never at a loss for words to extoll David and hold him up as the perfect king, but they do not tend to repeat themselves by using the same vocabulary to convey their message. Consequently, there isn't a stock set of words or phrases that are commonly used in support of the Davidic perspective.

Agenda

The two aspects of his story—God's endorsement of David and David's endorsement of Saul—work hand in hand to suggest that David's ascent to the throne was God's doing rather than his own. If your answer to the question "What is the text's intended effect on the reader's beliefs or behavior?" supports this view of how David became king, then you've found the Clue of the Perspectival Bias in its Davidic form.

Maybe detectives are just naturally suspicious types, but it doesn't quite pass the smell test for us. We'll never be able to prove it, but we're just not convinced David was the choirboy he's made out to be. For one thing, he shows several dark sides in his relationship with Bathsheba (2 Sam. 11) when he forces himself on a woman who's married to another man and then has the husband (who's out fighting David's battle for him) bumped off to cover his tracks. If that's the way he acted when he had all the power, what would he have done to reach the top of the heap? And then there's the issue of David's swan song. The deathbed scene in 1 Kings 2 reports his final words of advice to his son Solomon. It starts off on a pious note about following the law, and you don't have to look too hard to find the Deuteronomistic perspective in the chapter's first four verses. But then David's tone changes and he advises Solomon about how to take care of some unfinished business, including settling the score with a few enemies he had made over the years. To the very end, the man after God's own heart was also looking after his own best interests. Which one was the real David? We think probably both.

The Pauline perspective

The apostle Paul (a.k.a. Saul of Tarsus) was such an influential figure that he's sometimes referred to as the second founder of Christianity. He's earned that title primarily because in his writings he does something the gospel authors rarely do; they mostly describe the events of Jesus's life and leave it at that, but Paul attempts to explain and interpret what those events mean. He is therefore the rare New Testament author who explicitly addresses the issue of Jesus's significance. The Pauline perspective on Jesus is complex, and we can't possibly cover it all here, so we'll limit ourselves to an overview of some of the key points of his Christology as presented in one of his most important letters. It goes without saying that this perspective is different from the others we've considered, because we know for certain the identity of the author of the texts in which it is found. This means the writings that articulate the Pauline perspective are not the products of a group or movement, unlike those associated with the other three perspectives we discussed.

One of the biggest issues the early Christian community had to deal with concerned the relationship between Jewish Christians and gentile Christians, and the sources indicate that the community's leaders didn't always agree with each other on the matter and factions developed over it. Paul refers to this controversy in one of his letters when he rebukes Peter for caving in to those telling him not to eat with gentiles, even though that had been his practice previously (Gal. 2:11–14). We're not sure exactly how the situation was resolved, but the episode (as well as other statements he makes in his writings) indicates that Paul was clearly in the corner of those who believed Jewish and gentile Christians should fully interact with one another.

Hangouts

Thirteen of the twenty-seven works in the New Testament claim Paul as their author, but biblical detectives have determined that nearly one-half of them are forgeries. Since original copies of the letters don't exist, this conclusion wasn't arrived at through handwriting analysis. Based on a comparative study of the vocabulary they use, the themes they treat, and the Christologies they contain, the general consensus is that only seven of the letters actually come from Paul himself—1 Thessalonians, Galatians, 1 Corinthians, Philippians, Philemon, 2 Corinthians, and Romans (that's the likely order in which they were written).

Paul rarely talks about himself in these works, so beyond his occasional autobiographical references it's hard to get a good feel for who he was. That gap appears to be filled in another New Testament book, because Paul is the main character throughout the second half of the Acts of the Apostles, where his travels and attempts to spread the message of Christianity are documented in some detail (Acts 13–28). But careful investigative work on the relationship between the authentic letters of Paul and the Paul of Acts has determined that the latter book is not a reliable source for information about him and should therefore be used cautiously, if at all. This means that any attempt to piece together the Pauline perspective should be based only on the information provided in the seven undisputed letters listed above, because what he says about Jesus in Acts might not be an accurate reflection of what Paul himself actually thought.

Known acquaintances of Paul

Paul mentions many people by name in his letters, especially in their final sections when he offers his greetings to various individuals living in the place he is writing to. In most cases, it's hard to know the precise nature of Paul's relationship with those individuals and how well he knew them. Nonetheless, we can identify three people who were among his closest associates because Paul makes it clear that he spent quite a bit of time with them: Timothy, Titus, and Barnabas. These three are also mentioned in Acts as people who accompanied Paul on his journeys, and his references to them in his own letters validate the claim Acts makes that Paul knew them.

> But Timothy's worth you know, how like a son with a father he has served with me in the work of the gospel. (Phil. 2:22)

> Then after fourteen years I went up again to Jerusalem with Barnabas, taking Titus along with me. (Gal. 2:1)

Interests and tendencies

As the last of his writings, Paul's letter to the Romans contains the most fully developed expression of his Christology. It's therefore the perfect writing for a biblical sleuth to sift through in the search for examples of the Clue of the Perspectival Bias. Here we identify a few that have been particularly influential in shaping Christian views about the meaning of Jesus's life and death. Paul is fairly uninterested in the details of that life, because he rarely quotes from Jesus's teachings or recounts anything he did. It wasn't Jesus's words or works that demonstrated his divinity for Paul, but rather what happened after his death. "The gospel concerning his Son, who was descended from David according to the flesh and was *declared to be Son of God* with power according to the spirit of holiness *by resurrection from the dead,* Jesus Christ our Lord" (Rom. 1:3-4).

In Paul's view, there was a sacrificial dimension to Jesus's death that not only made him divine but also had an effect on the lives of others. He taught that all it takes for someone to be saved is to believe in Jesus, and this formed the basis of his well-known concept known as "justification by faith." This idea undercut one of the foundational elements of

Judaism because it challenged the importance of obeying the law as the means to salvation. *"They are now justified by his grace as a gift*, through the redemption that is in Christ Jesus, *whom God put forward as a sacrifice of atonement by his blood*, effective through faith. He did this to show his righteousness, because in his divine forbearance he had passed over the sins previously committed; it was to prove at the present time that he himself is righteous and that *he justifies the one who has faith in Jesus"* (Rom. 3:24–26). This understanding of Jesus's death as sacrificial gives it an expiatory quality for Paul that suggests that humanity is essentially flawed and imperfect. "For while we were still weak, at the right time *Christ died for the ungodly.* Indeed, rarely will anyone die for a righteous person—though perhaps for a good person someone might actually dare to die. But God proves his love for us in that *while we still were sinners Christ died for us"* (Rom. 5:6–8).

This has universal implications for Paul, who believes Jesus's death reversed the negative effect of Adam's sin that had plagued humanity since the beginning of time. "Therefore just as one man's trespass led to condemnation for all, so *one man's act of righteousness leads to justification and life for all"* (Rom. 5:18). According to Paul, the solution to the problem caused by the first human being is for Christians to participate in the death of Jesus through baptism so that they might overcome death the way he did. "For if we have been united with him in a death like his, *we will certainly be united with him in a resurrection like his"* (Rom. 6:5).

This means that Jesus resides in his followers, who have conquered death and can live a Spirit-filled existence. "But if *Christ is in you*, though the body is dead because of sin, the Spirit is life because of righteousness. If the Spirit of him who raised Jesus from the dead dwells in you, *he who raised Christ from the dead will give life to your mortal bodies also through his Spirit that dwells in you"* (Rom. 8:10–11). This indwelling is reciprocal because just as Jesus resides in them, his followers also reside in him, a belief that gave rise to Paul's idea of the church as the body of Christ in which no member is superior and all are dependent upon one another. "For as in one body we have many members, and not all the members have the same function, so *we, who are many, are one body in Christ*, and individually we are members one of another" (Rom. 12:4–5).

These passages help us sketch out the general outline of the Pauline perspective on the meaning of Jesus's death—it was a sacrifice that makes possible the salvation of those who have faith in him by uniting themselves with him to form a community of believers.

Favorite words/expressions

body of Christ
Christ died for us
dying in Christ
living in Christ
justification by faith
sacrifice of atonement

Agenda

The primary purpose of the Pauline perspective is to give meaning to the events of Jesus's life. If in reading one of his writings your answer to the question "What is the text's intended effect on the reader's beliefs or behavior?" indicates that it is trying to offer such a meaning, then you have found an example of the Clue of the Perspectival Bias in its Pauline guise. We have considered only one dimension of Paul's Christology as found in just one source, but the presence of the clue is still clear and unmistakable. The Pauline perspective is typically an easy one to identify because of the style of writing it's presented in—Paul doesn't communicate via narratives, but in letters whose sole purpose is to persuade readers about the truth of their messages. This is the ideal medium for propaganda, because a letter writer can be extremely blunt and get right to the point.

One final aspect of the Pauline perspective concerns how incredibly influential it has been. Because the Gospels simply report the events of Jesus's life and hardly ever explicitly interpret them, the Christian community has relied on Paul's writings to inform their understanding of what those events mean. Christians are indebted to Paul for such concepts as justification by faith, Jesus's sacrificial death, the church as the body of Christ, and many others. If Paul hadn't written his letters, those ideas might not exist today and Christianity would look very different. That shows us the power of a perspective.

WHY THIS CLUE MATTERS

The Clue of the Perspectival Bias is important for two main reasons. In the first place, it forces us to acknowledge something about the biblical writings that most readers either don't know or would rather not admit—that their authors had agendas and tried to influence how their readers thought and behaved. The idea of the Bible as propaganda literature is contrary to the way most people are taught to view the text, but once we get used to thinking about it in those terms, it becomes clear that there may not be a better way to describe the Bible. A second reason why this clue is important is that the authors have often been quite successful at pushing those agendas and getting readers to accept their propaganda. This clue lets us identify and learn from the rhetorical techniques and strategies the authors employed to achieve that success rate, and that knowledge will come in handy when we encounter other biblical perspectives.

THE CLUE OF THE PERSPECTIVAL BIAS CAN HELP US . . .

1. Discover the different perspectives found in the biblical literature.
2. Recognize that the Bible contains propaganda.
3. Become aware of the ways biblical authors attempt to persuade their readers.
4. Realize that biblical authors often represent groups that share their views.
5. Develop a set of skills to identify how texts influence our beliefs and behavior.
6. Think more critically about how and why the Bible was written.

THE CASEBOOK

1. Find examples of the priestly perspective in the following chapters:

   Exodus 35-40
   Joshua 3
   Joshua 6

2. Find examples of the Deuteronomistic perspective in the following chapters:

> Deuteronomy 12–26
> Judges 1–12
> 1 Kings 12–16

3. Find examples of the Davidic perspective in the following chapters:

> 1 Samuel 18–20
> 2 Samuel 9
> 1 Chronicles 11–29

4. Find examples of the Pauline perspective in the following chapters:

> 1 Corinthians 1
> Philippians 2
> 1 Thessalonians 4

A Postmortem Postscript

Our examination of the biblical body of literature has come to an end, and now that you've strolled through some of its most notorious neighborhoods, you're prepared to embark on your own career as a Bible detective. Congratulations! Despite its advanced age, the corpus is in remarkably good shape, so it should be around for many generations of sleuths to come. That's what makes this crime scene and the body it contains so unusual—they will long outlive the people who investigate them. Puts things in perspective, doesn't it? Each of us is one point in a long blue line that stretches as far as the eye can see in either direction, and we each have a limited amount of time to snoop around before handing off the baton to the next person in line. That's a big reason why teamwork is so important in Bible detective work. In this manual we've tried to explain how sleuths of the past and present have used clues to solve many mysteries of the biblical text, but many more cases are waiting to be cracked by tomorrow's Bible cops. Your contribution to the future of biblical police work will be a significant one as long as you keep things in perspective and have the big picture in mind. Crime fiction writer Ross Macdonald (a.k.a. Kenneth Millar) said it best with his observation, "The detective's job is to seek justice for the corpse. It's the corpse's story, first and foremost." That's a fitting motto for Bible detectives everywhere, and one we leave you with as you join our ranks. May justice be served!

Further Reading

The Bible

We recommend the following books that provide helpful overviews of the biblical literature and some of the ways it can be studied.

Carr, David M., and Colleen M. Conway. *An Introduction to the Bible: Sacred Texts and Imperial Contexts*. Malden, MA: Wiley-Blackwell, 2010.

Carvalho, Corrine L. *Primer on Biblical Methods*. Winona, MN: Anselm Academic, 2009.

Kugler, Robert, and Patrick Hartin. *An Introduction to the Bible*. Grand Rapids: Eerdmans, 2009.

McKenzie, Steven L., and John Kaltner. *New Meanings for Ancient Texts: Recent Approaches to Biblical Criticisms and Their Applications*. Louisville: Westminster John Knox, 2013.

The Bible and detective work

These are creative attempts to engage with the Bible from the detective angle, but we're not ready to give expert testimony in a court of law on the quality of their scholarship.

Bailey, Len. *Sherlock Holmes and the Needle's Eye: The World's Greatest Detective Tackles the Bible's Ultimate Mysteries*. Nashville: Nelson, 2013. A time-traveling Holmes and Watson try to solve ten mysteries that are found in the pages of the Bible.

Blyth, Caroline, and Alison Jack, editors. *The Bible in Crime Fiction and Drama: Murderous Texts*. London/New York: T & T Clark, 2019. A set of essays written by Bible scholars, literary critics, media experts, and criminologists that discuss how crime narratives implicitly and explicitly make reference to biblical texts.

Kalas, J. Ellsworth. *Detective Stories from the Bible*. Nashville: Abingdon, 2009. Written by a former seminary president, this book investigates some of the "life mysteries" contained in the Bible.

Smith, Carol. *The Bible Detective: Mixed-Up Stories to Test Your Bible Knowledge*. Ulrichsville, OH: Barbour, 2000. Expand your command of Bible trivia with these imaginary scenes that include biblical characters, quotations, and events that you have to sort your way through to unravel various riddles.

Other case files

Here are some authors of detective novels we recommend, both classic and contemporary, who can help you unwind after a long day spent sleuthing the Bible.

Sir Arthur Conan Doyle, *The Complete Sherlock Holmes*. The definitive collection of stories about the world's most famous detective is available in various formats. Still a great way to sharpen deductive skills and to move from identifying with the befuddled Dr. Watson to picking out the clues that lead Holmes to his unimpeachable deductions.

Agatha Christie. Unfortunately, there is no definitive collection of her works that we could find. But it is possible to get sets of novels about the cases of her Miss Marple and Hercule Poirot, who are almost as well known as Sherlock Holmes. Her second husband, Max Mallowan, was an archaeologist who dug in Mesopotamia (ancient Iraq), so it's no accident that two of her Poirot books are set in the ancient Middle East—*Death on the Nile* and *Murder in Mesopotamia*.

Kareem Abdul-Jabbar and Anna Waterhouse, *Mycroft Holmes* (London: Titan Books, 2015). The all-time leading scorer of the National Basketball Association is a big Sherlock Holmes fan, but in this novel the focus is on the famous detective's older brother as he attempts to solve a case that takes him from London to Trinidad.

Patricia Cornwell, *Portrait of a Killer: Jack the Ripper—Case Closed* (New York: Penguin Books, 2002). We like her novels about the Italian American forensic pathologist Dr. Kay Scarpetta for their attention to detail and depth of research. Her book on Jack the Ripper is nonfiction, but it exhibits the same detailed research applied to building a case for finally identifying Jack the Ripper beyond a shadow of a doubt.

Henning Mankell (http://henningmankell.se/). This Swedish writer's most famous creation was Kurt Wallander, a policeman featured in thirteen novels and an acclaimed television series.

Arnaldur Indridason (https://crimefictionlover.com/2018/05/a-guide-to-arnaldur-indridasons-detective-erlendur/). He is the author of more than a dozen books that describe the adventures of Inspector Erlendur, an Icelandic cop with a past he can't shake that continues to haunt him.

Index of Scripture References